M. L.

GENEALOGY COLLECTION

3-2-60

THE HARINGTON FAMILY

HENRY FREDERICK, PRINCE OF WALES, AND
JOHN, SECOND LORD HARINGTON OF EXTON, 1591-1614
Unknown British Painter, Early XVII century

THE
HARINGTON FAMILY

IAN GRIMBLE

ST MARTIN'S PRESS
NEW YORK

PRINTED IN GREAT BRITAIN

CONTENTS

ILLUSTRATIONS

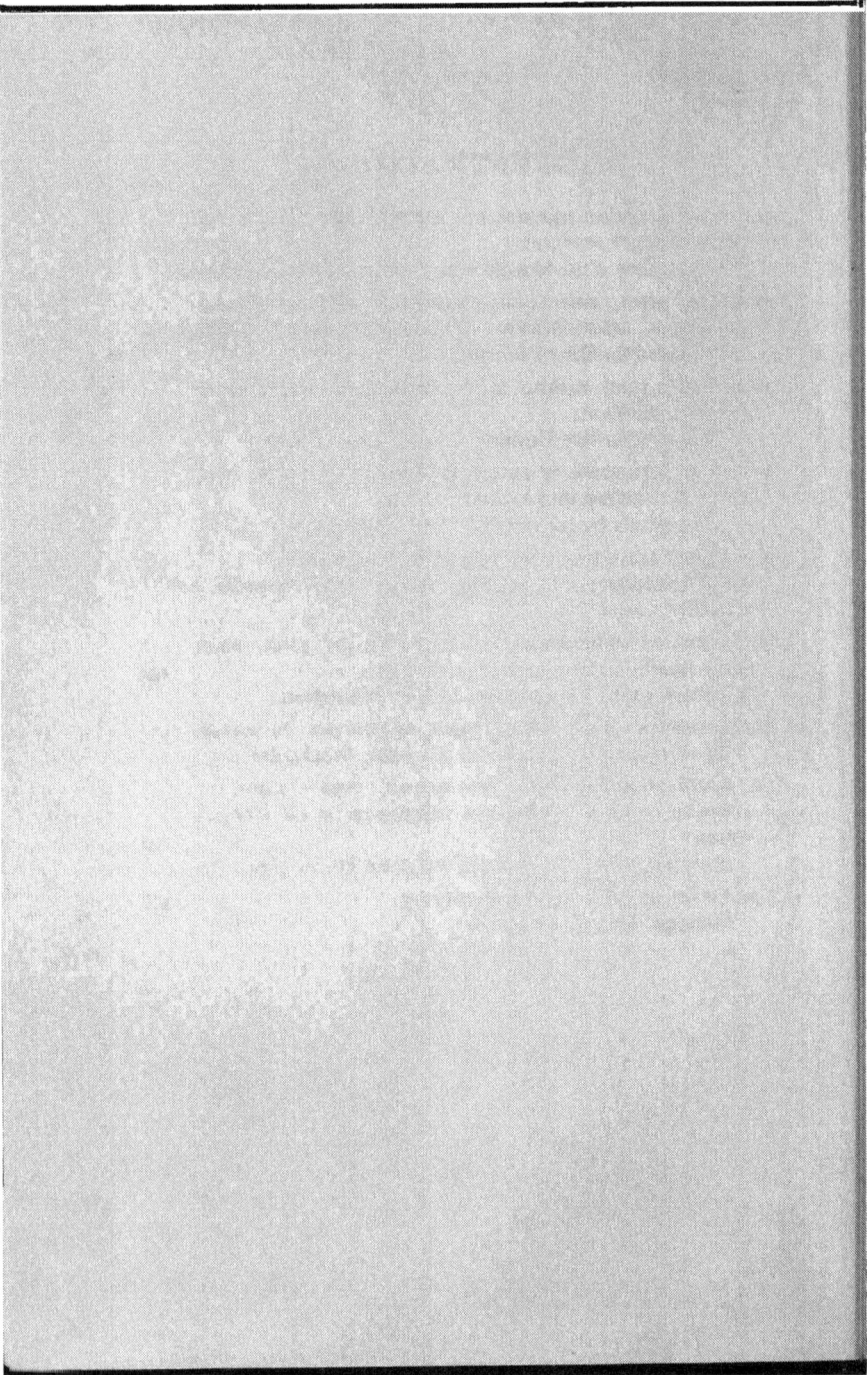

PREFACE

I wish to express my gratitude to Mrs H. V. More, the papers of whose father the late Herbert Harington formed the basis of my own researches; and to her cousin Miss Philippa Harington, the last of her family to own the Kelston portraits and manuscripts. I have also received more help than I know how to acknowledge from Mr John Harington, heir to the senior representative of the family.

I am also deeply grateful to many people who live in the places where Haringtons once held sway and whose care for the heritage of England has filled me with admiration. I have been greatly helped by Mr King-Smith, Kelston, by Sir Harold Parkinson of Hornby Castle, and by Mr Midgley, Farleton.

My translations from the Latin I owe to Mr T. S. Gregory, and from the Italian to Mr A. P. Philipson. In both these tongues I am profoundly ignorant. The staff of the Public Record Office of the British Museum, and of the National Portrait Gallery have shown me the greatest patience and helpfulness. So have many historians whose names it would be impertinent to recite. But I must acknowledge my immense debt to Professor Sir John Neale.

Finally, I would like to thank Miss Patricia Stanyon for all her help over the preparation of this book, and particularly for helping me to conceal the fact that I cannot spell.

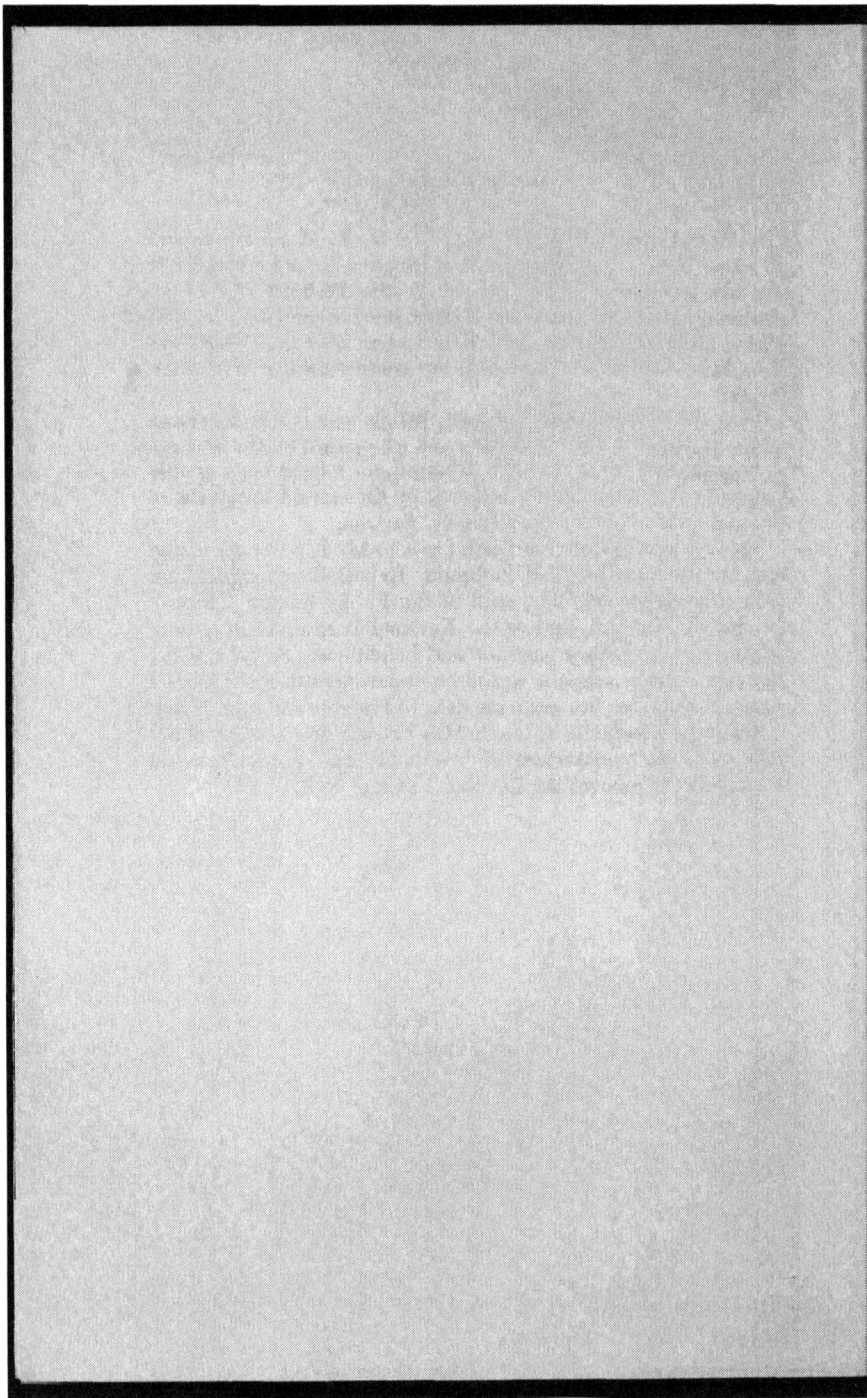

For
NICHOLAS JOHN HARINGTON
born 1942
who will one day be the
senior representative
of this family

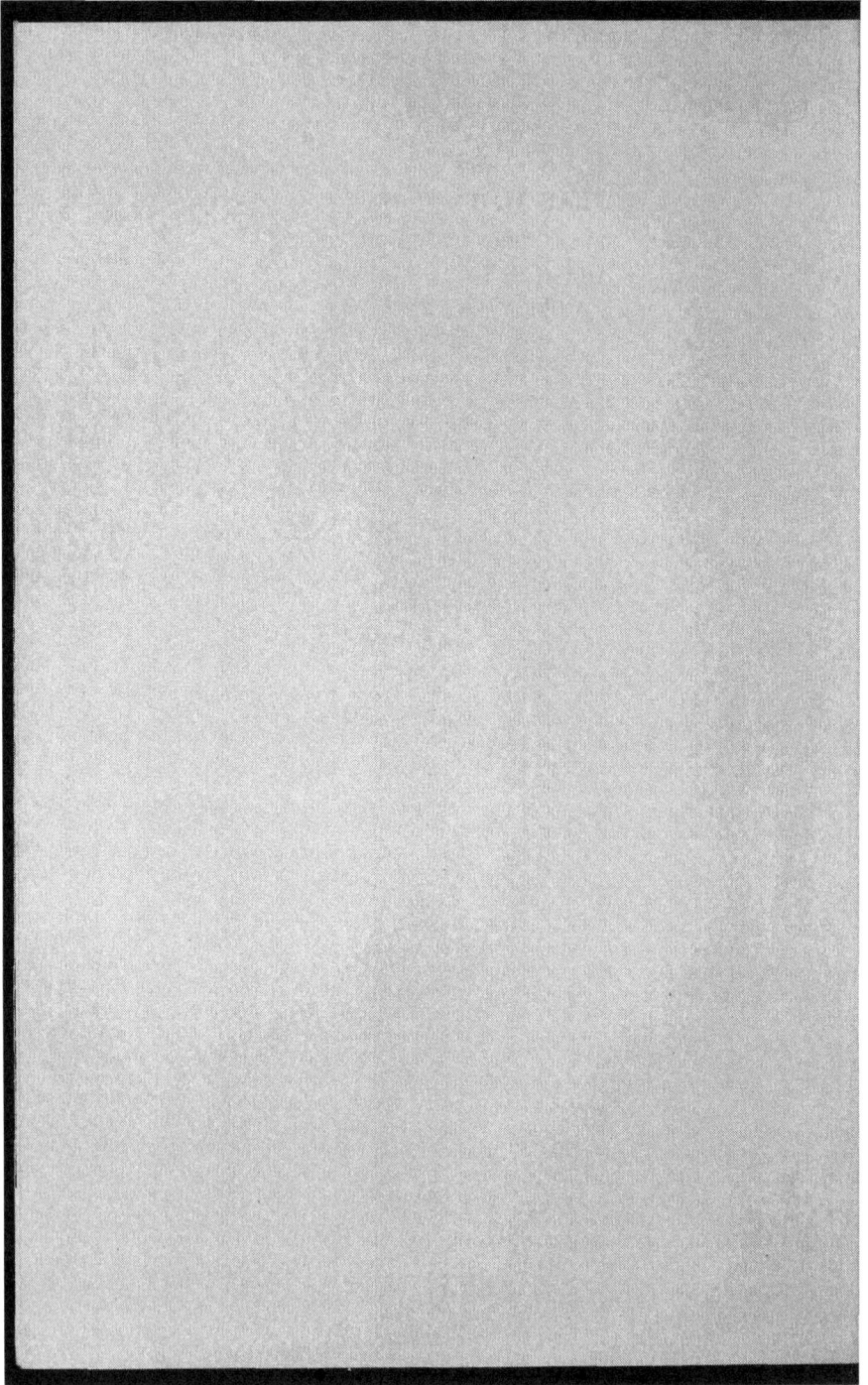

INTRODUCTION

IN 1656 Mr James Harington published *Oceana*. It was a blueprint for a model republic. Some who disagreed with his political thought argued with him. Others incensed by his attack on the divine right of kings abused him. One of his assailants accused him of disloyalty to his family since he was descended from the Norman kings.

'What moveth James Harington to provoke the wrath of Kings? His own lineage is derived from the blood of the Anointed, as will truly appear in the following account, which I have much laboured to obtain from Sir Andrew Markham, and be it now marked with the eye of shame and sorrow. The marriage of your ancestor with a descendant from Matilda, niece to William the Conqueror, is the first derivation of royalty. Another was granted large rewards by state acts for valiantly making prisoner Henry the Sixth, in obedience to the Powers that were then ruling . . .' The author of this letter does not seem to have paused to reflect on the family tradition embracing this earlier attack on an anointed King. He hurries on:

'The great King Henry the Eighth matched his darling daughter to John Harington, and, though a bastard, dowered her with the rich lands of Bath's priory; and Queen Elizabeth affected these faithful servants so much, as to become godmother to their son, and made him a knight for his wit and his valour. Our blessed King James did ennoble your great uncle the Lord Harington of Exton, and entrusted to his care and wisdom the renowned Princess Elizabeth for tuition. Yourself was caressed by the blessed martyr Charles, and honoured with his words, and even his princely favours from his own hands on the scaffold. And shall then any one branch of such noble stock, endowed with such rare gifts and graces, as all have been for the most part, and so many of you countenanced by Kings, shall any espouse such evil principles as you have now set forth in your book? If this be learning, give me to know only righteousness, and seek the Lord by obeying those whom he hath appointed. Why do you thus

13

stir up the people to imagine a vain thing, and set themselves against the Anointed, to whom you claim such glorious affinity, nay consanguinity? Had Prince Henry had presage of your boldness, he would not have chosen young Lord Harington, your cousin, to tennis withal, and write Latin epistles to in Germany . . .'

The author of the letter was a certain J. Lesley, and it came into the possession of a man described as a nobleman, who added at the top the noble comment: 'a slap on the snout of the republican swine'. With this superscription it was published by Henry Harington in his *Nugae Antiquae*. There it has lain neglected, and the officious Thomas Park, re-editing the *Nugae Antiquae* in 1804, omitted it altogether.[1]

Lesley's letter deserved better. With all its inaccuracy and venom, it came nearer to the truth about one of England's great political thinkers than many other critics of his time or since have done. It understood how a plain country gentleman of modest means moved among kings from his youth up, without embarrassment or reverence. What its author failed to understand was the traditional character of this irreverence. He had not considered that a family closely related to kings for many centuries was more likely to regard the sovereign as *primus inter pares* than the newly ennobled, and less likely to be impressed by a doctrine of divine right. Nor did he bother to notice that the central theme of James Harington's *Oceana* was the need to secure good government, rather than to maintain anyone's hereditary right to govern.

It is a preoccupation of thoughtful Englishmen down the centuries commonly neglected by historians. The deposition of Richard II may be attributed today to the private wrongs of Bolingbroke, that of Henry VI to the dynastic claims of York. Charles I's execution has been hailed as a triumph for the rule of law over tyranny. It has even been interpreted as the desperate sortie of a declining gentry, of whom James Harington is cited as an example; as though the younger sons of the family have not been able to furnish examples of a declining gentry ever since the principle of primogeniture was observed.[2]

The thoughts and actions of the Harington family were not so subtle. The family had helped to make and unmake kings, but never once had they held high office under the Crown. Its members played a long and important part in the local government of England, and when kings ruled well they were prominent in their support, and when they ruled badly the Haringtons were not inhibited by their respect for the anointed.

So the story of the Haringtons is not unworthy of the attention of historians. Nor will it disappoint those who honour men who have enriched the heritage of England.

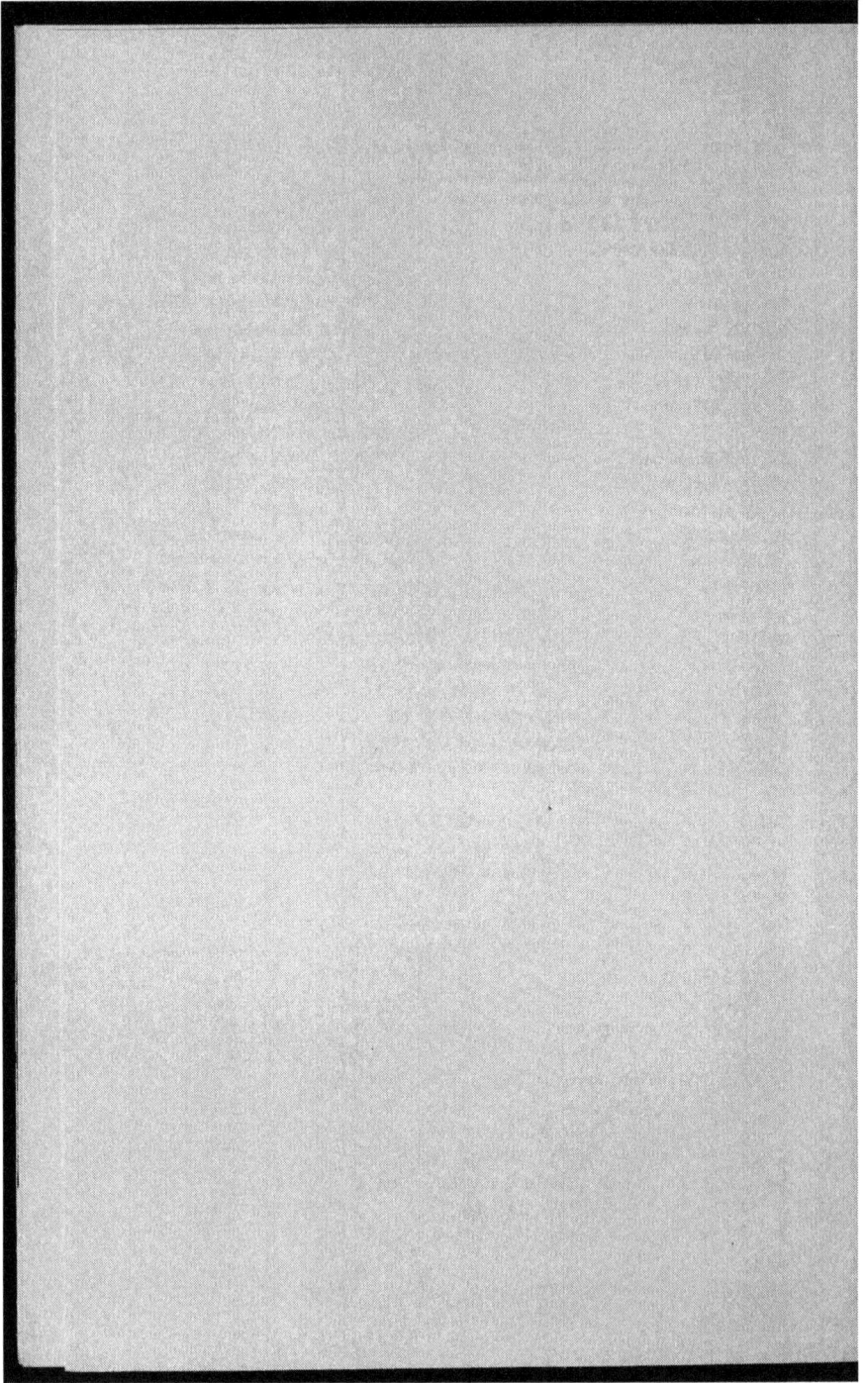

THE HARINGTON FAMILY

B

Osulf of Flemingby
Temp. Richard I

|

Robert (of Harrington)
Marr. Christiana

|

Thomas Harington

|

Michael Harington

|

Sir Robert Harington
Marr. Agnes, dau. of Sir Richard
Cansfield of Aldingham

|

John, first Lord Harington of Aldingham, 1281-1347
Marr. Joan, ? dau. of
Sir William Dacre

ONE

THE FOUNDERS

JUST before the cold dawn of history which scatters the enchanted night of legend, Osulf established himself in the manor of Flemingby in Cumberland. The long coast where he lived, stretching south from the Solway Firth between the mountains and the Irish Sea, had witnessed strange things. The Celtic founders of the kingdom of Strathclyde had trodden its fields. The Norsemen had sailed past it to their kingdoms of Dublin and Man. Missionaries from Iona had explored it on their missions to Northumbria.

All that energy was spent. The memory of it was being enshrined in the Irish annals and the Norse sagas. Osulf of Flemingby steps into the daylight of history in a grant of land made to the Priory of Carlisle, eighty years after Magnus Barelegs perished in Ireland. Iona had long lost the contest with Rome. The Normans controlled England, and an English Pope had recently bestowed on them the overlordship of Ireland also. The centre of the new dynamic society lay in the south, and the story of Osulf's descendants is of their move to that centre.

It would be foolish to speculate whether Osulf was in origin Celtic or Norse or Saxon. Intermarriage was general between these races. His name is that of a Northumbrian king, murdered four hundred years before, and the surname of his descendants became established in the time of his son. Robert son of Osulf was a benefactor of the Priory of St Bee's. The Register of the Priory[1] preserves a grant that he made with the advice of his wife Christiana, by which he gave a church and two hides of land in Hafrinctuna to the Priory. Robertus de Hafrinctuna, he is styled in the grant: so the descendants of Osulf have been called ever since. And the church at Harrington on the coast of Cumberland remains, though it was rebuilt in 1905.

Robert and Christiana's son Thomas, and their grandson Michael, must have continued to live at Harrington because they were described in the Register of St Bee's as 'de Haverington', as their fathers had been. Osulf's property of Flemingby had perhaps been whittled away in grants to the Church: at least, that is what appears from the action of Michael's son Robert in 1277. He laid a claim to the manor of Flemingby against the Abbot of Holm Culton.

Robert was claiming lands that had belonged to his great-great-grandfather Osulf. So the Plea Roll of 1277 contains a pedigree of his descent, confirming the evidence of the Register of St Bee's. Robert's case was heard before the itinerant justices two years later, and the two deeds which settled it are set out in Dugdale's *Monasticum*. Robert was compelled to yield all of the manor to the Abbot, except three hundred and eighty acres.

But if Robert was disappointed by this result, he was amply compensated by the death of his wife's brother. His wife Agnes was the daughter of Sir Richard Cansfield, on whose death the rich manor of Aldingham passed to Agnes's brother William. But William was drowned in the River Severn, and through this sad event Robert and Agnes were translated to the moated manor of Aldingham, on the shores of Morecambe Bay in Lancashire.

Only a square moat below Mote Hill remains today as the probable site of the original manor house. The inquisition of 1347 described it as possessing a garden and a dove-house, two hundred and forty acres of demesne land, one-third fallow, a third meadow and a third pasture. There were also an enclosed park and three mills, two water corn mills and one fulling mill. It was a pleasant seat to which Sir Robert and Agnes removed, beside the encroaching sea. But today no trace remains of their family's residence there except a stained-glass window, containing the Harington device of the silver fret, in the ancient church. The fret, as it has been worn by the Haringtons ever since, is an interlace identical to the pattern carved on bone Viking combs at Jarlshof in Shetland.[4]

The son of Sir Robert and Lady Agnes Harington was called John. He was born in 1281, a hundred years after his ancestor Osulf of Flemingby stepped out of the night of legend. John, first Lord Harington of Aldingham, is the founder of his family's greatness, and the progenitor of everyone of his name who appears in this record of its fortunes.

When John was only twelve years old his mother Agnes died, and four years later his father died also; Sir William Dacre became his guardian during the five remaining years of John's minority.

He would have been wise to marry John to his daughter Joan. But there is no historical evidence that he did so. On John's tomb

JOHN LORD HARINGTON, 1281-1347
CARTMEL

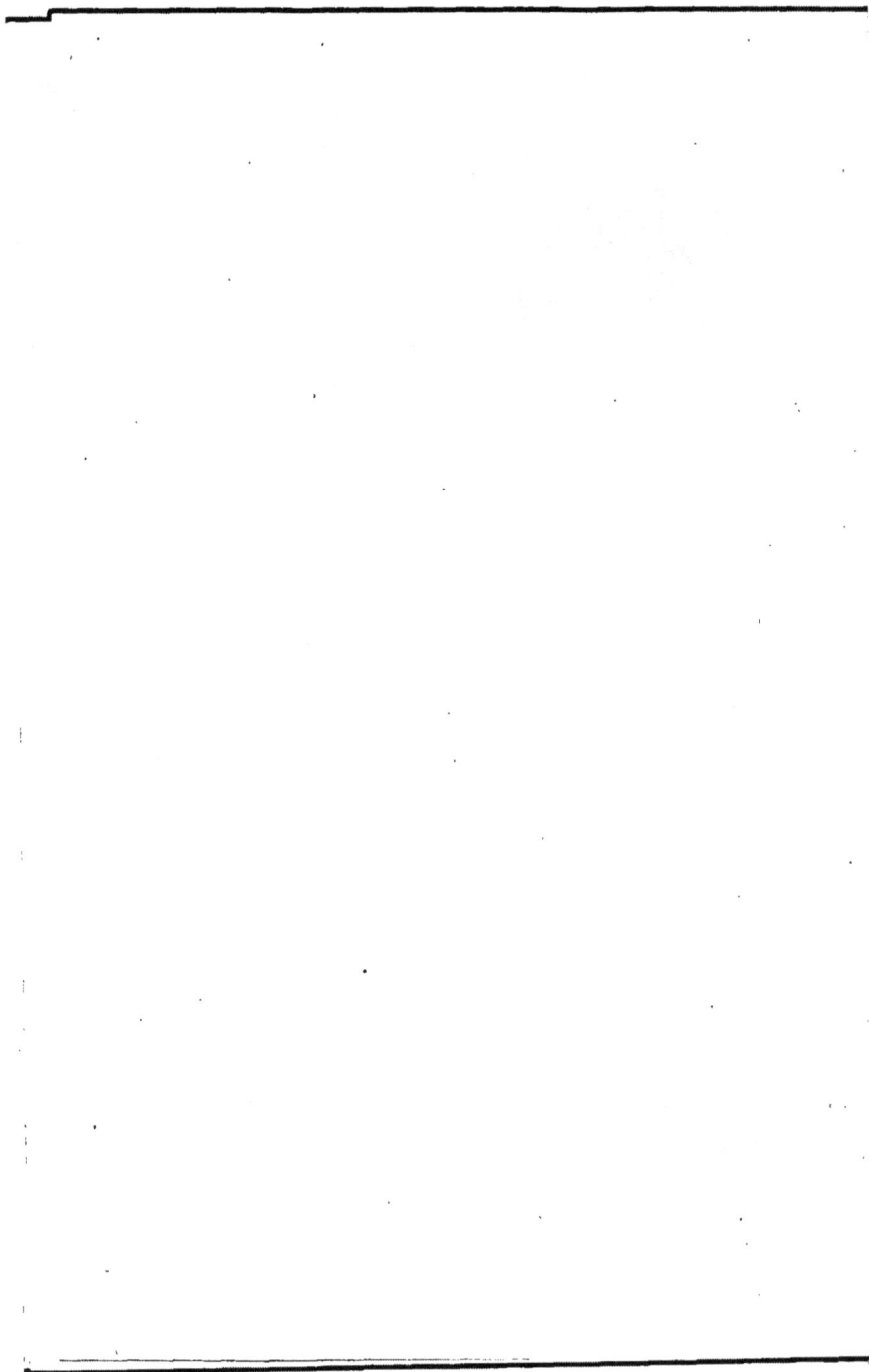

in Cartmel Priory church the escallops of Dacre alternate with the Harington fret, but the heraldic evidence is not conclusive. The pedigree of the College of Heralds gives to Lord John the wife of his grandson.[1]

On 22 May 1306 John Harington of Aldingham attended a ceremony in London, whose splendour he could not have seen equalled in the north. He was ceremonially knighted in the Palace of Westminster in the company of Edward Prince of Wales, after which, according to the *Rishanger Chronicle*, he accompanied the elder Edward, hammer of the Scots, across the northern border.

Edward I died in the following year, and was succeeded by a son who had little taste or aptitude for war. John was summoned for military service from 1309 to 1335, so he may have been present at the field of Bannockburn. He took part with the Earl of Lancaster in the treasons which culminated in the murder of the King's favourite Piers Gaveston, and received the wretched King's pardon. He was cautious in his adherence to Lancaster. When he was forbidden to attend the Earl's meeting of 'good peers' at Doncaster in 1321 he stood aside, and so escaped Lancaster's fate after the rising of the following spring. When he was outlawed for treason in the Scottish marches two years later, he once again secured a royal pardon. John Harington kept himself just, and only just, within the bounds of safety during those unruly times.

He was summoned as a man of weight and judgment to the Council of Magnates at Winchester in 1324 and to Parliament, as a Baron, from 1326 until his death in 1347. So the peerage of Harington was founded, by writ of summons. Up in the north, John led the busy administrative life of the fourteenth-century magnate. He was the custodian of a truce with the Scots. He was appointed to various commissions of the north to decide causes, and to array the local forces. At Aldingham he improved his estate, and obtained a king's licence to enclose three hundred acres of land, wood, moor, and marsh to make the park upon which the inquisition commented at his death.

When he died, he was buried in the magnificent tomb that has now come to rest under a makeshift arch in Cartmel church. His effigy was cut by a sculptor on a solid block of sandstone nearly seven feet long. The surcoat bears the fretty device of his house that must have identified him in the Scots wars. The interlaced chain mail is minutely carved, and its folds at the elbows and other loose places are defined with masterly skill. Where the right leg crosses the left the calf is flattened as in life, and there is a slight depression where the massive sword-belt crosses over the right flank. The effigy of Lord John provides excellent evidence of a form of armour that was just going out of fashion at his death.[6]

His features are now indecipherable, and so are those of his lady, who lies beside him in wimple and veil and long gown. In 1832 the tomb was opened during restorations to its screen and some of Lord John's bones, together with the bones of his hawk and a part of his leather doublet, were removed. These remain in the possession of his senior descendant today.[7]

But Lord John left to his descendants a great deal more than the usual heritage of bones, and the clothing in which they were wrapped, and the tomb in which these were interred. He left a lively family tradition which his descendants were to follow to their great gain and their greater loss. The form which this tradition was to take is outlined in the bare facts of Lord John's own career. He had inherited wealth, and therefore power, through the provident marriage of his father. He had supported the house of Lancaster to the point of treason. Above all he, the first of his name ever to have been summoned as a baron to Parliament, had shown no more respect for an anointed king than for any of his subjects. It was this irreverent attitude to kingship which was to distinguish his descendants above all else, and ultimately to cause their ruin.

THE BUILDERS

John, first Lord Harington
of Aldingham, 1281-1347

Sir Robert Harington, died
c. 1334
Marr. Elizabeth Moulton
of Egremont

Sir John Harington of
Farleton, died 1359
Marr. Katherine, dau. of
Sir Adam Banastre

John, second Lord Harington
of Aldingham, died 1363
Marr. Joan, dau. of
Sir Walter Berningham

Sir Nicholas Harington of
Farleton, died 1403
Marr. Isabella, dau. of
Sir William English

Robert, third Lord Harington
of Aldingham, 1356-1406
Marr. (1) Alice, dau. of
        Lord Greystoke
     (2) Isabel Loring

Sir William Harington of
Farleton, died 1440
Marr. Margaret, dau. of
Sir Robert Neville of
Hornby

John, fourth Lord Harington
of Aldingham, died 1418
Marr. Elizabeth, dau. of
the Earl of Devon

William, fifth Lord Harington of Aldingham, died 1457
Marr. Margaret Hill

TWO

THE BUILDERS

THE part of Lancashire in which Aldingham is situated is separate from the rest of the county, and surrounded by Cumberland, Westmorland, and the sea. But in times when the roads were few it was not cut off from Lancaster, on the other shore of Morecambe Bay. A safe route lay across the sands, as it still does today. And across those sands, almost in view of the manor of Aldingham, lay other possessions that the first Lord John had inherited from his mother. There was Tunstall in Westmorland, some of whose leases, made by Lord John, still survive at Longleat by a caprice of Providence, the property of the Marquess of Bath. Not far from Tunstall there was the manor of Farleton in the beautiful rich valley of the Lune, in Lancashire.[8]

Farleton was twice in dispute between Lord John and his Cansfield cousins, whereby, as a later Harington was to say in similar circumstances, they got nothing but lost labour. At Farleton Lord John established his younger son John, with results that were to make kings tremble. But Sir John Harington of Farleton himself lived quietly in that still untroubled valley. He married Katherine, the daughter of Sir Adam Banastre, executed by Edward II, and he held his patrimony, by the service of a rose yearly, of his nephew the second Lord John, and he died in 1359.[9]

The first Lord John's heir Robert had died before his father, in Ireland. But he had lived long enough to receive his knighthood and to marry a great heiress, Elizabeth Moulton of Egremont Castle in Cumberland. So when their son the second Lord John succeeded his grandfather, he was heir not merely to the lands of Flemingby, Harrington, and Aldingham, but to manors in Limerick, Suffolk, and Lincolnshire as well.

But his power lay in Lancashire, and there he consolidated it. He moved inland from the manor of Aldingham where his grandfather had lived, alarmed in all probability by the inroads of the sea. The manor of Gleaston was parcel of the manor of Aldingham, though the capital messuage was distinct, and here the new baron built himself a castle. He did so in a hurry — according to Thomas West, the author of *The Antiquities of Furness*, 1744, 'after the sea had swallowed up their seat at Aldingham, with the village, leaving only the church at the east end of the town, and the mote at the west end that serve to shew what the extent of Aldingham has been . . . Although the accident cannot now be ascertained, yet it may be conjectured, from the nature of the building, that the castle of Gleaston was built on the occasion, and in such haste, as obliged them to substitute mud mortar instead of lime, in a site that abounds with lime stone, and by a family so powerful'. The sudden catastrophe reads rather as the account of an eye-witness than as a conjecture.

Gleaston Castle stands close to the present village with a hill to the north of it and the high Beacon Hill to the south, between the castle and the sea. It consists of four towers, connected by curtain walls that enclose a ward two hundred and forty feet long, and varying from a hundred and twenty to a hundred and fifty feet in width. The northernmost tower is by far the largest, and beside it is the entrance gate. But this gate appears to have been ornamental rather than defensive, for no north curtain wall was ever built. Where it should have stood there lay the widest possible entry to the ward through a pleasure garden.[10]

'Gleaston is situated in a fertile vale,' wrote Camden in his *Britannia* two centuries later, 'amongst rich meadows, and sheltered from the sea by fruitful hills; all which render it one of the most pleasant seats in this country.' But when he penned these words the medieval barons had already vanished like the sea kings and the monks from Iona. Leland had visited Gleaston earlier than Camden, and described it as only 'the ruin and walls of a castle'. So it remains today.

Built all at one time of roughly dressed limestone with some dressings of red sandstone in the towers, it was probably completed by 1350, when the second Lord John was summoned as a peer to Parliament. His widowed mother will have been an early visitor there, with her second husband Sir Walter de Berningham, a widower. And Sir Walter will have brought with him his daughter Joan, by his first marriage, whom Lord John took to be his wife.

The multiplication of Johns in the Harington family has led almost every work that refers to them into error. On the two occasions when Haringtons of the same name married wives of the same name, the confusion has been complete. The first of these occasions occurred when the second Lord John took Joan to wife, as his grandfather the first Lord John had done.

How this sort of confusion occurs can be illustrated by one of the documents of the time, a conveyance that is preserved in the *Furness Coucher Book*. 'Placitum inter Johannem de Haveringtona de Aldingham, Chivaler, seniorem, et Johannam uxorem ejus . . .' The identity of John and Joan is not impossible to establish; but it is possible to confuse.[11]

To John and Joan their heir Robert was born at the new castle of Gleaston, and here the second Lord John died in 1363. At this time the barons lived quietly, consolidating rather than dissipating the fortune to which Lady Jane Grey would one day be heir. It was their junior cousins of Farleton who provided the impetus of the next two generations.

When Lord Robert succeeded as third baron, his cousin Nicholas was twenty years old, and had already been four years master of Farleton. Nicholas inherited this property unexpectedly when his elder brother died abroad. It seems that he had already had time to develop the ambitions of the younger son who must seek his own fortune, and their horizon was suddenly enlarged when first his father Sir John Harington of Farleton died, then, two years later his elder brother.[12]

It seems almost certain that Sir Nicholas lived at the manor of Farleton in the Lune valley as his father had done. But not a trace of a medieval manor house remains there. Outside the present village the square ditch or moat of a Roman camp that has not been excavated lies in a field of pasture, and near by stands Camp House, a large farm of great antiquity. When it was built, or where its stones were taken from, are matters of surmise. The village itself possesses a large tithe barn and other farm buildings of stone whose date is difficult to guess, so little have their architectural forms altered down the centuries. From the maelstrom that was to engulf the Haringtons of Farleton nothing certain remains in that once more peaceful valley of their earliest home there.

In 1362, the year of Sir Nicholas's succession to Farleton, there occurred an event of the utmost significance to the Haringtons, to Lancashire, and to the throne of England. John of Gaunt was created Duke of Lancaster by virtue of his marriage with the late Duke's daughter. 'Our very dear and well beloved' Nicholas Harington, 'our Sheriff of Lancaster': so John of Gaunt would address Sir Nicholas in the many letters enrolled among the Duchy records. The first evidence of his advance to a position of such trust and power occurs in 1367, when Sir Nicholas came of age. He received leave by writ to go overseas from Dover with a servant, a hackney, and a sum of ten marks.

Sir Nicholas took care to support the foreign war that John of Gaunt continued in the wake of the Black Prince, without becoming closely involved in it himself. In December 1368 he was a member of the commission that raised a hundred archers in Lancashire for the army with which Gaunt landed at Calais. But he himself went to Ireland in the King's service. Then, in 1372, he went to Parliament as one of the two knights of the shire representing the county of Lancaster. He had taken the first step that was to lead to the complete domination of the representation of Lancashire by his descendants.

The career of Sir Nicholas Harington is one of the most fascinating success stories in the fashion of the Middle Ages. His co-operation in foreign wars was judicious, his representation in Parliament indefatigable at a time when others sought to be excused. In his matrimonial alliances he was unerring. He married first a daughter of Sir Thomas Lathom, and secondly Isabella, daughter of Sir William English. By Isabella he begat his two remarkable sons, and by either or both of his wives he obtained the lands in Cumberland, Yorkshire, Westmorland, and South Lancashire of which he was found to be the owner in 1400. The marriages he arranged for his children were more spectacular still.

But above all, he laid his strong hand on the local administration of Gaunt's Duchy.

How powerful he had become by the time he was twenty-seven years old appears in an incident that occurred the year after he first entered Parliament. On 1 March 1373 a Dacre laid complaint that Sir Nicholas had come to Beaumond in Cumberland with a following of three hundred armed men, and had there destroyed houses, assaulted servants and tenants, and driven away horses, cattle, and sheep worth £50. Whatever the cause of this turbulence may have been, it is not without significance that a Dacre complained in vain. In 1375 Sir Nicholas was a member of two commissions appointed by the King to apprehend murderers. In 1377 he again returned to Parliament at the accession of Richard II: and there he will have witnessed the ceremony when his more placid cousin Robert, third Lord Harington, was knighted at the King's coronation.

27

So Sir Nicholas reached the highest offices of Lancaster, and helped to cement the power that was to deprive King Richard of his throne. The year after the coronation, being thirty-two years old, he first held the office of Sheriff of Lancaster for a year. Then he returned to Westminster for the Parliament of April 1379, and by the summer he was sheriff again, petitioning for the customary allowance for parchment and ink. In days when men must combine such responsibilities with such feats of physical endurance as all those journeys on horseback involved, it is no wonder that young men were preferred.

The appointment of Sir Nicholas as sheriff was renewed during pleasure and lasted four years. So he held the office during the Peasants' Revolt that turned against John of Gaunt with such special fury. Perhaps it was partly due to Sir Nicholas that it did not do so within Gaunt's own Duchy.

During this period of office he was also appointed 'Chief Warden of our forest of Quernmore'. Forests were among the most important assets of a medieval estate, and the head foresters were generally men of the first importance, already holding other high office.

Sir Nicholas left his post at his own request, as Gaunt explained in a mandate dated 24 February 1384 to the Chancellor, Justices, and Receiver of Lancaster, requiring them to recommend a successor: 'because we are informed that our Sheriff of Lancaster ... wishes to be discharged from the said office of Sheriff'.

Only three days earlier, Sir Nicholas had been appointed by Gaunt to a commission which brought him again into contact, in novel circumstances, with his cousin Robert of Gleaston. A Genoese ship had been wrecked on the coast near Furness Abbey on the detached segment of Lancashire, the other side of Morecambe Bay. The cargo had been plundered by the men of Furness, and the commission was authorized to restore all their merchandise to its Genoese owners. The chief culprits were the Abbot of Furness and Robert, Lord Harington of Gleaston. Perhaps the strong arm of Sir Nicholas was weakened by the claims of kinship, for no restitution had been made four years later.

But of the intercourse between the two branches of the family either side of Morecambe Bay (an association that has continued in their descendants to this century) no evidence remains. A Paston might write letters, but certainly not a Harington in this century. And the parchment for which Sir Nicholas indented as

Sheriff saw only his signature or seal. Such is the document among the muniments of the Dean and Canons of Windsor, to which Lord Harington and Sir Nicholas attached their seals in 1384 with sixteen other witnesses. The subject of the document does not concern this history. What is of such unique interest is the two perfect seals of the cousins side by side, that of Sir Nicholas showing clearly the label of difference borne by the junior branch and having his signature above.[11]

The silver fret of the junior branch with its label of difference had already received the first quartering adopted by the Farleton branch, three lions representing the blood and property of Sir Nicholas's second wife, Isabella English. The second quartering was to be more splendid, signifying nothing less than the capture of a castle. It was the saltire of the house of Neville.

Hornby lies a mile up the level Lune valley from Farleton, and its castle rises above the trees on a high eminence encircled by the river. The earlier Norman castle had guarded a different passage of the river some miles away, and the tactical strength of this former site is emphasized by the concrete gun emplacement built during the war of 1939-45 below the artificial mound of the Norman keep. But this site had been abandoned, and Sir Nicholas's neighbour Sir Robert Neville of Hornby lived in his castle on the wooded hill above the village. In one direction he could see for miles past Farleton down the Lune valley, and in the other he looked up the steepening fells to the tall summit of Ingleborough.

Sir Robert Neville of Hornby possessed an only son, whose only daughter John of Gaunt married to his own son, the Duke of Exeter. Hornby was to be the inheritance of a king's grandson. Nevertheless Sir Nicholas saw fit to marry his elder son and heir, William, to Sir Robert Neville's daughter Margaret. The chances that the Haringtons would ever succeed to Hornby Castle must then have appeared slight, and they were only slightly improved by the death of Sir Robert Neville's son in 1387, without leaving any other heirs than the Duchess of Exeter.

Meanwhile Sir Nicholas continued to serve the Duke of Lancaster in the administration of his Duchy, and the deposition of Richard II by Gaunt's son left him undisturbed. It was the rebellion of Owen Glendower and Harry Hotspur that gave him his most decisive opportunity to serve Henry IV as he had served his father. On 7 August 1402 a royal mandate commissioned Sir

Nicholas with eight others, including the sheriff and steward of
the county, 'to supervise and try all the fencible men of the
county'. This force was to meet the King at Shrewsbury and
march with him into Wales against Glendower. The same
September Sir Nicholas rode to the Parliament at Westminster
for the last time. He was now fifty-six years old but he was to end
his days as energetically as he had ever lived them.

The following spring King Henry moved north to do battle
with the Percies at Shrewsbury. And six days after their defeat
on July 21 an order was sent to eight great men of Lancaster,
including Sir Nicholas, to assemble all the knights, esquires, and
yeomen of the county to meet the King at Pontefract and do battle
with Percy, Earl of Northumberland, as he advanced to the aid
of his son. Sir Nicholas witnessed the Earl's submission: then he
died, leaving his son William heir to Farleton.

Two years later Robert, third Lord Harington died, also,
leaving another John to be the fourth Lord Harington at Gleaston.
He left a younger son William also who married Margaret Hill.
Their names are inscribed on a bell in Urswick church, Lancashire, which was their joint gift; the very same names as those of
their cousins William and Margaret his wife, of Farleton.

Then, in 1413, two deaths occurred which were to transform
the lives of the Harington family. Sir Robert Neville of Hornby
Castle died, his grand-daughter the Duchess of Exeter being thirty
years old and without an heir. And King Henry Bolingbroke died
and was succeeded by his son, Henry V.

So the first nine generations of the Haringtons live still in the
remaining records of those two hundred years of English history.
Their features and their thoughts are indistinct: only the per-
sonalities of the first Lord John and of Sir Nicholas of Farleton
emerge with any clarity. The ruins of their castles and their
scattered memorials in churches do not help to bring the others
back to life. But collectively they were invoked by their descendants constantly in times of prosperity, and particularly when
misfortune befell the inheritors of their proud name. That is
their most conspicuous memorial, the conscious family tradition
which they bequeathed to their posterity. The nature of this
tradition begins to show more clearly in the reign that began at
Henry IV's death.

THE HARINGTONS OF AGINCOURT

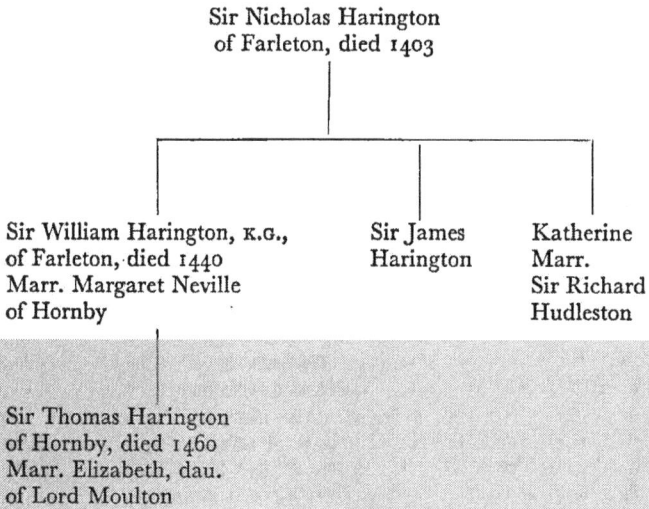

Sir Nicholas Harington
of Farleton, died 1403

Sir William Harington, K.G.,   Sir James   Katherine
of Farleton, died 1440   Harington   Marr.
Marr. Margaret Neville   Sir Richard
of Hornby   Hudleston

Sir Thomas Harington
of Hornby, died 1460
Marr. Elizabeth, dau.
of Lord Moulton

THREE

THE HARINGTONS OF AGINCOURT

KING HENRY V succeeded his father in March 1413. Up in the castle of Gleaston near Morecambe Bay that his grandfather had built, John fourth Lord Harington heard the news that Henry of Bolingbroke was dead. His first duty on succeeding to the barony had been to fix his seal at Westminster to the Act of Succession whose fulfilment he was witnessing. He had married Elizabeth, daughter of the third Earl of Devon, and settled upon her the manor of Porlock in the far south that he had inherited from his mother. He was under thirty years old, and his younger brother William was less than twenty-five years of age. That was the age of the new King.

The great-grandchildren of the first Lord John in the junior branch were likewise young. William, heir to Sir Nicholas of Farleton, was under thirty and had suddenly become a person of as much consequence as his senior cousin. For in the very month of Henry IV's death the Duchess of Exeter died also, without leaving an heir. Hornby, castle of the Nevilles, remained the Duke's property during his life 'by the courtesy of England', after which it would descend to William. In fact Exeter demised it to him in 1424.

William also possessed a promising younger brother James, who had begun his career early as Member of Parliament for Lancashire in 1404, the year of his father's death, and had joined the late king's retinue in 1412. Four Haringtons, two brothers of the senior branch and two of the junior, young, prosperous, already versed in affairs of state, waited to learn what the new reign would bring.

It brought to the throne the greatest sovereign of the house of Lancaster and the outstanding Englishman of his generation. Henry was an attractive person to meet as all accounts bear witness; though there were repellent qualities, too, in his character. He was hard to the point of cruelty, but his enemies the French remarked how just he was. He was sanctimonious and self-righteous, but then he was a young man personally governing a kingdom and personally conducting a war. No one left franker or more moving evidence than a later John Harington of his attitude to that even greater exponent of personal rule, Queen Elizabeth. In the case of Henry V the feelings of these four Haringtons of his own age can only be guessed from the record of their actions.

From the scanty pages of that record the four cousins spring into life, as their ancestors had failed to do. King Henry lost no time in organizing an expedition to sail to France, and every man was summoned according to his duty: Lord John and his brother Sir William, Sir William of Farleton and his brother Sir James. A curtain rises on the part that each of them played.[14]

The old feudal tie of military service between lord and vassal had broken down by this time. It was above all unenforceable for an expedition overseas, because the obligatory term of forty days between the sowing and the mowing was far too short. So now every captain made his own agreement with the King to bring to his service a certain number of men according to his status, and to keep them provided with arms, horses, and food. The King undertook for his part to transport them by sea and to pay their wages quarterly according to a recognized scale varying with the rank of each fighting unit, whether archers or men-of-arms. On an appointed day the captain presented himself with his retinue at the point of departure, bringing with him a list recording each individual man's name. Here he was met by an official from the Exchequer, who verified the name and numbers of the men; and their wages began from the day on which this muster had been satisfactorily passed. Many of the indentures which passed to the Exchequer, or their contents, have survived; but of all the duplicates that the captains held, those scrappy lists that commander and official scanned while the men fidgeted, only one has reached the pages of history. It was referred to by an antiquary of Lancashire in 1878, and it was James Harington's.

Sir James had an accident as he brought his contingent down from the north. The muster had originally been fixed at Southampton on Midsummer Day, but the date was postponed until July 1. Lancashire was committed to finding five hundred archers under ten captains, and James, with his fifty, halted at Fisherton on the Avon. There was a collision with the local townsfolk on the bridge, the sort of scuffle that may result when a serviceman obstructs a civilian in any age. James's troops started to shoot at the townspeople with their arrows, and then drew their swords

C 33

on them. The town bell was tolled. John Levesham the Mayor lost his hood 'in defence of the town'. Four townsmen were killed and fourteen others thrown from the bridge into the river. Finally peace was restored by a Welsh minstrel who got the Mayor another hood, and the troop passed on, to vent its high spirits on the French. The whole incident has the spirit of one of the old ballads, with its brutality, its humour, its *deus ex machina* in the guise of a Welsh minstrel.[14]

Lord John was responsible for a larger force, and accompanied the King in August with a retinue of thirty-four lances and ninety-four archers. His young brother William crossed to France in the Duke of Gloucester's train with thirteen lances and twenty-eight archers. William, the heir to Hornby Castle, was to be nothing less than the standard bearer to the King; his own standard bearer was Sir Richard Hudleston of Millum Castle, who was married to his sister.

And what of their men, the yeomen of England? Trevelyan has described them in his *Social History* as any sort of countrymen of the middling classes, usually farmers, but sometimes servants or armed retainers. They were the new order that had evolved with the gradual disappearance of the old servile status. They provided the bowmen who made such havoc of the chivalry of France. And there was a spirit of new-won freedom in these men, the terrible weapon of Henry's victories. It was a fruitful mixture of the old and the new that streamed into Southampton that summer of 1415, the hundreds of archers representing the new, and Haringtons caparisoned from head to foot in the silver fret flaunting the ancient splendour of feudal magnificence.

Over all hovered a cloud. It was almost certainly dysentery that killed King Henry later, so causing England to lose France when she did; and the bloody flux broke out while all this force lay before Harfleur. Wells are easily contaminated in time of war and King Henry's captains appear to have given none of the careful attention to food that they devoted to their heraldry. Men were allowed to devour the cockles and mussels that swarmed in muddy creeks. They lay where offal of slaughtered animals lay putrefying in swamps. The disease struck high and low alike, for there was no medical science for either rich or poor.

During this September of epidemic, wine, beef, and flour were served out freely to the sufferers from the royal stores. Sir James Harington's bowmen were given a hundred and seven quarterns of flour, twenty-three hundredweight of beef, and over eighteen casks of wine. It was well meant. Over two thousand men died in that melancholy place, edified by priests who spoke of the judgment of God on their sins. Henry lost perhaps the closest friend he ever possessed, young Bishop Courtney. Lord John Harington fell victim to the disease, and was given permission to return home on October 5, with ten of his lances. The feast of the martyr cobblers of Soissons, Crispin and Crispinian, fell on the twenty-fifth.   1108880

With an army in these straits the twenty-seven-year-old King captured Harfleur and fought the battle of Agincourt. It was fought against immensely superior numbers according to strict rules like a tourney, and the date of it was the subject of negotiation between heralds. Always, in the Middle Ages, there is this strange mixture of splendour and squalor. When the battle seemed over, and the English held prisoners in greater numbers than their own, an alarm was raised of a second attack. Henry at once ordered the murder of every prisoner. Men hesitated. Henry threatened to hang any man who disobeyed, and so began the hideous massacre. It is impossible to discover the extent of the danger when Henry gave that order. Illumination falls only on the character of the man who enforced it.

One of Sir James's men, Roger Hunt by name, earned posthumous fame at the battle of Agincourt. Henry almost certainly had no guns there; and the only evidence that the French did possess them is the report that Roger Hunt was killed by one. Sir James lost four of his retinue altogether, and supervised the embarkation of the remainder for Portsmouth before sailing himself for Dover. A year later he was still settling the arrears of payment to his archers, £253 14s. 6d. in all.[14]

But for Sir William of Farleton, who had carried the King's banner at Agincourt, there was to be other payment. The following spring, in the company of an emperor and two earls, there was bestowed on him the highest honour in contemporary estimation, the Order of the Garter.

While the presence of the Emperor Sigismund at this investiture caused it to be one of the most resplendent in the history of the order, it nevertheless represents Henry's greatest error of judgment. As King of Hungary, elected King of Bohemia, and Emperor of the Germans he doubtless appeared a less vain and empty creature to those who had not met him than to those who had.

But it was possible to obtain information from those who had seen Sigismund in the grandiose role of peacemaker between England and France that he adopted after Agincourt. He had begun his self-imposed duties in Paris, where his shabby clothing, his sexual promiscuity, and his meanness and greed soon filled everyone with disgust. When Sigismund set off for the English court he left a Canon of Notre-Dame busy chronicling his indecencies in malicious detail, while such were the rumours of his rapacity that Boulogne would not even open its gates to him.

But King Henry sent his brother Gloucester, with Lords Salisbury, Talbot, and Harington, to meet him at Dover. They rode into the sea with drawn swords and inquired the intentions of the royal visitor: then they escorted him to London.

It was not hard for the English to prejudice Sigismund in their favour with a welcome warmer than his French leave-taking. But it was a worthless objective. The French lost whatever faith they may have retained in Sigismund's impartiality as an arbitrator, the English gained only a treaty with Sigismund from which he carried away the spoils without ever fulfilling one of his obligations under it, and the Emperor himself proved almost impossible to get rid of. His own kingdom of Hungary was at that moment menaced by the Turks, but he was living far too comfortably at English expense to bestir himself on that account.

His installation as a Knight of the Garter, in company with the Earls of Huntingdon and Oxford and Sir William Harington of Farleton, was a striking feature of this entertainment. Well might it be. Sigismund had not only founded a corresponding Order of the Dragon some years earlier: he had brought as a present to King Henry the very heart of St George. The English at this time possessed only some of the bones of their saint, with a piece of his arm and a part of his skull. The addition of some offal as an object of veneration was naturally welcomed with enthusiasm, and indeed it continued to be borne in procession until the Reformation, when it vanished.

But the statutes promulgated at this chapter have survived as the earliest authority regulating the Order of the Garter. On 18 May 1416 instructions were given for the best lodgings at Windsor to be prepared for Sigismund and his suite. The Garter and blue silk mantle were supplied. Four days later all the existing knights and those who were to be installed rode down. The installations took place on Sunday the twenty-fourth in St George's Chapel.

36

At the ceremony King Henry was careful to occupy the chief place, both in the procession and at the mass, but at the feast which followed in the great hall Sigismund was invited to preside at the table. The two kings alone were served with three 'subtleties' which represented St George being armed by the Virgin, fighting the dragon, and entering the castle accompanied by a king's daughter leading a lamb. With such sumptuous ceremony did Sir William Harington receive the highest honour of his time.

At last, over three months after his arrival in England, Sigismund was escorted reluctantly back to Dover by King Henry, and dispatched to Calais with a fair wind. Henry now himself made a truce with France, while he prepared for the next expedition.

A greater force was expected of Sir William of Farleton this time. With his brother James, recently appointed Constable of Liverpool Castle, he was commissioned to assemble four hundred archers from Lancashire, two-thirds of whom were to be mounted and the rest on foot, and to bring them to Southampton by May 10. The atmosphere of preparation had changed from that of the previous May. Agents were dispatched to Wales in search of subsidies, and there was a muddle between the Receiver in Lancashire and the Treasurer in London over archers' wages which resulted in an order from the Treasury to return a sum of money, just when it had completed its precarious journey to the north. Lord John went to France in the King's train in July, and so began the conquest of Normandy.

As that winter of 1417 approached, the outstanding obstacle to the conquest of lower Normandy was Falaise, the great rock fortress near which Arlette the tanner's daughter had lived and given birth to William the Conqueror. Its fortifications were all but impregnable, the garrison determined. The weather turned bitter, with ground frozen and frequent hailstorms. Lord John fell ill again and was forced to return to England. To many of his companions in arms who remained throughout that harsh winter surveying Falaise with its walls and towers and the majestic castle on the cliff, the siege must have appeared a hopeless one. And entering that scene of voluntary discomfort helps to an understanding of the quality demanded of medieval kingship, the particular kind of pre-eminence, of which Garter ceremonies and banquets were but the show.

37

Henry's countrymen understood and were roused by it, though no Harington considered it proper as yet to express his thoughts on such a subject. It was left to such as John Page, a private soldier, to do so, and Gregory the Skinner, who later became Lord Mayor of London.[15]

Gregory's entries about the war in his journal are brief and matter of fact, not at all like his descriptions of goings on in London. 'And that same year the King laid siege unto Falaise the first day of November, and that siege continued unto the twentieth day of December, the year of grace 1417. Then the town descended for to treat with the King, and the King committed the treaty unto Thomas Earl of Shrewsbury, and to Harry Lord FitzHugh, and to Sir John Cornwall, and to Sir William Harington, knights and commissioners for his party.' So the treaty was signed on December 20, and sealed with the fret among all the other curious devices. But the King had to remain until February, when the castle also was reduced. Then he returned to Caen.

On February 11 of that year Lord John died. He had no children, and his widow Elizabeth, the Earl of Devon's daughter, retired to live at the manor of Porlock that had been bestowed on her at her marriage settlement. And in the little parish church in which her husband had endowed a chantry either she or her successors raised the stately tomb with its alabaster effigy that is still to be seen in Porlock church today. Lord John lies in plate armour, wearing the collar and badge of his order of knighthood, and his head rests on a lion's head erased, the crest of the Haringtons. The tomb, like that of the first Lord John, has been thrust under an arch to the considerable damage of its canopy, and all evidence of its identity except the crest and a tradition repeated by an aged sexton had vanished, when Maria Halliday re-identified it in 1882 in her *Description of the Monument in Porlock Church*.[16]

Lord John was succeeded in title, and in all his property except the manor of Porlock, by his brother William. At the same time the news reached Sir William of Farleton in France that his younger brother Sir James had died early in December. It is possible to feel touched, five hundred years later, by the special sorrow of James's death. He was only the younger son of a junior branch in an age when status was all important. Yet the hand of oblivion has been especially kind to him. It is as though he

38

possessed some quality that could charm a Welsh minstrel to come to his assistance when he was alive, and posterity to preserve a solitary muster roll bearing his name after he was dead.

But his own posterity crossed the Channel no more until the Field of the Cloth of Gold. They preserved, it seems, a sense of occasion.

King Henry pursued his campaigns with the energy of an age in which life was short. He summoned Rouen to surrender; his heralds were manhandled by the citizens and many of them killed. On August 1 the King and his captains took up their appointed stations to besiege the city.

> It was a sight of solemnity
> For to behold both party;
> To see the rich in their array,
> And on the walls the people that lay,
> And on our people that were without,
> How thick that they walked about:
> And the heralds seemly to seen,
> How that they went aye between,
> The King's heralds and pursuivants . . .

The hurried vivid narrative of Private John Page sweeps on, until the glory of war fades and only its misery remains.

> And women holding in their arm
> A dead child, and nothing warm,
> And children sucking on the pap
> Within a dead woman's lap.

One of the Paston letters gives the disposition of the forces drawn up at the castle gate, and it agrees exactly with the eye-witness account of John Page.

> Between him [that is, Exeter] and Clarence then
> Lay the Earl Marshal, a manful man;
> He lodged him next the Castle gate,
> And kept it both early and late:
> And so forth in that same way
> The Lord Harington then he lay:
> And Talbot, from Domfront when he come,
> He lodged him next that worthy gome.
> And then Harington, Sir William,
> When he was dead, his retinue he nam [took].

Domfront had capitulated in the spring. Talbot died before Rouen on October 19, and Sir William took over his force.

By that time the citizens were starving. In their confidence they had admitted hundreds of refugees at the approach of Henry's army, and now there was nothing left to eat save the vermin. Messengers stole out of the town, and making their way to Paris implored for aid from the Council. There was much sympathy for the gallant people of Rouen, and a subscription was opened to pay for troops to relieve them. But they never came. In December starving citizens began to trickle out to the English lines, women and children whom the defenders were eager to get off their hands. They did not know Henry. He had shown at Agincourt that he would never allow a military objective to be jeopardized by the restraints of humanity. He ordered those refugees, so piteously described by John Page, to be fed and then driven back to the town. But the defenders refused to readmit them; and so they died, in the incessant rain, in ditches beneath the walls.

On New Year's Eve Sir William and his cousin the new Lord William heard a great cry in the middle of the night from the castle gate. It was taken up at every gate in turn, that weird invitation from the beleaguered town to discuss terms of surrender. Still the poor people continued to suffer, because their leaders thought they could make terms with the man they had angered in August. When Henry finally obtained the abject submission they might have offered him in the first place, he did nothing to add to the miseries of the townspeople. He rode through Rouen seriously on a black horse with gold breast-cloth and housings of black damask. Behind him came a page, bearing on his lance a fox's brush 'whereby some wise men noted many things'. They might merely have noted the astonishing attention people then devoted to their heraldic emblems. The fox's brush was one of the badges of the King's family that he had found time to choose as the appropriate insignia for his entry into Rouen.

Sir William of Farleton returned home. The Duke of Exeter with whom he had served at the castle gate, and whose life stood between him and the ownership of Hornby Castle, was made Captain of Rouen.

Sir William's son Thomas was ten years old and it was time for him to marry. On his return from Rouen, Sir William obtained the wardship of Elizabeth, daughter and heiress of Lord

Moulton and Dacre, and married her to his son within three months. Her father owed his barony of Moulton to a Dacre ancestor who had snatched an infant heiress out of Warwick Castle in the middle of the night. Sir William's action was relatively unhurried. But they are among the most pathetic figures of the Middle Ages, the little heiresses, locked away until they were sold or snatched, to be married off to strangers while they were still children. Once married, they sometimes enjoyed great freedom and power. The French Dauphin's mother was showing all Europe how a woman could revenge herself for being married to a verminous madman. After the fall of Rouen she herself signed the Treaty of Troyes which contained the words 'the supposed Dauphin'. It was not the least achievement of Joan of Arc that she persuaded the Dauphin of his legitimacy after it had been denied by his own mother in a state treaty.

Immediately after the Treaty of Troyes had been signed, King Henry was married there to Catherine of France. The wooing can have borne little resemblance to the romantic scene in Shakespeare's play. It was a mere seal to the treaty that had just made him Regent of France. It would make him heir to France also unless the 'supposed Dauphin' should find evidence of his legitimacy to contradict his own mother. In his oratory Charles prayed for guidance, and presently Joan of Arc heard strange voices speaking to her at Domrémy.

King Henry returned to England with his queen, for her coronation. And now Gregory Skinner is in his element as he describes the banquet which followed. It is clear that he secured a social triumph in attending it. First he recites in his common-place book the noblemen who waited on the Queen. They included the Earls of Northumberland and Westmorland, and among the barons William, fifth Lord Harington. But Gregory is agog to recite the menu, and cuts short the list of notables with an et cetera, so that he can proceed with the 'serving of the first course'. This included brawn with mustard, lamprey powdered with eels, great crabs and a subtlety called pelican. The subtlety accompanying the second course was called 'a panter & a mayde before hym'. The third course was the most formidable of all. It was perhaps an irksome honour that befell Lord William, 'asygnyd for to do servyse ryallys before the quene'.

Immediately after these celebrations Henry was compelled by the reverses in France to return to his army. His sovereignty there depended, it seems, wholly on his personal presence; and there he died, fighting until he was too weak with dysentery even to sit on his horse. He was thirty-five years old, and he left as his heir a baby of only a few months. Everything he had striven for crumbled away.

The administration of Lancaster that his grandfather John of Gaunt had built up began to crumble. The government of his provinces crumbled. Finally his own dynasty of Lancaster fell before the legitimate line of York.

After Henry's death Lord William retired to Gleaston Castle, where he died in 1457. Sir William of the Garter inherited Hornby Castle and became Chief Steward of Lancashire in 1428, and lived until 1440. Up in that remote, almost autonomous corner of northern England the cousins will have witnessed many disturbing changes, a restlessness among the yeomen who had seen something of the world on their foreign service, and were now condemned once more to the home-acre, a slackening of local government. And from time to time little fragments of news will have reached them, staggering enough to their ears since they still tell the strangest tale in European history. Joan of Arc had appeared. Henry V's government and his conquests dissolved slowly, on both sides of the Channel. Finally, such pillars of the house of Lancaster as the Haringtons altered their allegiance, until they even laid violent hands on his anointed son.

When the Hundred Years War in France came to an end, the civil war known as the Wars of the Roses broke out in England. A battle in those days, if it was properly conducted, was still a tourney between a few hundred or thousand men, a display of elegance and courage. It was in the siege of towns that the rules of war proved inadequate, because civilians became involved.

Herein lay the chief difference between the foreign and the civil war. In the latter the towns were left almost entirely alone, until they became so prosperous that they could almost determine its course. Meanwhile there was a new hazard for those who took part. In a civil war, to lose is treason. All who lost, in every battle, forfeited their estates.

But Lord William and Sir William of Farleton, those pillars of the old Lancastrian order, did not live to see the mighty lottery in which their castles and manors were shortly to change hands as lightly as the crown of England.

THE HARINGTONS OF THE
WARS OF THE ROSES

Sir Thomas Harington of Hornby,
died 1460

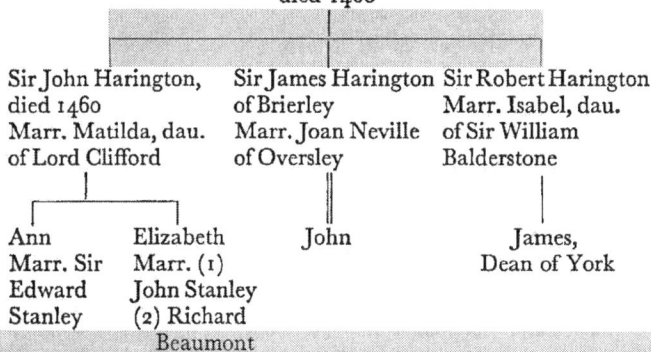

Sir John Harington,	Sir James Harington	Sir Robert Harington
died 1460	of Brierley	Marr. Isabel, dau.
Marr. Matilda, dau.	Marr. Joan Neville	of Sir William
of Lord Clifford	of Oversley	Balderstone

Ann	Elizabeth	John	James,
Marr. Sir	Marr. (1)		Dean of York
Edward	John Stanley		
Stanley	(2) Richard		
	Beaumont		

William, fifth Lord Harington
of Aldingham, died 1457

Elizabeth, Baroness Harington
Marr. Sir William Bonville,
died 1460, son of Lord
Bonville, executed 1461

William, sixth Lord Harington
of Aldingham, died 1460
Marr. Katherine Neville, dau. of the
Earl of Salisbury, died 1460

Cecile, Baroness Harington and Bonville,
died 1529
Marr. Thomas Grey, Marquess of Dorset

FOUR

THE HARINGTONS OF THE WARS OF THE ROSES

ENRY V's title to the throne of France had been consolidated by conquest and marriage. France did indeed
observe Salic law, while England did not. But even this
convenient difference in the systems of descent of the two
kingdoms would have availed Henry little, had his arm
been weaker.

And his father Henry IV had not placed the house of Lancaster
on the throne of England by right of descent alone. Like the
elected kings of an earlier age he had been accepted on terms. He
had offered constitutional government in place of personal rule;
and he had believed in the form of government he offered. He
continued to enunciate his theories of parliamentary rule with a
touch of pomposity long after they had served their purpose, and
the frequency and responsibility of Parliament advanced far under
the Lancastrian kings.

In particular the machinery for returning Members steadily
improved. One statute prohibited undue influence, and took
certain steps to prevent it. Another empowered assize judges to
inquire into suspicious returns. At Henry V's accession both
voters and candidates were limited to residents in the constituency.
In Henry VI's reign the vote was restricted to that now famous
category of Englishmen, the forty-shilling freeholder. But the
secret ballot, which a Harington was to propose two hundred
years later, was then an unknown heresy. Acclaimed by his
dependants, Sir Thomas Harington of Hornby was returned as a
Knight of the Shire of Lancashire in the year in which he attained
his majority and in which his father Sir William died.[17]

Sir Thomas was a small child when his family moved to Hornby
Castle, his mother's home. Hornby is not a ruin today, but it has
been so extensively rebuilt in later times that little remains
visible of the medieval castle. Only the central tower seen on its
eminence from a distance, rising above the encircling trees, evokes
the scene of Sir Thomas's upbringing. To the lordships of Hornby,
Farleton and Brierley in Yorkshire, and their annexed manors
there was added Heysham, through his marriage with Elizabeth,
daughter of Lord Moulton and Dacre. It is perhaps strange that

44

he was not summoned by writ as a baron to sit in the upper house.

William, fifth Lord Harington of Gleaston, was summoned to attend the Parliament of 1439 in which his cousin represented Lancashire. Lord William possessed an only daughter Elizabeth whom he married to William, the heir of Lord Bonville. In this there is plainly to be seen the activity of the Lady of Porlock, the fourth Lord Harington's widow, for she married a second time and her husband was Lord Bonville, a widower. Nothing, as a rule, remains from this period of the lives of the wives of the Haringtons, save the portions they brought to their husbands and the children they bore them. Only the Lady of Porlock shows faintly in the role of a matchmaking aunt, contriving the marriage of her niece to her stepson. Had she possessed a son, he would have succeeded to the title. She may have felt consoled when her step-grandson succeeded as sixth Lord Harington on his maternal grandfather's death. But all this lay in the future, for William Bonville the younger was not yet born when Lord William Harington and Sir Thomas met in Parliament to observe the breakdown of government whose repercussions occasionally troubled remote Lancashire.[18]

Lord William had known and Sir Thomas had heard of a king whom none dared contradict. They now saw a king without malice or guile, graciously pleased to accept advice from every contending group, conceiving it to be his whole duty to listen, reconcile and, as occasion increasingly demanded, to forgive. Such qualities were unsuited to fifteenth-century kingship. In 1440, when Sir Thomas succeeded to Hornby Castle, Henry VI had come of age worn out by the cares of his youth, and already showing signs of an insanity that he might have inherited from either of his grandfathers. In place of the splendour and misery of feudal war there was substituted a greater paradox. The King founded Eton College and King's College at Cambridge while political rivals accused one another of witchcraft and France was lost.

The Lancastrian kings had established their title as men who ruled well, in place of a king who ruled badly. It was a novel situation to possess a harmless king who did not rule at all. Gradually there was created a belligerent body of opinion that a man who failed to govern must cease to reign. How Sir Thomas and the Harington-Bonvilles came to share that opinion can only be seen at this distance in time through their public actions.

The situation created sharp rivalry between the Lancastrian supporters who sought to rule for Henry, and their rivals of York. At Sir Thomas's succession in 1440 the head of the first group was Cardinal Beaufort, labouring to preserve the administration of Lancashire whose revenues Sir Thomas was voting to the royal household in Parliament, and to secure peace. The leader of the Yorkists was Humphrey, Duke of Gloucester, heir to the throne as long as King Henry remained childless.

In 1447 Sir Thomas was summoned to a Parliament in which he witnessed strange doings in a strange place. Bury St Edmunds had been chosen, where Beaufort's power was strong, and as soon as Gloucester arrived he was arrested. Five days later his body was exhibited to the Members of Parliament assembled there. Lord William of Gleaston did not receive a writ of summons after 1439, so he presumably missed this ominous portent of things to come.

As for Sir Thomas, while he continued to represent Lancashire in Parliament, he became also Sheriff of Yorkshire, in which his Brierley properties lay. The decline of the Lancastrian cause was gradual and the falling away of its supporters equally gradual, with ample time for reflection. Beaufort died; the young king married, deeply in debt and periodically quite insane. Jack Cade staged his rebellion. Sir Thomas, '*notabilis armiger*' as the parliamentary returns quaintly style him, ceased to stand for election as a representative of Lancashire.

Then, in 1453, Queen Margaret bore to King Henry VI a son, after eight years of barren wedlock. The Duke of York, the Yorkist heir since Duke Humphrey's death, ceased to be the heir presumptive. He was either the rightful king or he was nothing. York drew the sword. The battle of St Albans in which he defeated the King's forces in 1455 marks the beginning of naked power which ended only with the coming of the Tudors. There is something symbolic in the pathetic King, wounded in the neck beside his banner at St Albans, and only rebuking his assailant: 'forsooth, forsooth, ye do foully to smite an anointed king so'.

After the battle York became Protector, while King Henry preserved all the honours belonging to the Crown. Parliament was summoned to meet at Westminster on July 9 and Sir Thomas attended it as a representative of Yorkshire. He had crossed the Rubicon.

In this act of abandonment of the ancient loyalties of his house he was following the lead of Neville, Earl of Warwick, who had been Henry VI's governor when he was a child, and who, in joining the Yorkists at St Albans, admitted the utter failure of his charge. Sir Thomas was himself half Neville, and lived in the Neville castle of Hornby. His second son James was married to Joan Neville, heiress of John Neville of Oversley.

The senior branch joined the same alliance. When Lord William, the fifth baron, died in 1457, he was succeeded by his sixteen-year-old grandson William Bonville. William's other grandfather still lived to enjoy the title of Lord Bonville, and the Lady of Porlock was still living also to smile on the succession of her step-grandson as sixth Lord Harington. She witnessed the nuptials of the young Lord William with Katherine Neville, the Earl of Salisbury's daughter, and she lived to grieve over the consequences of this alliance. For this is the threshold of the period of English history so poignantly mirrored in Shakespeare's *Richard III*, the age of widows.

That learned historian Joseph Hunter wrote in volume II of his *History of Doncaster*, 1831, 'although the Haringtons might be said to be bound to King Henry VI by a double tie, first, as their sovereign to whom they owed allegiance, and next as the chief lord to whom they were feudatories; yet when Richard Duke of York aspired to the Crown, they espoused his cause, and appeared with his army in the field'. This is a harsh judgment to pass on the men in whose hands lay the local government of England, and who had had so long to witness the breakdown of government, spreading from the centre, between Henry V's death and the battle of St Albans. Hunter insists on the duty of loyalty that the Haringtons owed to their feudal chief and their anointed King, and it is interesting that this was the very charge brought against the later Haringtons who turned from their allegiance to Charles I. It was not one which impressed the descendants of the first Lord Harington of Aldingham.

Sir Thomas Harington of Hornby was not an idle adventurer, looking for the main chance. He was an elderly public servant who attended nearly every Parliament between the age of twenty-one and his death, who filled some of the highest local government offices, and whose discharge of his military duties up to 1450 is thus described in a statute of that date.[19]

'Thomas Harington Knight, which with 3 Spears and 60 Bows,

at his great labour, costs and expenses, rode from his own County, not only to Crotoi to the rescue thereof; but also to the rescue of Calais, at siege late thereto laid, with 6 Spears and 26 Bows; and also was three half year together with 3 Bows, at his own costs, in your service in your Realm of France . . .'

He had been given a mission of high trust at Henry's marriage, for the statute speaks of 'the great and notable costs supported and borne for himself, 4 Gentlemen, and 12 Yeomen in fetching home the Queen . . .'

He played his part as his ancestors had done in the wars against the Scots, and 'herbages and pastures were late granted to the said Thomas, for his service done and to be done to Your Highness, and for the relief of him of the great hurt and losses that he had, by his late taking prisoner in Scotland in your service there'.

A man who had spent his life in such active support of a dynasty and government can have felt no slight disgust with either when, instead of retiring peacefully to his ample estates, he sacrificed his life to change them. But in Hunter's opinion Sir Thomas took a course 'opposite to that to which the more honourable and the gentler feelings of nature should have attached him'.

After the feast of All Hallows in 1458 Sir Thomas visited the Earl of Salisbury, father-in-law of William sixth Lord Harington, at Middleham in Yorkshire. There he engaged himself to the House of York, among many of the noblest and most patriotic men in England. Foreseeing the dangers of his act, he made a conveyance of his estates to men of the Lancastrian party. It throws a warm light on the personal loyalties which still survived political differences. 'Remembering himself of the great wars and troubles likely to fall', Sir Thomas made this conveyance to the Archbishop of York, the Earl of Shrewsbury, Lord Clifford, whose sister was wife to his eldest son and others: 'to the intent that the same lords were mighty and in consort with the contrary party, should be fair means, if God fortuned the field in the said wars to go against that party that the said Sir Thomas was upon, and if the law happened to proceed against him as others, and he be attainted, should save his lands unforfeited'. He also made his will, directing that he should be buried at Lancaster if he died in Lancashire, otherwise in the Priory of Monk Seaton. Among his executors he named his cousin Sir John Hudleston, whose grandfather had carried his own father's banner at Agincourt.[20]

His affairs in order, Sir Thomas acted with an energy worthy of

48

his predecessors. On September 23 forces of King Henry's indomitable queen pounced on those of York at Blore Heath, and were defeated. A Petition of the Commons against Lord Stanley in the following year contains Sir Thomas's sole surviving utterance, and it was made on that day. 'When the said Earl of Salisbury and his fellowship had distressed your said people at Blore Heath, the said Lord Stanley sent a letter to the said Earl at Drayton the same night, thanking God of the good speed of the said Earl ... which letter the said Earl sent to Sir Thomas Harington, and he showed it openly, saying "Sirs, be merry, for yet we have more friends".'[19]

He soon lost his merriment: pursuing the Lancastrians too far with two Neville knights, they were all captured. For months they waited in captivity for the Duke of York to follow up their victory, but the tide of battle turned. Instead of the expected delivery Sir Thomas found himself named in a graphic Act of Attainder that rang with the forensic eloquence of Sir John Fortescue, Chief Justice of the King's Bench. Hornby Castle was lost; Farleton, that the first Lord Harington had given his younger son, Brierley in Yorkshire, Heysham of the Dacres, and all the other manors. Henry VI busied himself in obtaining pardons for whom he could, and in exacting solemn empty oaths of fidelity. York, included in the Attainder, fled to Ireland.

The storm burst again in the following year when York and Warwick returned to win the victory of Northampton, and to reverse the attainders that lay, in such picturesque detail, among the statutes. Attainder and reversal of attainder were to become almost the chief functions of Parliament during the next few years, and they even set a parliamentary precedent. For they were the first kind of statute to be introduced in Parliament in the complete and final form in which they were enacted, as all Bills are today. Members casting their votes on such measures must have felt the piquancy of what they did, since a large number of the legislators of both Houses were taking a full part in the contest as well as distributing its rewards and punishments. But for the citizens of London the contest had the excitement of an increasingly uncertain monetary gamble, as they lent ever larger sums to one, and then another, of the contending armies.

> Treason doth never prosper; what's the reason?
> Why, if it prosper, none dare call it treason.

So a descendant of Sir Thomas wrote, years later, in his commonplace book, and another descendant noticed it there and sent it to Prince Henry, Charles I's elder brother. So this curious couplet links the two civil wars in England, that of 1460 and that of 1640, in both of which the Haringtons joined the forces of change, and in both of which they were ruined.

Sir Thomas was reinstated, and spent the last months of 1459 helping to restore peace and order in the north. His heir Sir John, husband of Lord Clifford's sister, was named in a commission dated October 14 at Westminster to arrest and commit to prison all persons guilty of unlawful gatherings, and to expel the evil-doers from three castles in the north, first by proclamation, but if necessary by storm. Sir Thomas and his second son Sir James were instructed in another commission of November 12 to prevent unlawful gatherings likewise, and to gather all the loyal men of Westmorland, Cumberland, and the adjacent counties to resist them.

For while King Henry had made the Duke of York Protector and heir to the Crown after the victory of Northampton, the Queen was at large with her dispossessed son. She sought help from France by letter. She went personally to Scotland. She wrote to the Common Council of London, which sent no reply but voted a thousand marks to the Duke of York. Yet the Queen succeeded in assembling a large army. She scoured the very estates of Salisbury and York for men, and threatened with loss of life or limb anyone between the ages of sixteen or sixty who did not come forward to deliver the King. The battle of Wakefield, the supreme holocaust of the Wars of the Roses, is the terrible monument of this woman who defended the rights of her son to the death.

There are fuller accounts of the battle than that of Gregory, but none more immediate. 'And the 9th day of December next following, the Duke of York, the Earl of Salisbury, the Earl Rutland (he was the Duke of York's second son, one the best disposed lord in this land), and Sir Thomas Harington, with many more knights and squires and great people with them, and so departed out of London toward York. And the same year, the 30th day of December, the Duke of Exeter, the Duke of Somerset, the Earl of Northumberland, the Lord Ros, the Lord Neville, the Lord Clifford, with many more lords, knights, squires, and gentles, and the commons of the queen's party met with the Duke of York at Wakefield, and there made a great journey upon the Lord and

50

Duke of York, and took him and the Earl of Salisbury, the Earl of Rutland, and the Lord Harington, and Sir Thomas Neville and Sir Thomas Harington, and many more knights were taken and slain beside all the commons. But this good Duke of York with his lords aforesaid lost their heads. God have mercy on their souls, for they lost in that journey the number of 2,500 men. And in the Queen's party were slain but 200 men.'

The Queen had broken the week's truce, made at Christmas time, and set on the Yorkists on New Year's Eve; and the Duke of York in his impetuous anger had sallied out of Sandal Castle to certain destruction. The seventeen-year-old William, sixth Lord Harington was killed, leaving only a newly born baby, Cecile, heiress to the barony of Harington. His father-in-law Salisbury was killed, and so was his father Sir William Bonville. His grandfather, Lord Bonville, was beheaded in the following year. Of the senior branch of the Harington family only the agèd Lady of Porlock and a tiny girl remained.

Sir Thomas was mortally wounded and died on the day following the battle, knowing that his eldest son John lay dead on the field. His head was set up on one of the gates of the city of York. Here it kept company with the heads of the good Duke of York, Salisbury, and York's young son Rutland whom Lord Clifford stabbed. It was Clifford's little joke that the Protector of England looked down on his city from the Micklegate Bar, crowned with a crown of paper and straw. But when the Queen's army moved south, plundering and slaughtering, London closed its gates to her. It opened them instead to the son of the Duke of York, Rutland's brother. In the great hall at Westminster where the first Lord John had been knighted with Edward II, this young man was arrayed in royal robes and acclaimed King Edward IV.

The new sovereign of the legitimate dynasty of York possessed energy, courage, and skill. He moved north, killing 'bloody Clifford' on the way, and inflicting on the Lancastrians at Towton as great a slaughter as the Yorkists had suffered at Wakefield. When he reached York he took down the heads of his father and his dead supporters, and substituted those of the Lancastrians that he had carried with him from Towton for this purpose. The elegance of medieval war was wearing threadbare. But while the provisions that Sir Thomas had made for the burial of his body were never carried out, his head was at least taken to where his body lay at Pontefract.

51

It was a rewarding time for those who had suffered so much in the Yorkist cause, provided, that is, that they were still alive to receive the rewards. In the Harington family the survivors of Wakefield were separated from their patrimony by the claims of tiny female heirs.

When the widow of William, sixth Lord Harington, and mother of Cecile remarried, it required a special Act of Parliament to solve the problems of inheritance involved. 'Considering that where Richard late Earl of Salisbury paid great and notable sums of money to William late Lord Bonville, and to William late Lord Harington the elder, for a marriage had between William Bonville the late Lord Harington the younger, cousin and heir to the said William late Lord Harington the elder, and cousin and heir apparent to the said late Lord Bonville, and Katherine, daughter of the said late Earl ...' It provides illuminating details of a marriage 'had' in the Middle Ages, with its exhaustive concern over property; 'the Lordship and Manor of Aldingham with the appurtenance, the Manor and Castle of Gleaston with the appurtenance' and all sorts of other 'Lands and Tenements, Rents and Services'. The tragedy of baby Cecile, deprived of her five male forebears at a single blow and left only with this snowball of accumulating property, is lost in the statute. It shows more clearly in the fate of her great-grand-daughter and ultimate heir, Lady Jane Grey.

There was a grave risk that the entire property of the junior branch also would pass out of the family, as most of it had come in to the family, through female heirs. When that *notabilis armiger* Sir Thomas died at Wakefield with his eldest son Sir John, the ultimate heirs were John's daughters Ann and Elizabeth, five and four years old. On the other hand Sir Thomas had outlived his eldest son by a day on the field of Wakefield, and it might be thought that this day was long enough to establish his second son Sir James as the new heir. It was long enough for Sir James. He took possession of Hornby Castle without loss of time and proceeded to fortify it. England was entering a period of violence and confusion, and the violence is exemplified by Sir James Harington's life, and the confusion by the train of mysteries into which the history of his family is suddenly plunged.

These mysteries cannot be perfectly solved by the documents at present known to exist. On the other hand, the evidence of these documents is sufficient to cast grave doubt on an interpretation of

52

Sir James Harington that represents him simply as a villain. And the character of Sir James is not merely of interest to a history of the Harington family. He became a close associate and finally remained a loyal supporter of Richard III, so that his character and career are relevant to the question, whether King Richard was, or was not, the victim of the most spectacular act of defamation in English history.

The surviving evidences for the facts of Sir James Harington's career, between the battle of Wakefield in 1460 and the battle of Bosworth in 1485, are these.

Among the Patent Rolls is enrolled a grant from Edward IV in 1461, to Geoffrey Middelton Esquire, of the custody and marriage of Ann, one of the daughters and heirs of Sir John Harington, a minor and in the King's custody. There is no evidence concerning the custody of her sister Elizabeth at this time.

Sir Thomas had conveyed his properties to trustees before the battle of Wakefield. On 12 March 1463 a charter of the Archbishop of York, Sir John Hudleston and others delivered to Sir James possession of all messuages, etc., in Brierley, Calthorn, Shafton, South Hindeley, and Cudworth, according to the form and effect of a charter already made to him. From 1463 Sir James Harington was indisputable lord of Brierley in Yorkshire.[21]

In 1465 King Henry's inexhaustible queen tried to recover the throne, and left him wandering in England, a fugitive. For some time he was given hospitality near Appleby; and at Furness he may have worn the monk's cowl that suited him so much better than a crown. Sir James rode in search of him, and discovered the poor King at Waddington Hall in Yorkshire. John Tempest and two Talbots were with Sir James, but it was he who received the chief reward, and who is therefore likely to have played the chief part.

King Henry's hosts made a determined stand against the intruders while Henry escaped to the woods. But soon he was captured and carried, his feet bound to the stirrups of his horse, to the Tower of London. 'Till he came to Furness Fells he was never known but there he was known and taken, and upon Saint James's Eve he was brought to the Tower of London.' Gregory Skinner, who had mentioned Sir James's father by name among the dukes and earls at Wakefield, omits from this pitying reference the part played by the son.

It was set out, however, in an Act of Parliament of 19 July 1465.

Sir James was rewarded with the castle, manor, and lordship of Thurland, and with other lands in the counties of Lancaster and York. In 1466 the Patent Rolls contain a grant to Sir James Harington of Brierley of £340 from the issues of the county of York.

Meanwhile Sir James's two nieces were growing up, and the succession to the lordship of Hornby remained unsettled. In 1468 two commissions were appointed under the royal seal, one to inquire what lands the late Sir Thomas Harington had held at his death and who was his heir, the other to make like inquiries concerning his eldest son, the late Sir John. And one Henry Sotehill was able to show in Chancery that Ann and Elizabeth, Sir Thomas's grand-daughters, were found at these inquests to be his heirs. They were aged eight and nine at the date of the inquests, and it was shown in Chancery that they were being kept by their uncle Sir James and by Sir John Hudleston. Sir James had held their manors and lands since their father's death without title or right. Sotehill's prayer in Chancery contains an endorsement dated November 29, to the effect that Sir James and his cousin Hudleston were committed by the Chancellor prisoners to the Fleet prison. It was a very different association from that of their two grandfathers at Agincourt.

There is another surviving document which bears on this episode; but it is undated. It is framed in the form of a petition to the King by the two girls against their uncle Sir James, who 'took the said complainants and them kept as prisoners contrary to their wills, in divers places by long space, intending the utter destruction and disinheritance of the said complainants until the time they were by your high commandment delivered out of his keeping into the keeping of the Lord Stanley. Also the said James hath occupied the said castle'. This is the disputed castle of Hornby.[11]

Such were the circumstances, as the scanty records reveal them, in which King Edward IV granted to Lord Stanley the custody of Ann and Elizabeth Harington of Hornby.

It need hardly be said that Thomas, Lord Stanley, was the girls' cousin. All the great families in the north were related, and not a few of them descended from the numerous progeny of John of Gaunt's sheriff, Sir Nicholas Harington. Lord Stanley was the eldest grandson of Sir Nicholas's daughter Isabel, wife of Sir John Stanley. Up to the battle of Wakefield the Haringtons and the Stanleys had been equal in power in Lancashire, and for more than a generation before the battle the two families had dominated the representation of the county in Parliament with their relatives and dependants. The Stanleys now prepared to monopolize that power and to seize, by perfidy and poison, by legal forms and legal fictions, the entire inheritance of the Haringtons.

The learned Hunter wrote in his *History of Doncaster*: 'no person could have been chosen who could have protected more effectually any rights of these young ladies, than Lord Stanley, the most potent man in the county of Lancaster. The grant of a wardship usually led to marriage, and Sir James Harington saw the fortunes of the great house of Stanley united with those of his nieces, Ann the elder being married to Edward Stanley, a younger son of Lord Stanley, and Elizabeth the younger to John Stanley of Hornford, a brother's son'. His account assumes that the Stanleys did protect the rights of Ann and Elizabeth against a wicked uncle. It assumes that the little girls were themselves the authors of the prayers for deliverance from Sir James's hands. The profitable perfidy of the Stanleys at Bosworth and the fatal loyalty of the Haringtons have helped to confirm this interpretation. The wicked uncle perished with the wicked king. The saviour of the heiresses triumphed with Henry Tudor, the saviour of the nation.

The evidence that has already been given for this interpretation is certainly formidable, and it is reinforced by something that happened in 1473. In that year it was found necessary to commission Richard, Duke of Gloucester, the King's brother, to take into the King's possession all castles, lordships, manors, and lands of the late Sir Thomas Harington and his son Sir John, belonging to the King by reason of the minority of the heiresses, and to remove Sir James Harington and his brother Sir Robert, who had taken possession. The lesson of the Fleet had proved inadequate.

Sir James had shared his previous misfortune with his cousin Hudleston: this one he shared with his younger brother, Sir Robert. Robert, the third son of Sir Thomas Harington, had married Isabel, heir to Sir William Balderstone, in 1461, which brought to him among other blessings the presentation to the rich church of Badsworth. Sir Robert was knighted on the field of Tewkesbury in 1471, and how active he was with his brother in local government is reflected in the commissions of oyer and terminer, commissions of array, commissions of the peace. Now Sir James, now Sir Robert, represented the county of Lancashire in Parliament. Presumably the brothers confined themselves to such legitimate pursuits after the lesson of 1473, for three years later

55

Sir James received a pardon for all offences committed by him, and all debts, fines, and amercements due from him to the King. He was described as of Brierley, late of Hornby, as though his pretensions to Hornby were not altogether without foundation, but were now extinguished. In 1480 he was licensed to build walls and towers with stone, lime, and sand around his manors of Farleton and Brierley, and to crenellate them, and to impark all his lands of Farleton and Brierley.

A particular family circumstance linked the two surviving sons of Sir Thomas Harington. Sir James Harington of Brierley possessed no legitimate son; only a bastard son John. Sir Robert had an only son James. And although Sir James had daughters, he was determined that what remained of the possessions of the house of Farleton should descend to a legitimate male heir. Perhaps it was the lesson of his nieces that had influenced this decision. On 12 July 1482 he made the only will that has survived, on the eve of an expedition against the Scots. In it he left all his property to his bastard son John for life, and then to his brother Sir Robert and Sir Robert's lawful heirs. It is the fate of the bastard John, some time after 1482, which first brings into question Hunter's interpretation of the behaviour of the Stanleys.[22]

The Stanleys had secured the castle and honour of Hornby when they obtained the wardship of the two heiresses, established the title of these girls to the property, and married them to Stanleys. But one of these Stanley husbands died, and his widow Elizabeth remarried a Beaumont. If her title were as secure as the Stanleys had maintained, then it was now lost to them. This is what Elizabeth wrote to her second husband Beaumont about the family of her first husband. The letter is undated, but it must have been written after 1482 when her cousin the bastard John was alive, because he was named in his father's will of that date.

'Right worshipful Sir, in my best manner that I can I recommend me to you, desiring heartily to hear of your welfare . . . Sir, I would advise you and my cousin John Harington's man be in no jeopardy of sickness to get all the evidence of him that you can before Sir James comes up, for he is purposed to come hastily. Also Sir James and the parson of Sladeborne think that my cousin John was poisoned, and that his servant was hired to do it by my brother Sir Edward [Stanley], and if it so be, then he forfeits all. Moreover I sent Nettleton for Sir James to meet me and speak with me, and he said that he would come home to me, and if he so do before we leave, you shall have word . . . Sir, pray you to keep out of all jeopardy and to make much of yourself, and the Holy Trinity have you in his blessed keeping . . .'[22]

The bastard John has apparently just died in mysterious circumstances, and Elizabeth is prepared to believe that her sister Ann's husband, Sir Edward Stanley, of the family that saved her from her wicked uncle, poisoned him. She has turned to her wicked uncle Sir James for counsel. A letter to her from the parson of Sladeborne throws further light on the real situation. This letter too is undated, but since it refers to Richard III, it must have been written after that King's accession in 1483.

'To my right worshipful and most heartily well beloved good Mistress Beaumont be these delivered. Mistress, as heartily as I can I recommend me to you, and of your good mind in all things I am right glad. And whereas you say Master Sir Edward Stanley has shewn that King Edward made award betwixt you and your uncle's title, King Edward made never none award, nor none such can be shewn under seals of authority. It was so laboured that King Richard commanded a note to be drawn, and caused the Chancellor of the Duchy to examine the true value of all the manors and livelihood the which your father was lawfully possessed and died seised of; and yet, this notwithstanding, King Richard never made award betwixt you and your uncles. And where you desire evidence of certain places, you know Sir James Harington has them . . .'[23]

The motives that the Stanleys might have had for poisoning the bastard John, their sudden concern over Sir James of Brierley's title to Hornby, these are inexplicable except on the assumption that the letters referring to them were both written after the battle of Bosworth in 1485. On such an assumption (and they are undated) they become horribly significant.

What happened at Bosworth is both well known and highly controversial. Richard III, the last Plantagenet king, was defeated and killed there by Henry Tudor. Henry belonged to an ancient family of minor Welsh chieftains, and possessed no claim to the throne that would not have been laughed out of a court of law. But he made an oath, in France, that he would place Elizabeth Plantagenet, sister of the 'Princes in the Tower', upon the throne and marry her. In the hour of victory he broke his promise, and only on the petition of Parliament did he take Elizabeth of York for his consort. It is thought by some that Richard III

57

murdered her brothers, the last male Plantagenet heirs; by others that Henry VII committed the crime and laid the guilt on his predecessor.

Such were the rivals who met on the field of Bosworth in 1485. On the side of Richard III were arrayed Sir James Harington and his younger brother Sir Robert, and Sir Robert's sole heir James. The Stanleys were on the same side, and glancing at their private rivals it cannot have escaped them how much they might gain if Richard were defeated. All the Haringtons who stood between the Stanleys and the properties they had so long coveted were present on Richard's side — all, that is, except Sir James's son John, who might have to be removed by some other means. At an opportune moment in the battle the Stanleys deserted the last Plantagenet king, and joined the victorious forces of Henry Tudor.

There is only one eye-witness account of the battle of Bosworth, the ballad known as 'The Most Pleasant Song of Lady Bessie'. There is no surviving transcription of it earlier than 1600, but on two facts that are important to this history the scholars are agreed. The original ballad must have been composed by someone who was present at the battle, and the person described in such heroic terms as Sir William Harington must be Sir James or his brother Sir Robert. But perhaps the irony is unconscious in the passage in which a Harington pleads with King Richard to spare the life of a Stanley.

> A knight to the King did appear,
> Good Sir William Harington,
> Says, 'let him have his life a while
> Till we have the father, the uncle, and the son.
>
> 'We shall have them soon on the field,
> The father, the uncle, the son, all three;
> Then may you deem them with your mouth,
> What kind of death that they shall die'.
>
> But a block on the ground was cast,
> Thereupon the Lord's head was laid;
> An axe over his head can stand,
> And out of passion it was braid [flourished].
>
> He saith, 'there is no other boot
> But that thou, Lord, needs must die'.
> Harington heard it, and was full woe
> When it would no better be.

> He saith, 'our ray breaketh on every side:
> We put our field in jeopardy'.
> Then they took up the Lord alive;
> King Richard did him never see.

Having succeeded in saving the life of a Stanley, Harington is next reported to have tried to save King Richard's life.

> A knight to King Richard can say,
> It was good Sir William Harington,
> He saith, 'we are like all here
> To the death soon to be done:
>
> 'There may no man their strokes abide,
> The Stanleys' dints they been so strong;
> Ye may come in another time,
> Therefore methinks ye tarry too long.
>
> 'Your horse is ready at your hand,
> Another day ye may your worship win,
> And to reign with royalty,
> And wear your crown, and be our King'.

But King Richard remained to face death in the field, and if Sir James did not remain with him, he galloped off into the realms of legend from which his ancestor Osulf had first emerged, just three centuries before.

At the Parliament of Leicester, held in the first year of King Henry VII's reign, Sir James Harington and his brother Sir Robert were attainted. Sir Edward Stanley, whose wife Ann Harington had died in 1480, was granted by the new King the castle, manor, and lands of Hornby, the manors of Farleton, the manor of Brierley, and all other manors and benefices 'which formerly belonged to James Harington, knight, in the counties aforesaid which by reason of the forfeiture and attainder of the said James are in our hands'.

There was to be no limit to the infamy of the Stanleys. Before the battle of Bosworth they had laid claim to Hornby through the child heiresses with whom they united themselves in marriage. Sir James Harington was accused of trying to appropriate the inheritance of these heiresses, to whom the Stanleys played the part of saviours. When Elizabeth's first husband died and she married a Beaumont, the role of saviour became exactly half as rewarding as it had been before. But after Sir James Harington's attainder there was a remedy. If Sir James could now be represented as the legitimate lord of Hornby until his forfeiture, the whole property might pass under the new King's grant to Sir Edward Stanley. And this is what Sir Edward Stanley contrived.

It is made abundantly clear by the inquisition which reported on the property held by Sir Edward Stanley, Lord Mounteagle, at his death in 1523. This consisted entirely of the vast estates belonging to Sir James when he was convicted of high treason. 'He was then seised in tail male of the castle or manor of Hornby and of 200 messuages or cottages, 2000 acres of land, 200 acres of meadow, 300 acres of pasture . . .' So the impressive catalogue continues. It was not without reason that Elizabeth Beaumont wrote as she did of her brother-in-law.

It was Sir Edward Stanley's father, created Earl of Derby by the grateful King, who had obtained the guardianship of the Harington heiresses. Derby himself extracted only one perquisite from the Harington properties; the presentation to the rich church of Badsworth. Here a Stanley rector would soon be celebrating the hero of Flodden in indifferent verse.

This presentation was a part of the Balderstone property that came to Sir Robert Harington at his marriage, and the fortunes of Bosworth did not place it immediately at the disposal of the Stanleys. But Sir Robert's son took the step that completed the ruin of his house. He rose in Lambert Simnel's rebellion, and in the third year of Henry VII's reign he too was attainted.[14]

He had been treated with leniency by the new King. A special pardon after the battle of Bosworth had provided that he might acquire land and bequeath it as though his blood had suffered no corruption by his father's attainder. He was admitted, through a commission, to the King's grace, took an oath of allegiance, and gave sureties for his good behaviour. On 17 August 1486 this last Sir James Harington, late of Brierley, was granted restitution of his properties.

It was not to be so, once they had fallen into the hands of a Stanley. By 1503 Sir James occupied a position altogether novel for a Harington. He was Dean of York, 'as sorrowful and repentant as any creature may be'. So he proclaimed in the Act of Parliament which enabled him to inherit the property of his mother 'Dame Isabel, late the wife of Sir Robert Harington Knight, father to your said suppliant'. But the statute contained the proviso that nothing contained in it should be prejudicial to the interests of the Earl of Derby or of Sir Edward Stanley, and Derby had already obtained the Balderstone living of Badsworth.[25]

So one of England's noble houses cemented its fortunes. Sir Edward Stanley, Lord Mounteagle, rebuilt Hornby Castle, and nothing of the castle of the Haringtons remained visible until the present owner of Hornby restored to view the base of the original keep. The manorial documents before 1500 seem to have been destroyed. It is as though every trace of the Haringtons had been deliberately erased in the valley of the Lune.

At Brierley there is no trace of them either. The village may or may not contain portions of farm buildings that once belonged to the medieval manor. But in the parish church at Felkirk, across the fields of tarnished corn surrounded by the slag-heaps of innumerable coal mines, no Harington found rest. From Brierley the Haringtons were beckoned by their lands in Lancashire, and the menace of the Stanleys. And as they galloped over to the north-west their horses' hooves were treading an underground fortune of which they knew nothing.

As for Mounteagle, he directed that his body should lie at Hornby Priory until the new church he was building in the village should be completed. It was never finished, and his body was never translated there. The Priory vanished, and on its site now stands a farm. Mounteagle is reputed to lie beneath its midden.

Before his death his own nephew, the second Earl of Derby, added his testimonial to that of Elizabeth Beaumont, by will. 'Whereas his uncle Sir Edward Stanley Knight, Lord Mounteagle, enjoyed of his gift and grant the castle and demesnes of Hornby Castle, and other manors, for the special love, trust, and kindness he then found, and supposed he had to him, which estates he held on conditions; he now wills, that for the great unkindness he since found and does find in his uncle, and for that he has not observed or performed the said conditions, he should have none of the rents and profits thereof . . .'

This will achieved nothing, unless it could make the ghost of Sir James Harington chuckle.[26]

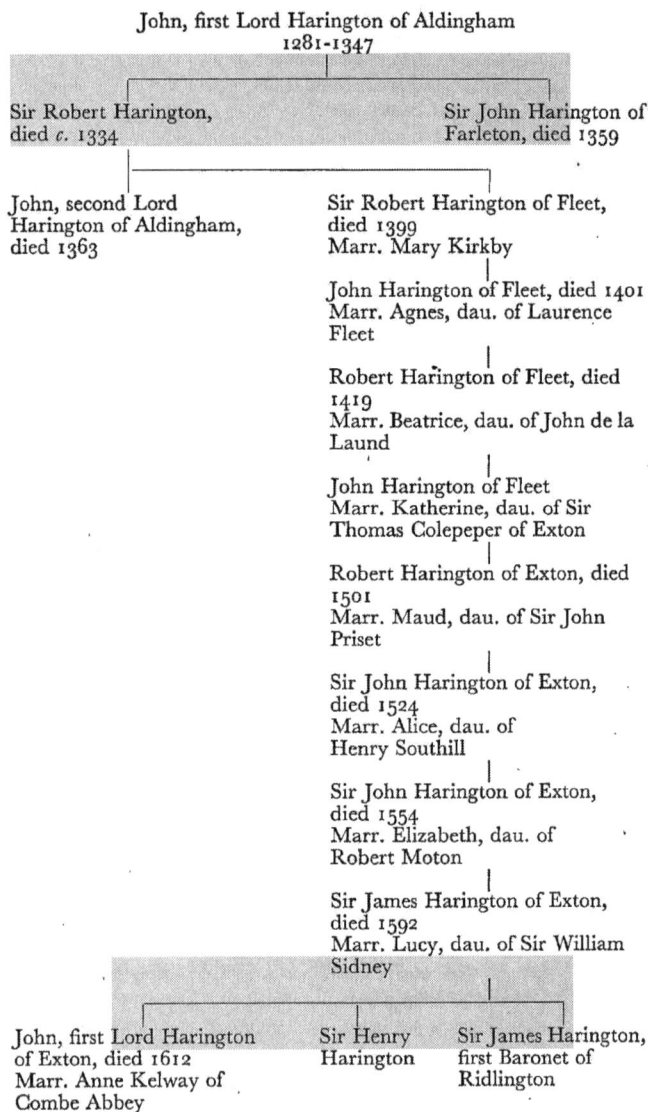

John, first Lord Harington of Aldingham
1281-1347

Sir Robert Harington,
died c. 1334

Sir John Harington of
Farleton, died 1359

John, second Lord
Harington of Aldingham,
died 1363

Sir Robert Harington of Fleet,
died 1399
Marr. Mary Kirkby

John Harington of Fleet, died 1401
Marr. Agnes, dau. of Laurence
Fleet

Robert Harington of Fleet, died
1419
Marr. Beatrice, dau. of John de la
Laund

John Harington of Fleet
Marr. Katherine, dau. of Sir
Thomas Colepeper of Exton

Robert Harington of Exton, died
1501
Marr. Maud, dau. of Sir John
Priset

Sir John Harington of Exton,
died 1524
Marr. Alice, dau. of
Henry Southill

Sir John Harington of Exton,
died 1554
Marr. Elizabeth, dau. of
Robert Moton

Sir James Harington of Exton,
died 1592
Marr. Lucy, dau. of Sir William
Sidney

John, first Lord Harington
of Exton, died 1612
Marr. Anne Kelway of
Combe Abbey

Sir Henry
Harington

Sir James Harington,
first Baronet of
Ridlington

FIVE

THE SLEEPING PARTNERS OF EXTON

IN the fertile face of modern Rutland there is little to hint how
late and slow its cultivation in the Middle Ages had been. The
relative absence of impressive medieval buildings is one of the
indications that in those days the few great men who were connected with the county were absentees, while the residents lived
modestly. In 1311, indeed, there was not a single knight resident
in the county to represent it in Parliament.

But during this century and the next two quite unrelated factors
transformed the economy of Rutland, and the status of its landowners. Sheep farming was introduced on a large scale: while
the men who prospered from it were protected by their county's
isolation from the hazards of foreign and domestic war. Such
were the Haringtons of Exton, the senior representatives of their
family after the battle of Bosworth.

While their cousins in the north were pursuing such eager and
adventurous lives, these Haringtons were content to follow the
quiet pastoral ways. They took the easy path to the summit their
more energetic cousins had assaulted in vain.

Their origins were identical to those of the Farleton branch,
only they began a generation later. John, first Lord Harington,
had given to his younger son the manor of Farleton that he
inherited from his Cansfield mother. Lord John's eldest son was
married to the heiress of Moulton, and her younger son was
likewise given a manor out of her inheritance.[17]

It was Fleet in Lincolnshire, and because Fleet contained three
manors, Robert Harington's became known as Fleet Harington.
His son John married into one of the neighbouring manors,
taking to wife the daughter of Laurence Fleet of Fleet. So the
process of settlement and accumulation began. John's son Robert
married Beatrice, the heiress of John de la Laund. The marriage
settlement, executed in 1405, is the oldest family document
remaining in the hands of their descendants today. It represents
a triumph compared with the marriage of the preceding generation, but compared with the next it was a bagatelle.[18]

The manor of Exton in Rutland descended, and still descends,

63

with the blood royal of Scotland. At the moment when Osulf entered the pages of English history, it was owned by the brother of William King of Scots. With the crown of Scotland it passed to the family of Bruce, and so to Sir Nicholas Greene, the husband of Jane Bruce. His tomb is the oldest in Exton church.· It was his great-grand-daughter Katherine Colepeper, heiress of Exton, who married the heir of Robert and Beatrice Harington.¹¹

His name was John Harington. He lived to see the death of his cousin John, fourth Lord Harington, and the extinction of the barony in the male line. He saw his cousin Sir John grow up, · heir to Hornby Castle, and saw him perish with his father at Wakefield. Compared with these, John Harington of Exton had been brought up in modest circumstances. Well may he have reflected on the vicissitudes of life when he found himself heir to the Bruces and senior representative of his house.

The little village of Exton still lives today undisturbed in its ancient tranquillity. It lies about five miles from the market town of Oakham amidst fields of arable and pasture, and considerable woodland. The village green is canopied with trees, and from it run lanes of houses built in warm weathered stone, almost all of them thatched. The church in which Sir Nicholas Greene was buried stands apart from the village, in the park of Exton Hall. Here John and Katherine Harington brought up Robert their heir.

In 1492, while his cousins were tasting the ruin that has blotted their very fates from the records of history, this Robert Harington of Exton became High Sheriff of Rutland.· He was sixth in descent from the first baron, buried in Cartmel church, and he was first of the six generations of Haringtons to hold the office of Sheriff of Rutland in unbroken succession. Robert himself was merely taking a lead for the first time in his county's affairs: it was to the sixth Harington Sheriff that the responsibility fell to raise ship-money for Charles I.

Robert became Sheriff of Rutland again in 1498, and he died in 1501. It was left to his son John to make the next advance.

First, Sir John obtained a knighthood. This may not have appeared to him a matter of great consequence, because he could not have known what part he was playing in preserving the title in the senior representative of his house for what is now over six hundred years. Secondly, Sir John became High Sheriff four times, but in this his father had set the precedent. He set one of

SIR JOHN HARINGTON, D. 1524
EXTON CHURCH

his own when, in 1517, he purchased the neighbouring manor of
Horn. Another manor adjoining Exton was settled on his daughter
Alice, at her marriage, by her father-in-law. But the significance
of the Horn transaction is that it was the first of the series of
purchases with which the Haringtons supplemented their marriage
settlements, to build up one of the largest landed fortunes in
England.[18]

Finally, Sir John Harington of Exton was buried at his death
in 1524 in Exton church, and his monument there is the earliest
after that of Sir Nicholas Greene. It is also of a beauty com-
parable with that of the tomb of John, fourth Lord Harington at
Porlock, and of John, first Lord Harington at Cartmel. Shafts of
light from the unstained window by the south door gleam on the
white alabaster effigies of John and his wife, he in plate armour,
she in hood and full length gown. John's head rests on a mantled
helmet surmounted by the collared lion's head of the Harington
crest, and his feet are supported by a dog, marvellously carved.
About the feet of his wife her gown lies lightly in innumerable
folds. There are sixteenth-century tombs of greater magnificence,
but not of more arresting art.

Sir John Harington who succeeded his father in 1524 took the
last decisive step in the dangerous road to greatness. He too
became four times Sheriff of Rutland. He too married an heiress,
Elizabeth Moton. But he also left the pleasant shades of Exton,
to try his fortune at the court of Henry VIII. And he certainly
found it there: the only question is how he did so.

There is a week at the end of August 1542 when the activities
of Sir John can still be seen in meticulous detail: all, that is,
except those that involved the public moneys committed to his
charge. It was the month in which Henry VIII opened his war
against Scotland, and the veteran soldier Thomas, Earl of Rutland
went to the Scottish border as warden of the marches. The council
appointed to assist him consisted of Sir John Markham, of a
family that had boasted kinship with the Plantagenets, and John
Uvedale, whose more uncertain origins were compensated by his
services at Flodden and during the Pilgrimage of Grace. These
are the men whose signatures are grouped round the name of
John Harington on the reports written to the King from August
25 to the end of the month.

Their first concern was to discover the fate of Sir Robert Bowes,
whose raid into Teviotdale earlier in the month had ended in

disaster for the English. At nine a.m. on the twenty-fifth they wrote to the King that Bowes was apparently a prisoner of the Scots, and that they were about to hasten north from Darneton to Newcastle. Presently they left, and arrived in Newcastle at seven p.m. the same evening.[20]

It was to the council that they wrote the following morning (Rutland phrased his reports in the first person singular, though they are all signed by Harington, Markham, and Uvedale): 'Please it your good and honourable lordships to be advertised that yesterday in the morning I despatched a post from Darneton with letters unto the King's Majesty concerning the occurrences on the borders, and that day I made such diligence as I arrived here at Newcastle at 7 o'clock at night.

'The same day I received letters at Darneton from the King's said Majesty of the 22nd of August instant, and have at length with good advisement considered and pondered the sundry devices, commandments, and charges contained in the same and shall apply myself with all diligence possible to put the effects thereof in . . . with such money as I have here already. But to have all things done, set forth, and ordered as his Majesty's pleasure is expressed in his said letters greater sums of money, as your lordships can well consider, be requisite to be had and sent hither with speed, for furniture of all the contents in the said letters expressed. And in the meantime I shall be doing with such money as I have here already until I know his Majesty's further pleasure therein. . . .

'All kinds of corn and grain be very dear in these parts, wherefore provision of the same must needs be made out of hand in other places and sent unto Berwick, or unto some other ports, creeks, and havens near thereunto; or else the garrisons there, and also such as be in my company (being once repaired thither) shall not be able to continue there any time without great danger to the town, because a great number of men will consume and spend most part of all the victual as well at Berwick as at Carlisle and in other places thereabouts, if they shall suddenly repair thither without good and great provision made before for the same. And here in Newcastle they be so destitute of grain that they cannot undertake to make provision thereof in any short time, and no provision is yet come hither of any such grain from the south . . .'[21]

Henry VIII possessed in full measure the Tudor flair for

successful personal rule, and an important part of this was his skill in choosing the agents of his government. All that is known (rather than guessed) about Sir John Harington's career indicates that King Henry was exercising this skill when he entrusted the responsibilities of treasurer to Sir John. He possessed financial acumen to the degree that easily gives rise to charges of malpractice.

'By the King. Trusty and well beloved, we greet you well. And where we have appointed you by virtue of our sundry warrants, directed to divers our treasurers and servants, to receive the sum of three score thousand pounds sterling; our pleasure and commandment is that you shall order and employ the said money in manner and form following. First, you shall of the same content and pay presently all such sums of money as you shall be commanded to disbourse by the letters of our right trusty and right entirely well beloved cousin and councillor the Duke of Norfolk' — it was he who had mobilized the north in the previous year for the Scots war — 'or by the letters of any four of our private council attendant on our person, for provisions of corn and all other kinds of victuals, for necessaries and for conduct, coats, and wages of such horsemen and footmen as we now send to our borders foranent Scotland, for the furniture and defence of the same, which payments to be so made, their several bills as is aforesaid with these presents shall be your warrant and discharge against us.

'And our further pleasure is that putting the rest of the three score thousand pounds which shall remain unpaid here, in order to be carried towards our said borders, you shall with the same repair to our town of York, and there deliver it with the bills of all the prests for coats and conduct, by you before paid, to our trusty and right well beloved councillor Sir John Harington, knight, whom we have appointed to be our treasurer for the payment of our garrison men of war now sent to the said borders. And the other for provisions of victuals and necessaries you shall reserve upon your charge, for that we have appointed you to receive the provisions to be made upon the said prests, and to see them uttered to our profit and renewed as you shall be commanded by our cousin the Duke of Norfolk, we bearing all the adventure in the conveyance of the same.

'And further we will that you shall content and pay the remain of all such money as shall come to your hands of the sale of the said victuals and necessaries, when you shall not be commanded eftsones to renew the said provisions, to the hands of the said Sir John Harington, for the payment of our said garrison, whose bill shall be your discharge in that behalf.'[32]

This instruction from the King does not belong to the week in which Sir John Harington hurried north to Newcastle with the Earl of Rutland, but it is important to an understanding of his actions there.

The constant preoccupations of the warden of the marches were the shortage of food along that ravaged frontier, and the uncertain news from beyond it, following Bowes's defeat. The reports he sent south this week are ominous with the approaching consequences of Henry's savage war against the Scots, the victory of Solway Moss, and the devastations by Hertford. He wrote on his second night in Newcastle:

'Please it your most excellent Majesty to be advised that this present night at 11 of the clock I have received letters and other news and occurrents of the borders and out of Scotland sent unto me by Sir William Ure, knight, all which I do send unto your Majesty here enclosed, to the intent your said Majesty may at length perceive the same. And having with me here at this time John Horsley and Robert Collingwood, I have communed with them touching the state of your borders and country of Northumberland, who plainly affirm unto me that there is such great scarcity of all manner of grain, as the like thereof hath not been seen in all their lives. And further, they do affirm that the country is not able to furnish themselves with grain, and that the poor people do live in such penury as they never saw before this time, for want of corn; of which thing, according to my most bounden duty, I can no less do but to advertise your Majesty.

'And as concerning the late mischance happened unto Sir Robert Bowes and to his company, I cannot yet ascertain your Majesty of the truth thereof, because of sundry varieties of reports of that matter. And thus Almighty God evermore have you in His most holy governance, my most singular good and gracious sovereign lord. Written at your town of Newcastle-upon-Tyne the 26th day of August at 12 of the clock at midnight.

'Your most humble and obedient subjects and servants Thomas Rutland

John Harington   John Markham   Jo. Uvedale.'[33]

Rutland did his best to provision Berwick, 'until such time as your Majesty's other provisions may be arrived there, the coming whereof shall be a great relief and comfort'. He also wrote to York for 'four hundred men out of Yorkshire to revive and renew the said borders again'. He was reporting these actions to the King on the afternoon of the twenty-eighth when there arrived at Newcastle 'one Ross, an herald of Scotland, who had letters addressed as well unto the ambassador of Scotland now with your Majesty, as unto your council at York, which letters so addressed to your said council at York I was bold, for many considerations, to open and look upon; and thinking the same necessary to be seen by your Majesty, I do send it also here enclosed unto the same your Majesty, and not unto your said council to York . . .'

After the four guardians of the border had signed this report they added a postscript on a separate sheet. Never did dry postscript reveal more clearly the things left unsaid, the expectation and uncertainty, the conversations broken off and resumed, the sound of horses' hooves in the courtyard that promised fresh news.

'The foresaid Scottish herald cometh not by post, but on his own horse, and said unto me here that one of the causes of his coming at this time unto your Majesty is to obtain a safe-conduct for two ambassadors to be sent forthwith out of Scotland unto your said Majesty. And also he showed me one packet of letters addressed unto their ambassadors now attending upon your said Majesty.

'Upon the receipt of Sir William Ure's letters concerning the entry of John Carr of Wark, I have sent thither one hundred men under the leading of Thomas Waterby and of Nicholas Tempest . . .'[34]

While Rutland or one of his councillors was dictating those words, Carr himself was writing them the warning which they forwarded to the King the following day: 'so far as I can get wit or knowledge by mine acquaintance in Scotland, that the first journey that the Earl of Huntly makes into England will be to lay siege to the King's castle of Wark. Wherefore I humbly beseech your good lordship that I might have some aid to maintain the King's grace's castle . . .' Carr's letter is written in his own hurried hand, and his spelling and grammar contrast sharply with those of the warden's reports.[35]

Rutland and his lieutenants had moved on to Morpeth by the time they forwarded Carr's letter to the King the next evening.

'. . . This day in the morning I received a letter from the said
John Carr, which at his return he wrote unto me; and I do send
the same herewith enclosed unto your lordships, by the tenor
whereof your lordships may perceive of what good courage he is
to keep the said house of Wark. And to enforce and encourage
him so to do I have granted unto him his fifty men in wages there,
such as he will name and appoint for the better defence of the
said castle.' At the same time Rutland reported that the ordnance
of the King of Scots was now only three miles from Wark.[16]

Two days later Rutland was at Alnwick. 'Please it your good
and honourable lordships to be advertised, that yesterday in my
journey from Morpeth hitherwards divers and many gentlemen
of these parts repaired unto me. And at my coming hither I
further consulted with them, not only for the bestowing of part
of my train in sundry houses in the county of Northumberland
which I have already done by their advice, as appeareth by a
schedule here enclosed, but also I have given straight charge and
commandment in the King's Majesty's name to every of the
captains of the said retinue, and also unto the gentlemen of the
county of Northumberland that they shall study, devise, and apply
themselves and all their forces only for defence of the border's
peace and people there, without seeking any means or ways to
revenge, like as it is contained in your letters . . .'

Such were the irregular forces that gathered to rout the Scots
at Solway Moss in November, when they entered England to
revenge Norfolk's destructive raid into Scotland in October. And
there is another passage of this dispatch from Alnwick that
contained a portent for the future. King Henry's costly wars were
emptying his treasury, and he had resorted to further debasement
of the coinage.

'Finally, my lords, you shall understand that there is sent
hither at this present a great number of French crowns and ducats,
of sundry strange coins whereof a great number be broken work,
and also do lack weight, some 12d., some 10d., some 8d., and
some 6d. And the people of the country being poor and destitute
of silver, and not acquainted with any such strange gold, do make
very much refusal of the same. The poor soldiers on the other side
have uttered a great sum of them, to their no little loss and
detriment . . .'[17]

The curtain falls again on this brief, eventful week of over four
hundred years ago in which a Harington is to be seen in the same

places, and playing the same kind of part, as so many of his name had done before him. Sir John was the first of the Haringtons of Exton to do so. As he travelled about the north he cannot have failed to find his family's past crowding about him, and to find the traditions that lingered on at Exton confirmed at every turn. And if he had time to ponder the fate of his cousins, just sixty years before, well may he have wondered if his own exertions would lead to a similar end.

He himself saw them lead only to ever greater prosperity.

On 14 July 1543 King Henry crossed to Calais to launch his war against France, and again Sir John Harington was appointed a military treasurer. It was at this time that Sir John took John Bradford into his service, who acted in the following year as deputy-paymaster at the siege of Montreuil. Such was the association that has so gravely injured Harington's reputation: though whether justly or not will perhaps never be known.[11]

In 1547 John Bradford entered the Middle Temple as a student of the common law, and falling under the religious influence of Thomas Sampson, a fellow student, he sold all his jewellery and gave the money to the poor. He was next moved by a sermon of Latimer to restore to the Crown money he had misappropriated while he was in the service of Sir John Harington. He became a preacher, and his preaching was commended by Knox. On the succession of Queen Mary he was thrown into the Tower, where he lodged in the same room with Cranmer, Ridley, and Latimer. Ridley testified: 'I thank God heartily that ever I was acquainted with our dear brother Bradford.' So he advanced in sanctity until he suffered the martyrdom related by Foxe.

But Thomas Sampson lived to become Dean of Christ Church, and to write the preface to the *Two Notable Sermons* of John Bradford which were published in 1574. In this preface Sampson took the trouble to state, long after Sir John Harington's death, that Bradford had committed the fraud of which he later repented without the knowledge of his master. And Strype, drawing on his enormous collection of Tudor documents in the following century, agreed with this verdict.

There the matter might be allowed to rest, but for a piece of evidence that appears to contradict it. Bradford was interrogated by Bishop Gardiner, created Lord High Chancellor in 1553, and as will appear in a later chapter Gardiner had a particular interest in the name of John Harington. The *Examination of Bradford* was

71

printed in 1561, and in it appears the statement of the martyr that he never deceived his master. This could be interpreted to mean that Harington collaborated in his fraud without being smitten later by a tender conscience. And it has recently been shown by a historian that Harington bought numerous estates that he can be presumed to have paid for out of the public money he had misappropriated.¹⁹

Such charges are nothing new. They were made at the time. Thomas Cromwell the parvenu was suspected of bribery and embezzlement on a scale that left men astonished at the smallness of his treasure at his execution. Surrey the aristocrat was driven to protest 'that Henry of Surrey was never for singular profit corrupted, nor never yet bribe closed his hand'. It is not easy to define corruption in the age that saw the abolition of the monasteries and the building of Knole, Hatfield, and Holdenby. But it is possible to relate the dates of Exton's enlargement to those of Sir John Harington's brief tenure of a public office.

Sir John's father had shown, in purchasing the manor of Horn in 1517, that such a luxury could be afforded by a fortune derived entirely from land. In 1539, while Sir John filled the unremunerative post of Esquire of the Royal Body, he bought from Lord Zouche the manor of Clipsham, and from the Crown the manor of Pickworth Stocking, formally the property of Oulston Priory. After Sir John had handled public money in the north of England and in France, he purchased the manor of Kettlethorpe in 1546, and in 1549 a third share of the manor of Burley. The evidence that his fortune sprang from the perquisites of office rather than a rich patrimony in land is no more impressive than that.²⁰

After the death of Henry VIII, the patent rolls of his young son Edward VI show Sir John busy again in the local offices that Haringtons had filled for so many centuries. There are the commissions of oyer and terminer, the commissions of the peace, the commissions to make inquisition post mortem. Only one commission recalled his previous employment. He was appointed with Sir Hugh Poulett to survey the state of the new king's towns, marches, castles, and fortresses in the parts beyond the sea, and, conferring with the deputies and councillors there, to take order for the safety of these towns and castles. In 1551 he was commissioned to inquire into the rising price of corn 'by the insatiable greediness of divers covetous persons'. It was perhaps his last public duty to make an inventory of all church goods, plate, jewels, and vestments in Rutland, and compare it with former inventories, to judge how thorough had been the work of Reformation in his county.

In 1553 he died, not at Exton, but in London. 'The 28th day of August died Sir John Harington, knight, of Rutlandshire, within St Ellens, Bishopgate Street. And from that day that he died till he was carried into his country was mass and dirge every day sung. And Monday the 4th day of September he went into the country in a horse litter, with his standard and his pennon of arms, and after his horse ... with 4 pennons of arms borne about him, and with a goodly helmet gilt, with target, sword, and crest, and a 10 dozen of scutcheons, and 10 dozen of pencils for a hearse, and staff torches, and a hearse of wax, and a fair majesty, and the vallance gilded and fringed, and so to Ware ...' So Henry Machyn, citizen of London, saw him on his last journey home, and preserved what he saw in the diary that passed into the hands of Strype.[10]

His heir, Sir James Harington, was content to remain at Exton. It is well that he did so, for he acquired five more manors in Rutland, besides the remaining two-thirds of Burley, and if he had held a single office under the Crown he would without question have fallen a prey to the modern economic historian with a theory. In the office of Rutland's sheriff, which he held three times, he is safe.

He married Lucy, daughter of Sir William Sidney of Penshurst, Sir Philip's grandfather. After their death their son commissioned Nicholas Stone to build the second Harington monument in Exton church to their memory. And their inscription on it is a sufficient record of their happy and uneventful lives.

It is in Latin, beneath figures of Sir James and Lady Lucy who are kneeling, with seemly reverence, under escutcheons of the arms of Harington and Sidney.

'Here is placed James Harington of Exton, knight, with his wife Lucy, daughter of Sir William Sidney, knight, by whom he had eighteen children, of whom three sons and eight daughters entered into marriage . . .' There follows a list of impressive alliances. 'The said James and Lucy lived fifty years in wedlock. She died first in her 72nd year. He departed this life when 80 years old, in the year of man's redemption 1592, the 34th of Queen Elizabeth. Both appointed as their sole executor their son James, who to perform his duty to his parents, and to leave testimony of his filial affection to posterity, erected and dedicated this monument to their lasting memory.

'If an old family and the ancient busts on the walls, if the badge of knighthood, the reward of peculiar virtue, if a numerous offspring and the absence of all complaint throughout fifty years of married life, if late decay and a rapid death, lastly if a happy estate, and more happy than any estate, a liberal hand, untainted honour, reverence for heaven, have made either a happy life or a blessed death, they have made both life and death blessed for us. Now, when the fates have bid us to have done with life, and the stars demand our spirits, the affection of our heir has gathered our ashes and bidden them rest under this mausoleum.'

Such was Exton's contribution to the first Elizabethan age. And Sir James made the following provisions for the future prosperity of his house. At the marriage of his eldest son John to Anne Kelway, sole heiress of Combe Abbey in Warwickshire, he settled on him the great manor of Burley adjoining Exton. To his third son and sole executor, James, he gave the smaller neighbouring manor of Ridlington. Perhaps he did not care for his second son Henry, or perhaps he considered that Henry should be satisfied with the Elmsthorpe property which he obtained by marriage.

Sir James also built the great hall at Exton whose ruins still stand among the trees, not far from the church. And so it was that when Sir James Harington died in 1592 his eldest son John became owner of the three mansions of Exton, Burley, and Combe Abbey, and ranked among the best barons in England. It was high summer for the Haringtons of Exton, and their fruit was ripe to fall to the ground.

THE PHOENIX OF KELSTON

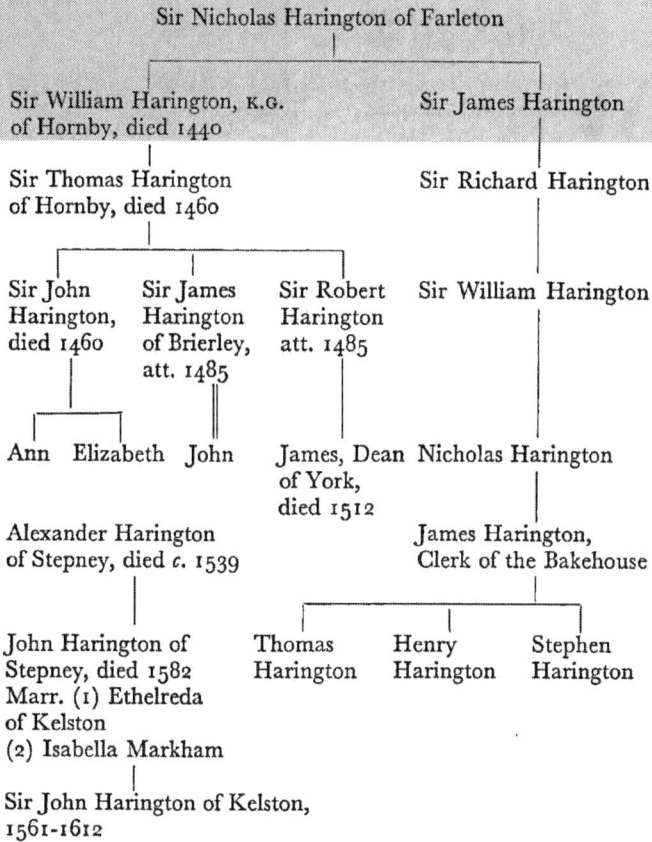

Sir Nicholas Harington of Farleton

Sir William Harington, K.G.
of Hornby, died 1440

Sir James Harington

Sir Thomas Harington
of Hornby, died 1460

Sir Richard Harington

Sir John
Harington,
died 1460

Sir James
Harington
of Brierley,
att. 1485

Sir Robert
Harington
att. 1485

Sir William Harington

Ann   Elizabeth   John

James, Dean
of York,
died 1512

Nicholas Harington

Alexander Harington
of Stepney, died c. 1539

James Harington,
Clerk of the Bakehouse

John Harington of
Stepney, died 1582
Marr. (1) Ethelreda
of Kelston
(2) Isabella Markham

Thomas
Harington

Henry
Harington

Stephen
Harington

Sir John Harington of Kelston,
1561-1612

SIX

THE PHOENIX OF KELSTON

WHEN King Henry's treasurer, Sir John Harington of Exton, rode down to London from Rutland he found that he was not the first Harington to have come to the court. A certain James Harington was there whose absence of fortune and honourable descent had earned him the now obsolete appellation 'Generosus'. James Generosus was the eldest in descent from Sir Nicholas's second son Sir James, who had fought at Agincourt. This fact was to be of the greatest significance in his life. It was Sir James's elder brother Sir William, Knight of the Garter, who had obtained Hornby Castle, *jure uxoris*, and James Generosus was now the senior living descendant of the Farleton branch only if no descendants of Sir William remained alive. All the property of this branch had passed to the King by attainder after the battle of Bosworth, and it had been granted to the Stanleys. But it had been granted to them in tail male, with reversion to the crown on the failure of a male heir.

James Generosus was present on the field of the cloth of gold, and he played a part in the wedding ceremonies of Anne Boleyn. His part was more novel even than that of his cousin the Dean of York: he was Clerk to the Bakehouse. In January 1522 the King granted him the reversion of all the possessions formerly belonging to Sir James Harington attainted, except the moiety of the manors of Hemsworth and Hornby, on the failure of the Lord Mount-eagle to beget a male heir. [41]

This grant did not assume the senior branch to be extinct: the King could grant the reversion to whom he chose. But taken in conjunction with the Dean of York's will, it raises a strong presumption. The Dean of York had died in 1512, leaving James Generosus his sole heir. And the Dean had been the ultimate heir in the will of his uncle Sir James, attainted, made at Brierley on 12 July 1482. Sir James had left his property to his bastard son John, 'and after the decease of the same John, to remain to the right heirs of the said Sir James'. It might appear that James Generosus had been granted what was his by right, as well as by the King's gift. [42]

76

It did not, however, appear so to the Tudor Heralds. It did not appear so to Queen Elizabeth, the Sidneys, the Cecils, William Camden, or finally, to Charles I. These all assumed that the senior branch of Farleton was not extinct.

It is significant that although all of these people expressed their views on the subject, and some at great length, not one of them disclosed exactly how the senior branch remained in being: that is, who gave birth to whom. It was not until over a hundred years after the battle of Bosworth that the explanation emerged which is now repeated as an unquestioned fact. James, Dean of York, according to this explanation, must have been married before he entered holy orders; he must have left a legitimate son. The statement appears among the Middlesex pedigrees in volume LXV of the Harleian Society, and its latest appearances are in Mr John Pudney's *The Smallest Room* and Mr John Buxton's *Sir Philip Sidney and the English Renaissance*, books published in 1954, and amongst the concentration of errors about the Harington family issued in *History Today* in November 1956. It is an interesting example of the method of seeking truth by reaffirmation rather than by evidence.

Both the public records and the local records contain evidence of many Haringtons living in Cumberland, Yorkshire, Lancashire, and Lincolnshire after the coming of the Tudors. Some of them can be related to the houses of Aldingham, Farleton, and Exton. Others cannot. Every family contains such off-shoots, the younger sons of younger sons, and the children born out of wedlock. But the man who is alleged to have been the Dean of York's legitimate son, although he was not mentioned in the Dean's will, lived in London. He was Alexander Harington, and he lived in a house of which all trace has now vanished, the prebend house in Stepney.

Because Alexander's son John lived there also, perhaps until his death, and left detailed rules for household servants, the size and shape of the prebend house is still possible to guess. It possessed an inner courtyard with a gate into it, which the porter was instructed to lock during meals. And an anecdote of Alexander's grandson shows it to have possessed a garden, into which guests wandered when they came to dine. Among Alexander's guests was Tallis, who taught his son to compose music in the form of the canon, and here came the Tudor poets whose manuscript poems, some written in their own hands, remained for centuries among the Harington papers. It may not have been Alexander himself

77

who entertained these poets: he died in about 1539, and the poet Surrey was not executed until 1546.

Such was the household of Alexander Harington, who possessed no landed property, and who never held office of profit, but who lived where wharves were springing up and men were making new fortunes from the Thames river trade. There is no evidence that he engaged in this trade, though a surviving bill due to a William Harington for victualling ships proves that at least one of his name was doing so.[42]

Whatever the source of his wealth, Alexander showed no concern, either over the terms of the Dean of York's will in 1512, or over the royal letters patent to James Generosus in 1522. Had he contested either, it is beyond peradventure that his descendants would have mentioned the fact.

Alexander appears to have been a sensible man, one who made his fortune in the context of the present, rather than seeking to recover it from the disastrous past, one who never flaunted the past importance of his name, but enjoyed quietly the present social advantages to which it entitled him. But this is pure surmise, for he left no evidence of his descent even to his son, and no evidence of his thoughts to posterity. But he left such a son that the Victorian prelate, writing in the *Dictionary of National Biography*, found it necessary to invest him with the offices of Sir John Harington of Exton in order to account for his position and influence at the Tudor court.

Alexander's son John Harington of Stepney, and his grandson Sir John Harington of Kelston, would require separate biographies to do them justice. In this history of their family it is necessary to confine each to a single chapter. It is also necessary to explain why they are included at all when the descent of Alexander Harington cannot be proved by historical evidence.

The nature of this uncertainty is outlined in the regrant of arms to Alexander's son in 1568: 'whereas John Harington of Kelston in the County of Somerset son of Alexander Harington, descended of a younger brother of the Haringtons of Brierley in the county of York, by right (as one abstract from such a stock and descended of such ancestors) ought to be in the number of the bearers of those tokens of honour: and yet, not knowing in what manner he ought to bear his Arms, the time being now so long since his ancestors first descended from out of the said house of Brierley . . .'[44]

There are several odd things about the wording of this grant.

78

In the first place, the time since anyone could have descended from a Harington of Brierley was a hundred years at the most. Sir Nicholas Harington had been 'of Farleton', his son Sir William 'of Hornby'. Only after the battle of Wakefield in 1460 did Sir James come to be described as 'of Brierley, late of Hornby'. And how long after that date Sir James lost Hornby, either *de jure* or *de facto*, it is impossible to be certain. So if this grant is not pure fabrication, Alexander must have been the grandson either of Sir James (who named only a bastard son John in his will) or of his brother Sir Robert (whose only known son was the Dean of York). If Alexander's father was the Dean, why was he not mentioned in the Dean's will, proved in 1512, and why did Alexander's son permit such an air of mystery to surround his descent in the grant of 1568? Whether Alexander was genuinely descended of the house of Brierley, either legitimately or illegitimately, he could hardly have been ignorant who his father was. There could only have been deliberate suppression.

The consistent claim of every one of Alexander's descendants to stem from Brierley constitutes at least a prima facie case. The possibility of legitimate descent from the Dean of York is eliminated by the terms of the Dean's will and the grant of 1568. The alternative of illegitimate descent, either from the Dean or from the bastard John who was believed to have been poisoned, is made a degree more feasible by the nature of the grant itself. This did not bestow on the Haringtons of Kelston the fret charged with a bend sinister. But the difference is scarcely less significant. It consists of a chequered border, not unlike that worn by illegitimate members of the house of Plantagenet before the Tudor usurpation. And what is perhaps more significant still is the distaste with which later Haringtons of Kelston were to regard this difference: as though it gave away a secret nowhere else disclosed.

For the time being Alexander's son John was content to have obtained official recognition as a Harington of the stock of Brierley. Sir Gilbert Dethick, Garter King-of-Arms, had committed himself. The College of Heralds, guardians of the nation's heraldry and genealogies, had issued a patent resplendent with pretentious phrases and painted blazon, a mixture of invention and hearsay. The fact was exposed ten years later when John made further inquiries as to why he had been granted the silver fret with a difference if he were genuinely descended from the Brierley branch. Sir Gilbert Dethick was still Garter King-of-Arms when his colleagues contradicted his statements in 1578.

'Whereas we Clarenceux and Norroy King-of-Arms have been earnestly requested by Thomas Baldwin, Gentleman, to make search in our records whether there are any issue of Haverington of Hornby, otherwise called Harington, left alive; these are therefore to signify, unto all those to whom these presents shall come, that we can find none, and for a further declaration of the truth thereof we have thought good to set down the true and perfect copy of the descent of the foresaid Harington of Hornby, as the same remaineth in our records.' What the records of the Heralds' college might reveal must await the time when they are sent to the Public Record Office for the proper convenience of scholar and student.[44]

The historical usefulness of the heraldic grant of 1568, and of the contradictory statement of 1578, is that they prove that Alexander concealed his own parentage from his son. Only genuine ignorance and curiosity could have inspired the inquiry of 1578. The advantages of his supposed descent had already been secured by the grant of 1568. The claim of James Generosus to be the senior descendant of the house of Farleton was doomed.

James Generosus left three sons, of whom Stephen, the youngest, bought out his two brothers, and obtained in 1563 fresh letters patent, confirming to him the reversion that had been granted to his father by Henry VIII. Stephen's panic after the heraldic grant of 1568 is reflected in his petition to Sir William Cecil the following year, preserved among the State Papers. Stephen prayed Cecil to procure the Queen's licence for him to purchase the reversion of the manors of Farleton, Brierley, and Hemsworth, or to have them otherwise assured to him. He prayed in vain.[46]

In 1570 Queen Elizabeth issued fresh letters patent in favour of Alexander's son, whose lengthy Latin explanations throw the most light in those places where they are most ambiguous. They set out the disasters of Bosworth and after. They mention the ultimate heir, James, Dean of York. They recite the grant of Henry VIII to James Generosus, Clerk of the Bakehouse, and show his descent from Sir James, younger son of Sir Nicholas of Farleton.

They then proceed either to a casual error or a deliberate

falsification. If it was deliberate, then it is worth exposing what it was intended to conceal.

When the letters have finished with the misdeeds of the Dean, have mentioned James Generosus, and have carried his antecedents back to Sir Nicholas and down the senior branch to Sir James Harington, attainted, they then refer to him as 'idem Jacobus Harington Miles'. But this is not the same Sir James as the one who became Dean of York. It is his uncle, who disappeared after Bosworth. Either this confusion was inadvertent or it was purposeful, and the only purpose it could serve is this.

One of them died in holy orders, mentioned no son in his will, and named his remote cousin James Generosus as his heir. The other named only a bastard son in his will. To claim descent impartially from either while confusing the two was to exercise a certain sensibility. It continues, as the letters slowly unfold their purpose. After stating the pedigree of James Generosus exactly, they name John of Stepney as his supplanter without even mentioning his father Alexander: 'which Letters Patent the same Stephen Harington . . . gave back and restored to us in our chancery aforesaid, there to be cancelled and utterly left . . . with intention that we should deign and grant our other Letters Patent to John Harington of Stepney'.

It will probably never be known whether Alexander's son had exploited his influence with Queen Elizabeth, or whether he compensated Stephen as Stephen had bought out the other sons of James Generosus. In either case Stephen was freed of a dangerous encumbrance. For no Harington ever succeeded in recovering those twenty-five rich manors in the north, and almost all the Haringtons of Kelston inherited from those letters of 1570 were care and bitterness.

The heraldic grant of 1568 that seems to have played such an important part in their claim to the manors remained a source of separate worry. It is as if it were only necessary to expunge the difference of the chequered border surrounding the silver fret, to establish the legitimate descent of Alexander's branch. The *Orlando Furioso* of Alexander's grandson contains a portrait of its author, dated 1591, and displaying the fret without a difference. The tombs of Alexander's descendants at Kelston, and the one in Bath Abbey, show the fret with never a difference. A small gold seal which dates from about 1550, and which remains in the family to this day, bears the fret without a difference. " Alexander's grandson did have a new seal cut, containing the difference: its impression remains on a lease of 1594, beneath his signature. But his descendants have not preserved this seal.[47]

William Camden learned of the distaste with which Alexander's descendants regarded the chequered border as soon as he was appointed Clarenceux King-of-Arms in 1597. Alexander's grandson wrote to Garter:

'June 14, 1597. Master Garter. I have dealt effectually with Master Clarenceux, who hath taken some pains in searching the pedigrees, and hath found in the right line from Nicholas Harington to James Harington, Dean of York, matches of Neville, of Egremont, and others, whereby he thinketh that not only by the adoption of my cousin Stephen (which he seemeth to make no great account of) and by the testimony of my father's patent of arms, witnessing him of the house of Brierley, and our last patent from her Majesty, that gives us the right to the Haringtons' land, I say Master Clarenceux thinketh that there may with your consent some other coat be added to this I now give, and this with some less difference, or none at all.'[48]

In this letter Alexander's grandson had suggested he was descended from the Dean of York, without precisely saying so. In 1609 he wrote, 'my ancestor Sir James Harington did once take prisoner, with his party, this poor Prince', speaking of the capture of Henry VI. It is the 'idem Jacobus Harington Miles' myth again. Alexander's grandson was in fact claiming to descend both from the uncle and the nephew.[49]

Now if he were legitimately descended from either, the following letter that Sir Philip Sidney's brother Robert wrote to him in 1600 would defy interpretation. If he were the illegitimate descendant of either, it becomes intelligible. 'Our lawyers say your title is well grounded in conscience, but that strict law doth not countenance your recovering those lands of your ancestors, as the Queen's right is somewhat extinguished by your cousins Stephen and James, who left issue; and hereby it cometh not straight to the Queen, whose good will toward you is ever apparent.'[50]

So the references continue down the centuries, often strengthening an assumption, never supplying the historical evidence. And it must be emphasized that Alexander's descent from the house of Brierley is no more than an assumption, and that it is the only descent in this history of the family that is not based on incontrovertible evidence.

It must be remembered, too, that such a presumption is particularly dangerous within the period in which Alexander lived. Pedigree mania had broken out in Tudor England. The elder Cecil, Lord Burghley, wasted an extraordinary amount of his busy life, doing what he could to festoon his family tree. Sir Christopher Hatton is perhaps the most thorough ancestor hunter of them all. He engaged scholars to undertake years of research on his behalf, bribed obscure Hattons who possessed a coat-of-arms to address him as cousin, and having claimed no arms as a young man, left twelve quite fictitious quarterings on his tomb. Others engaged lawyers to put them on the track of 'concealed lands', the titles to which had become obscure, and to which they laid claim by fictitious descent. This is the background against which the behaviour of the Kelston Haringtons must be judged.

For they did not themselves remain in the background. Alexander's son went to the court of King Henry VIII, as James Generosus had done years earlier, and Sir John Harington of Exton. James knew his descent back to a baron of Edward II's reign, and Sir John of Exton was one of the greatest men of his county. Alexander's son came obscurely from Stepney, and did not know who his grandfather was. But the name of Harington, and his conscious pride in it, was enough.

It is on these grounds, in the last resort, that Alexander's son and grandson deserve to be included in the family history in which their exact place remains uncertain. Indeed, it would be impossible fully to understand their characters, their actions, or their utterances, except in the context of this family history.

Alexander Harington of Stepney,
died *c.* 1539

|

John Harington of Stepney, died 1582
Marr. (1) Ethelreda of Kelston
    (2) Isabella, dau. of Sir John Markham

|

Sir John Harington of Kelston, 1561-1612

SEVEN

TUDOR POET

ALEXANDER's son is an object of special curiosity to us, and except in the matter of his descent he did much to satisfy it. Hitherto the members of his family had left little more record of themselves than the first Lord John, that recumbent figure within his splendid tomb, had done. The proud surcoat, the watchful arms, these may appear to stir in his sleep. But the features remain blank, and the thoughts behind them can only be faintly guessed. John of Stepney is the first of his house to have left a living picture of himself, his hopes, his fears, and his loves.

It is not certain that his features are preserved in the portrait that remained in the possession of his descendants until 1942, and now hangs in the Victoria Art Gallery at Bath. This picture was probably painted several decades after his death. The line engraving made by Turston in 1828 for *Effigies Poeticae* used only this portrait, and used it with licence. John's features, like his descent, must remain in doubt.

Probably he was born in the prebend house at Stepney, and all that is known of his mother is that she outlived his father and was the sort of person to whom, in 1540, her son wrote:

There was a battle fought of late,
Nor was the slaughter small.
The strife was, whether I should write
Or send no thing at all.

Of one side were the captains' names
Short Time and Little Skill;
One fought alone against them both,
Whose name was Great Goodwill.

Short Time enforced me in a strait,
And bad me hold my hand;
Small Skill also withstood desire,
My writing to withstand.

But Great Goodwill, in show though small,
To write encouraged me,
And to the battle held on still,
No common thing to see.

Thus gan these busy warriors three
Between themselves to fight
As valiantly as though they had
Been of much greater might;

Till Fortune, that unconstant dame,
Which rules such things alway,
Did cause the weaker part in fight
To bear the greater sway.

And then the victor caused me,
However was my skill,
To write these verses unto you,
To shew my great *goodwill*.[11]

This, John's earliest extant poem, was written soon after his father's death. We do not know how old John was when this occurred, and the fact that he lived for another forty-two years does not prove that he was either a youth or a grown man in 1540. His son's biographer in the *Dictionary of National Biography*, who bestowed upon him the treasurership held by his cousin of Exton at that time, presumably thought him old enough for such responsibilities. Mr John Buxton, in his book on the English Renaissance, added Sir John of Exton's knighthood for good measure.

The person lurking behind all this uncertainty and confusion was old enough to have written that apparently rather adolescent poem in 1540; and to have listened to Tallis at some time during the next seven years with sufficient attention to learn how to construct a canon. That is all that is known of him positively at this time. His name does not appear among the State Papers, like those of James Generosus or Sir John of Exton, as having held any office in the reign of Henry VIII.

But he went to court towards the end of the King's reign, and made his mark there in three singular ways. It might appear that, coming obscurely from Stepney, he would have needed all the help his cousins could give him to secure his introduction there. But it is fanciful to suppose that the rich and powerful Exton Haringtons would have bothered to advance an obscure namesake who claimed kinship. Either they would have rejected his claim as unfounded, or they would have accepted John when he appeared at court with the casual politeness, with which rich people sometimes protect themselves against their unimportant relatives. As for James Generosus, he cannot possibly have felt inclined to advance the fortunes of a Harington of his branch, for he would only be encouraging competition for the twenty-five manors in the north.

John can only have come to court as a young man at the end of Henry VIII's reign because it was an acceptable thing for one of his name to do. His success there was that of the young David, when first he came to sing his songs before King Saul. If Joab, his older and more important kinsman, was pleased with his success, that is not to say that he did anything to promote it.

John had composed a Black Sanctus, or Monk's Hymn to Satan, 'that King Henry was used in pleasant mood to sing'. He set his humorous Latin verses to a canon, following the manner of Tallis, and his descendant published both in the *Nugae Antiquae*. This is the only musical composition of his to have survived, and it may be the only one he ever wrote. For his enthusiasm had meanwhile found its object in the new court poetry of the English Renaissance.[52]

It was nearly a hundred and fifty years since Chaucer's death, and England's genius for lyric poetry, which had been quietly smouldering for so long, was now bursting out in sudden blaze. The beacon light was Tottell's *Miscellany*, published in 1557, an anthology to which nearly all the poets of the day contributed. But John had started his own manuscript anthology long before this, where poems by Sir Thomas Wyatt, the Earls of Surrey and Rochford, and others, perhaps his own, perhaps by another hand, are all mingled. There was one manuscript volume among the Harington papers containing over two hundred pages devoted entirely to Wyatt's poems, half of them written in his own hand, and the remainder corrected and initialled by him. The horrible fate of this unique manuscript will appear later.[53]

When some of these poems were first published by John's descendant in the *Nugae Antiquae*, it was soon noticed, by Bishop Percy and Dr Nott, that the versions of those poems which had appeared in Tottell's *Miscellany* two centuries before were in many cases different. John's manuscript preserved the earliest versions of them. Another curious circumstance, too, suggests that he gave advice, and acted in a sense as editor. For there is an extremely rare publication of Surrey's poems, in which the name John Harington appears with that of the printer Raynauld on the title-page. The dictionary of printers does not couple Raynauld's name with any other, nor does a Harington appear in it. So it does not seem unreasonable to conclude that John's name was added to a collection that he had helped to prepare for publication.

Nott was prepared to go further than this, and stated in his definitive edition of the poems of Wyatt and Surrey in 1815 that John was 'the person who first gave both Surrey's and Wyatt's poems to the public'. Nott was equally struck by John's quality as a poet. He wrote to Henry Harington in 1811: 'I have ascertained so many beautiful poems in Tottel's original collection of "Uncertain Authors" to have been written by your illustrious ancestor (he really deserves that name) John Harington, the first owner of Kelston, that it would please me very much to discover a sufficient number of his poems to form a little volume, whose name I should have a pride and pleasure in first introducing to the world with the encomium it deserves.' But in 1820 he was writing less purposefully of 'John Harington, to whom I consider our literature has the greatest obligations ... I am solicitous for nothing but to do justice to a person too little known.'[54]

The poet who has been awaiting recognition these four hundred years made his first truly remarkable utterance in 1543. It is natural that his thoughts should have been turning to love and marriage, but the treatment he gave to this eternal theme is altogether unusual. In not so very bygone days girls of his class had been browbeaten into marriage with men with whom they were not in love, and the Haringtons had been prominent bidders in the market in which heiresses (if they had not already been abducted from their castles) were bought and sold. Now John turned his imagination to the feelings of the girls themselves, denied the fortune of their pleasant choice.

> O happy dames, that may embrace
> The fruit of your delight,
> Help to bewail the woeful case,
> And eke the heavy plight

TUDOR POET

Of me that wonted to rejoice
The fortune of my pleasant choice:
Good ladies help to fill my mourning voice.

In a ship fraught with remembrance
Of words and pleasures past,
He sails, that hath in governance
My life while it will last;
With scalding sighs for lack of gale,
Furthering his hope, that is his sail,
Toward me, the sweet port of his avail.

Alas, how oft, in dreams, I see
Those eyes that were my food;
Which sometime so rejoiced me
That yet they do me good:
Wherewith I wake with his return,
Whose absent flame did make me burn,
But when I find the lack, Lord! how I mourn.

When other lovers in arms across
Rejoice their chief delight,
Drowned in tears I mourn my loss.
I stand the bitter night
In my window, where I may see
Before the winds how the clouds flee —
Lo! What a mariner Love hath made me.

And in green waves, when the salt flood
Doth rise by rage of wind,
A thousand fancies in that mood
Assail my restless mind.
Now fear it drencheth my sweet foe,
That with the spoil of my heart did go,
And left me; but alas! Why did he so?

And when the seas wax calm again
To chase from me annoy,
My doubtful hope doth cause me 'plain;
So dread cuts off my joy.

Thus is my wealth mingled with woe,
And of each thought a doubt doth grow,
Now he comes; will he come? Alas! No, no.[55]

The surging imagery of the sea in this poem brings back the
mystery of Alexander Harington's life and fortune. Its passion
provides a curious background to the mystery of John's first
marriage.

The legend concerning this marriage has been repeated as a
historical fact ever since Lesley wrote in 1656: 'the great King
Henry VIII matched his darling daughter to John Harington,
and, though a bastard, dowered her with the rich lands of Bath's
priory'. The date of this girl's marriage and the date of her
death are demonstrably false in almost every reference, and it may
have been partly on this account that Pollard ignored her completely in his study of Henry VIII's illegitimate children.

Her name was Ethelreda, or Audrey; her mother's name was
Dingley, or it might have been Dobson; her father was John
Malte, unless he was Henry VIII. And unless her father were the
King it would be very odd indeed that a girl in her circumstances
should have been so richly endowed, quite apart from the family
tradition on the subject. Nevertheless Pollard was right: there is
no historical evidence, only a strong presumption.

John Malte was the King's tailor. In 1546 he settled the manor
of Watchfield on Ethelreda, describing her as his illegitimate
daughter, in view of her proposed marriage with an illegitimate
son of Sir Richard Southwell. Later the same year the King made
a grant to Malte of the former church lands of Bath Priory and
Shaftsbury abbey, Kelston, Easton, and St Catherine, all near
Bath. This was a formidable gift, and it was made to Malte and
Ethelreda, then to the heirs of her body. Only on the failure of
such heirs was it to revert to the right heirs of Malte. Both
Henry VIII and Malte died in the following year, when Ethelreda
obtained by Malte's will the manor of Nyland as well.[56]

Such were the origins, and such the fortune, of John Harington's
first wife. Henry VIII did not give him Kelston with the hand of
his daughter: there is no evidence or likelihood that John married
Ethelreda before the death of Henry or Malte, and the properties
that Ethelreda had obtained in quite other circumstances she did
not settle on her husband until 1555. By that time the purveyors
of the legend, assuming poor Ethelreda to be dead, are busy

quoting John's sonnets to his second wife. For Ethelreda there were to be no sonnets. She who founded the fortune of the Haringtons of Kelston aroused no strong emotion in the passionate poet she had married. But perhaps she met kindness, for which her settlement of 1555 was an expression of gratitude. She is said to have died in childbirth, and to have left a daughter Hester, who is last heard of in a legal transaction of 1567.[57]

Ethelreda will have stood in need of a strong protector during the troubled years that followed Henry VIII's death. The great act of state of his reign had been the breach with Rome, and the dissolution of the monasteries. But Henry would have none of the Protestantism of the continental reformers. At the same time that he denied the Pope's authority in the Act of Supremacy, he preserved the Six Articles of the Catholic religion. In doing this he reached a solution offensive both to Papists and Protestants; but the fate of the Pilgrimage of Grace had warned people to keep their consciences to themselves. By dying when he suddenly did, Henry enabled each religious group to take its revenge. He was succeeded first by a precocious boy, ably instructed in the teachings of the reformed religion, and then by the sad Catholic daughter of his first marriage.

It was one of those periods of history when to possess convictions was hazardous. John, who had laughed at the monks and the old liturgy in his Black Sanctus, was to have ample opportunity to decide whether they were not indeed too great a luxury.

Edward VI, Jane Seymour's son, ascended the throne and his uncle the Duke of Somerset became Protector. The Bishops Bonner and Gardiner presently found themselves in the Tower, while Latimer and Cranmer enjoyed the first advantage in the religious contest.

King Edward's mother had another brother, Seymour, who was promoted to the office of Lord Admiral, and the first upheaval was political, rather than religious, precipitated by the matrimonial plans of the Lord High Admiral. His sister had married a king, and he was determined to marry a queen. He had his eye on the young Princess Elizabeth, but King Edward suggested Anne of Cleves, and then reflected: 'Nay, nay; wot you what? I would he married my sister Mary, to change her opinions.' The course of English history might have been different if Seymour had followed this advice: but he secretly married Queen Catharine Parr instead.

While he was intriguing to secure possession of the young King's person, to the neglect of his naval duties, Queen Catharine died. Seymour renewed his suit to the Princess Elizabeth, while he obtained a promise from the Lady Jane Grey's father that she should be his wife. He was in a dilemma. There were so many possible queens that even an abler judgment than Seymour's might have hesitated between them. In 1549 he was released from his dilemma by attainder and the executioner's axe — the only person in English history except the equally unfortunate James II whose power rested in the Navy, rather than the Army, of this maritime nation.

John Harington was in Admiral Seymour's service. How deeply he was involved in the pursuit of queens will never be known, but he may at least have claimed kinship with both the principal quarries, as Elizabeth's brother-in-law, and Jane's cousin. On Seymour's arrest he was lodged in the Tower.

The Lieutenant of the Tower at this time was Sir John Markham, the late colleague of Sir John Harington of Exton in the Scottish marches. If Markham sometimes consorted with his old companion 'within St Ellens, Bishopgate Street', on his visits to London from Exton, it is not impossible that he made inquiries about his new prisoner of the same name. If the evidence against John pointed to Princess Elizabeth, Markham will have been able to make further inquiries of his daughter Isabella, who was a lady-in-waiting of the Princess. In neither case can Markham have learned anything greatly to John's detriment, for he was to accept him as his son-in-law one day.

Under Sir John Markham's lieutenancy the Tower was becoming a fashionable place of residence, offering, as John was to describe later, the most varied company. In addition to the victims of Seymour's fall it contained those who objected to the new prayer book of 1549. The list of prisoners for October of that year contains fifty-five names. There was Bishop Gardiner, with whom John sometimes conversed, Thomas, Duke of Norfolk, the fallen Protector Somerset, and James, Earl of Morton. John was more fortunate for the present than some of his companions. There was no charge to prefer against him and he was soon released.

But at no time either now or later did he waver in his loyalty to the Lord Admiral, or to his memory. The historian Froude, who treated Seymour with such lengthy severity in his detailed history of this period, preferred to ignore John's testimony. Doubtless he was right to reject such partial comment. But at least it was evidence of a steadfast character; for John expressed it when it was unpopular and dangerous to do so, in a letter to Bishop Gardiner that will be quoted, and he referred to it again on his death-bed over thirty years later. And at some time in the interval he scribbled:

> Sumptuous abroad for honour of the land,
> Temperate at home, yet kept great state with stay,
> And noble house that fed more mouths with meat
> Than some, advanced on higher steps to stand . . .

Seymour's love of grandeur was not a quality over which a Harington would cavil. John concluded his defence of his dead master,

> Yet, against nature, reason, and just laws,
> His blood was spilt, guiltless, without just cause.

This poem is painted round the head of Seymour in a portrait that John was said by his son to have presented to Queen Elizabeth. The portrait was purchased by an ancestor of the Marquess of Bath early in the eighteenth century, and now hangs at Longleat.[58]

John was to have further opportunity to show his capacity for loyalty, as he drew closer to those objects of dead Seymour's ambitions, the Greys and Princess Elizabeth. In 1552 he received the grant of a half share of the Minories in London. The other joint owner under this grant was the man who bore the title Lord Harington, Henry Grey, Duke of Suffolk. In 1553 Edward VI died and Suffolk's daughter embarked on her nine unwilling days of rule. Then both father and daughter were imprisoned in the Tower while Mary became Queen.[59]

At Mary's accession Elizabeth could scarcely count herself more legitimate than Ethelreda. Her mother Anne Boleyn had indeed been a queen at the time of her birth, but she had been executed for adultery shortly afterwards. And if, as appears in her character so strongly, she was nevertheless King Henry's daughter, that made her no more legitimate in the eyes of Christendom. A Christian marriage cannot be sundered. Henry VIII could only have made Anne Boleyn his wife if the Pope had declared his previous marriage with Catharine of Aragon void from the beginning. In the first place the Pope had refused to do this; in the second, if the marriage had been void despite the Pope's refusal to say so, the child of this marriage could not have been legitimate herself. Either Mary was legitimate, or Elizabeth, but not both, irrespective of the breach with Rome. Elizabeth's status was secured by her father's Act of Succession. But now there were Mary's private feelings to reckon with, and the advice of Bishops Bonner and Gardiner, matured by long reflection in the Tower.

Here, where John had once shared those reflections, he now found himself a prisoner once more in other company. The precise reason for his arrest was set down by John himself, by Gardiner, John's persecutor, and by John's son. John carried letters to Princess Elizabeth and was personally involved with the fallen family of Grey. If the letters and the meetings were not treasonable, then John was unjustly imprisoned: but if they were, then it seems that Elizabeth herself was implicated in the conspiracy that culminated in Wyatt's rebellion.

Gardiner wrote to Secretary Petre: 'in the morning I thought good to search the Minories and Medles lodging there for letters, and among others, found a letter lately written by Harington, which Harington came to me this night, and after examination I have taken him tardy by occasion of that letter, and keep him with me as prisoner this night, intending in the morning to send him to the Tower. For he hath confessed how upon Friday at night the Lord John Grey came to Cheston, where Master Wroth and he was, and spake with Master Wroth and him to get a guide to lead him the way to St Albans, because he was commanded by the Queen, he said, to levy men in his country in all haste; and more I cannot get yet . . .'[40]

So John returned to the Tower, a few months before his namesake of Exton died in London, and his remains were carried back with such pomp to his family's mausoleum. And so Gardiner developed his distrust of the name of John Harington, which he seems to have recalled during his interrogation of John Bradford. If Gardiner transferred the supposed guilt of the one John Harington to the other, he was only doing what a king of England would do a hundred years later, with more tragic results.

The Register of the Privy Council shows that on 24 June 1553 John was among those ordered to be removed from the Tower to the Fleet, but as he was still in the Tower the following January, this order does not seem to have been carried out. Perhaps this was due to Sir John Markham's intervention, though Markham cannot have intervened as John's father-in-law, because Ethelreda was still alive. It is necessary to point this out, since John's son has left an account of his father's troubles that speaks of John's wife at this time as 'my mother'. This was a casual error: Ethelreda was not his mother.

'I may truly say,' wrote John's son of Bishop Gardiner, 'this prelate did persecute me before I was born; for my father was by his command imprisoned in the Tower for eleven months, for only carrying a letter to the Princess Elizabeth; and my mother was taken from her presence, and obliged to dwell with Mr Topcliff, as an heretic. My poor father did send many petitions to the Bishop, but in vain, as he expended one thousand pounds to get his liberty. Nor had they any comfort but their consciences to beguile this affliction, and the sweet words and sweeter deeds of their mistress and fellow prisoner. But, not to rail only, I will inform your Highness what old Sir Matthew Arundel was wont to say, touching those times — "that Bonner was more to blame than Gardiner, who used to call him ass, and other scurvy names, for dealing so cruelly by honest men". I was moved to say so much against this judgment that Sir Matthew said my father ought to have lain in prison much longer, for sending such a saucy sonnet to Gardiner. In truth it was not over civil, but after fair words ill taken, such deeds are not foul; and considering those unrefined times, the poetry is not badly conceived . . .' England's earliest literary critic has chosen an odd context in which to appraise his father's verse.[11]

John had been placed in the Tower first by the Protestant faction, sharing its amenities with Bishop Gardiner. He treated his second confinement by the Papists philosophically, and applied himself to the translation of Marcus Tullius Cicero's treatise on friendship, *De Amicitia*. He wrote to Jane Grey's mother: 'as my prisonment and adversity, most honourable lady, was (of their own nature) joined with great and sundry miseries, so was the sufferance of the same eased by the chance of divers and many commodities. For thereby found I a great soul-profit, a little mind-knowledge, some hollow hearts, and a few faithful friends. Whereby I tried prisonment of the body to be the liberty of spirit; adversity of fortune, the touchstone of friendship; exemption from the world, to be a contempt of vanities; and in the end, quietness of mind, the occasion of study. And thus somewhat altered, to

95

avoid my old idleness, to recompense my lost time, and to take profit of my calamity, I gave myself, among other things, to study and learn the French tongue, having both skilful prisoners to instruct me, and thereto plenty of books to learn the language. Among which, as there were divers notable, and for their sundry matter worthy reading, so none liked me above Tullius' book of Friendship; nor for the argument any with it to be compared. The whole whereof when I had perused, and saw the goodly rules, the natural order, and civil use of friendship; where before I but liked, then was I ravished, and in a certain wonder with the heathen learning, which chiefly for itself I phantasied, and for my state I deemed good to be embraced as a glass to discern my friends in, and a civil rule to lead my life by; these causes moved me to think it meet for more. Whereupon I (as I could) translated it'. The earliest edition of John's *De Amicitia*, the only prose work he published, is that of 1562.[62]

While the opposing religious factions tore one another to pieces for the love of the Lord, John, persecuted by each in turn, found solace in the ancient writers. It is an interesting picture. So is the opinion of a man who possessed in such exceptional measure the gift of friendship, that it is an art, to be cultivated with effort and study. Of John's pre-eminence in this art, some of his most distinguished contemporaries bore witness. Sir John Cheke, Edward VI's tutor, wrote to him before leaving England in 1554: 'I could not take my leave of you at my departure, and give you such thanks as your friendship in mine adversity deserved ... yet is it all I have, and therefore the greatest thing I can give you; not worthy your friendship, but not unfit for my offer.' Burghley later wrote to John's son a letter 'from your father's friend that loves you'. Elizabeth, after she became queen, sent John one of her own translations on the same subject.[63]

But the most important person to convince of the duties of friendship was Bishop Gardiner. John wrote to him from the Tower: 'My Lord, this mine humble prayer doth come with much sorrow for any deed of evil that I have done to your lordship. But alas! I know of none, save such duty to the Lady Elizabeth as I am bounden to pay her at all times: and, if this matter breedeth in you such wrath towards her and me, I shall not in this mine imprisonment repent thereof. My wife is her servant, and doth but rejoice in this our misery, when we look with whom we are holden in bondage. Our gracious King Henry did ever advance our

family's good estate, as did his pious father aforetime; wherefore
our service is in remembrance of such good kindness. Albeit there
needeth none other cause to render our tendance, sith the Lady
Elizabeth beareth such piety and goodly affection to all virtue.
Consider, that your lordship aforetime hath combated with much
like affliction: why then should not our state cause you to recount
the same, and breed pity to usward? . . . May God incline you
to amend all this cruelty, and ever and anon turn our prayer in
good and merciful consideration. My Lord Admiral Seymour did
truly win my love amidst this hard and deadly annoyance: now,
may the same like pity touch your heart, and deal us better usage.
His service was ever joyful, and why must this be afflicting? Mine
ancient kindred have ever held their duty and liege obeysance,
nor will I do them such dishonour as may blot out their worthy
deeds, but will ever abide in all honesty and love. If you should
give ear to mine complaint, it will bind me to thankfully repay
this kindness; but if not, will continue to suffer, and rest ourselves
in God, whose mercy is sure and safe; and in all true love to *her*,
who doth honour us in tender sort, and scorneth not to shed her
tears with ours. I commend your lordship to God's appointment,
and rest sorely afflicted. John Harington.'⁹⁴

Fair words? On the contrary, a proud self-justification and
superb reproof. And when, not unnaturally, it had been ill-taken,
John dropped the pose of humility and returned to the fray with
the weapon he could use best. He sent Gardiner the 'saucy
sonnet' that his son thought not badly conceived for those
unrefined times.

> At least withdraw your cruelty,
> Or force the time to work your will;
> It is too much extremity
> To keep me pent in prison still,
> Free from all fault, void of all cause,
> Without all right, against all laws.
> How can you do more cruel spite
> Than profer wrong, and promise right,
> Nor can accuse, nor will acquite?
>
> Eleven months past, and longer space,
> I have abid your devilish drifts,
> While you have sought both man and place,
> And set your snares with all your shifts,

The faultless foot to wrap in wile,
With any guilt, by any guile:
And now you see it will not be,
How can you thus for shame agree
To keep him bound you ought set free?

Your chance was once as mine is now,
To keep this hold against your will,
And then you swore, you know well how,
Though now you swerve, I know how ill.
But thus the world his course doth pass.
The priest forgets that clerk he was,
And you that then cried 'Justice' still,
And now have justice at your will,
Wrest justice wrong, against all skill.

But why do I thus coldly plain,
As though it were my cause alone?
When cause doth each man so constrain,
As England through hath cause to moan,
To see your bloody search of Such,
As all the earth can no way touch:
And better 'twere that all your kind,
Like hounds in hell, with shame were shrined,
Then you had might unto your mind.

But as the stone that strikes the wall
Sometimes rebounds on th' hurler's head,
So your foul fetch to your foul fall
May turn, and 'noy the breast it bred.
And then such measure as you gave
Of right and justice, look to have;
If good or ill, if short or long,
If false or true, if right or wrong:
And thus, till then, I end my song.[65]

If John had to pay a thousand pounds to get out of the Tower as a result of this poem, it must rank among the more expensive libels. But it could have cost John a great deal more than that. Bishop Gardiner, who had learnt statecraft from Wolsey, had destroyed Thomas Cromwell, and was out to destroy Elizabeth, was not a man to trifle with. Perhaps this added to the zest of composition. When Gardiner died in the following year, John must have felt relieved that he had been able to give him a piece of his mind in time. In doing so, he also left the only surviving evidence of his feelings about his descent. He was strongly moved by pride in an ancient kindred whom he would not dishonour, and this pride of descent is implicit in his rebuke to my lord bishop: 'the priest forgets that clerk he was'. Such undesigning phrases perhaps reveal more than the fabrications of the kings-of-arms.

In his literary output in prison John ranks with John Bunyan and Sir Walter Ralegh. He wrote less than either of these because the time he spent in prison was comparatively slight. But those few months' captivity in 1549 and the eleven months in the Tower in 1554 left an indelible mark on his character.

> When I look back, and in myself behold
> The wandering ways that youth could not descry,
> And see the fearful course that youth did hold,
> And meet in mind each step I strayed awry,
> My knees I bow, and from my heart I call:
> My God! forget youth's fault and follies all.
>
> The humble heart hath daunted the proud mind,
> Knowledge hath given ignorance the fall,
> Wisdom hath taught what folly could not find,
> And age hath youth, his captive, brought in thrall:
> Wherefore I pray, O Lord of life and truth,
> Cancel those crimes committed in my youth.
>
> Thou that didst grant the wise king his request,
> Thou that of grace didst bring the blind to sight,
> Thou that forgav'st the wounding of thy breast,
> Thou that in favour cam'st the world to light;
> Thou only good dispenser of all grace,
> Wipe out the guilt that grew in youth's green race.
>
> But now, since hope by grace with doubtless mind
> Doth press to Thee by prayer to assuage thine ire;
> And since, with trust to speed, I seek to find,
> Waiting, through faith, to attain this just desire;
> Lord, mind no more youth's error nor unskill,
> But able age to do thine holy will.[11]

And thus somewhat altered, and comforted by what is best in the Christian and classical traditions, John passed through those unquiet times.

At some time between 1555 and 1560 his first wife died, and he wrote of his love for Sir John Markham's daughter Isabella, 'when I first thought her fair as she stood at the Princess's window in goodly attire, and talked to divers in the court-yard'.

> Whence comes my love? O heart, disclose.
> 'Twas from cheeks that shame the rose,
> From lips that spoil the ruby's praise,
> From eyes that mock the diamond's blaze.
> Whence comes my love? As freely own:
> Ah me! 'Twas from a heart like stone.
>
> The blushing cheek speaks modest mind,
> The lips befitting words most kind;
> The eye does tempt to love's desire,
> And seems to say, 'tis Cupid's fire.
> Yet all so fair but speak my moan,
> Sith nought doth say the heart of stone.
>
> Why thus, my love, so kind bespeak
> Sweet lip, sweet eye, sweet blushing cheek,
> Yet not a heart to save my pain?
> O Venus, take thy gifts again;
> Make not so fair to cause our moan,
> Or make a heart that's like our own.[67]

Isabella yielded to John's passionate protestations, and her mistress succeeded to the throne of England. His cup was full.

> I am not dead, although I had a fall.
> The sun returns that was hid under cloud,
> And, when fortune hath spit out all her gall,
> I trust good luck shall be to me allowed.
> For I have seen a ship into the haven fall
> When storm hath broke both mast and also shroud;
> And eke the willow that stoopeth with the wind
> Doth rise again, and greater wood doth bind.[68]

So it came to pass. On 29 June 1559 the new Queen granted
to John for life, as a reward for his services to her, the office of
receiver-general of lands in the counties of Nottingham and
Derby. He was allowed to exchange these counties by surrender
and new grant in 1561, for Somerset and Dorset. These counties
were more rewarding, and in Somerset lay the properties that he
had inherited from Ethelreda. Out of his revenues, John was to
pay the Queen £51 in every £100.

On 12 March 1563 Elizabeth further granted to her servant
John and Isabella his wife, gentlewoman of the privy chamber,
the manor and former priory site of Lenton in Nottinghamshire
in tail male. This last provision was in favour of the son who had
been born to John and Isabella two years earlier, and who was to
be known, among her hundred and two godchildren, as Queen
Elizabeth's godson.[68]

The Duke of Norfolk and the Earl of Pembroke were the child's
godfathers, and at his baptism he was sprinkled with water from
a miniature font of gold, the gift of the Queen. It was an auspicious beginning for the son of John and Isabella. But the luck of
the Haringtons soon overtook his golden font. It was sent to
Bristol Castle for safety during the Civil War, and when the
castle surrendered after its seige, the font had disappeared.[70]

Many other gifts were exchanged between the Queen, and John
and Isabella. On New Year's Day 1572 they presented her with
a heart of gold, garnished with sparks of rubies, three pearls, and
with another pearl pendant from it. Out of the heart grew a
branch of red and white roses composed of diamonds, rubies,
emeralds, and pearls. Elizabeth's present to them on this occasion
was a gilt plate weighing forty ounces. Other presents to the
Queen are recorded up to the year of Isabella's death in 1579; an
agate salt cellar, six yards of black cloth of silver, and a crystal
bowl. The only present from the Queen that remains in the
family is a round wooden box on whose lid the royal arms are
painted, between her monogram and the date 1600.

The exceptional value of John's New Year gift in 1572 has been
attributed to motives other than gratitude or affection. His
descendant Henry Harington must be held partly responsible for
this, in publishing only the fragment of a letter in his *Nugae
Antiquae*. He headed it: 'the following extract may serve to confirm the general idea given us of Queen Elizabeth's passion for
rich clothes and personal ornaments. A law-suit was depending to

recover some lands which had been forfeited by Sir James Harington, for espousing the cause of Richard the Third, and a reversion granted to his family by Henry the Eighth'. Henry Harington placed beneath these remarks the following passage, without attributing it to anyone: because it was only a copy of a letter, and therefore unsigned.

'Yet I will adventure to give her Majesty five hundred pounds in money, and some pretty jewel or garment as you shall advise, only praying her Majesty to further my suit with some of her learned Counsel; which I pray you to find some proper time to move in. This some hold as a dangerous adventure, but five and twenty manors do well warrant my trying it.'

Anyone who had inspected Queen Elizabeth's list of New Year presents might be forgiven for pausing at the mention of that pretty jewel. It was the scholarly John Nichols who swallowed the bait, and added another legend to those that have been current for so long. In 1823, in his *Progresses and Processions of Queen Elizabeth*, he transmitted the familiar fictions; that John had held considerable office under Henry VIII, and that Henry had given him Kelston as a dowry with the hand of Ethelreda. He added an unkinder one. He said that John gave Elizabeth the New Year's gift in 1572 as a bribe, and he quoted the undated and unsigned fragment in the *Nugae Antiquae* as evidence. Elizabeth had granted to John the reversion of the manors in 1570, and Nichols did not explain how a bribe could operate whose object had been gained two years earlier.

But Professor McClure dissipated this legend in 1930 in *The Letters and Epigrams of Sir John Harington*, where he added an important sentence to the fragment already published. 'If I make anything at all of the title, I must acknowledge it only of her Majesty's goodness that first gave it my father.' John's father Alexander died in about 1539; Elizabeth succeeded in 1558.

Such are the errors, often trivial in themselves, that the Harington family have succeeded in attracting to themselves down the centuries.

John continued to live for twenty-four years under the government of the great Queen. He lived as a gentleman of moderate means, playing his part in local administration, and attending court without leaving any evidence that he sought to exploit the favour he enjoyed there. Nothing he said or did after 1558 hints at any attempt to raise himself above the Tudor gentry to which, to all appearances, he belonged. Only in the heraldic grant of 1568, the letters patent of 1570, and in his son's godparents, is a social superiority implicit.

The house that he began to build at Kelston has not the same significance. Many families, new and old, were doing the same at this time, whether a Harington whose castles Leland had seen in ruins on his itinerary, or a Cecil, whose grandfather was the younger son of a yeoman. If John really employed Vignola to design his new home, this is certainly evidence of taste in a new field. Mr Buxton, in his book on the English Renaissance, says that he did; and his statement appears to derive from a remark of the eighteenth-century Bishop Pococke, repeated by Poynton in his *Memoranda of Kelston*. The house, that was said to have once been the largest in Somerset, has vanished almost without a trace like the golden font. It is no longer possible to judge from its style whether it was Vignola's work, and neither among the master's papers nor those of the Haringtons is there any surviving evidence that he prepared the plans for Kelston.

John almost certainly continued to live in London, and when his official duties or estate management drew him to Somerset he may have visited his relative Thomas Harington, whom he had placed in the rectory which still serves its ancient purpose at Kelston. Or he may have gone to his manor house of St Catherine's Court, one of Somerset's most beautiful Elizabethan monuments.

He grew more serious with the passing of the years. To Isabella, whose cheeks had shamed the rose, he wrote, perhaps in 1564:

> If duty, wife, lead thee to deem
> That trade most fit I hold most dear,
> First God regard, next me esteem,
> Our children then respect, though near.
>
> Our house both sweet and cleanly see,
> Order our fare, thy maids keep short;
> Thy mirth with mean well mixed be,
> Thy courteous parts in chaste wise sort.
>
> In sober weeds thee cleanly dress.
> When joys me raise, thy cares down cast,
> When griefs me grieve, thy solace cease.
> Whoso my friends, friend them as fast.

In peace give place, whatso I say;
Apart complain if cause thou find.
Let liberal lips no trust betray,
Nor jealous humour pain thy mind.

If I thee wrong, thy griefs unfold.
If thou me vex, thine error grant.
To seek strange toils be not too bold;
The strifeless bed no jars may haunt.

Small sleep and early prayer intend;
The idle life as poison hate.
No credit light nor much speech spend;
In open place no cause debate.

No thwarts, no frowns, no grudge, no strife;
Eschew the bad, embrace the best.
To truth of word join honest life,
And in my bosom build thy nest. [71]

The contrast between this poem and those passionate declarations of love he had once addressed to Isabella is quite extraordinary. One might sympathize with her if it did not appear extremely likely that she herself was responsible for the change. In 1572 an author of some repute in those days called Thomas Paulfreyman dedicated a book to her in a long and revealing epistle. The book consisted of divine meditations. Let no one detract from the excellence of such a theme, nor from the worth of character Isabella reveals in the one anecdote that her son permitted himself to relate concerning her. Lord Hastings had come to dine, and 'walked out into the garden while prayers were saying'. Isabella, sorting her courteous parts in chaste wise, declared that guests who 'scorned to pray with her, she would scorn they should eat with her'. When she died, her son revered her memory in verses which emphasized her chastity and spotless fame, but contained little of the warmth that he did not know how to conceal when he felt it. [72]

No, there seems to be little doubt that it was Isabella's devout and estimable character that had tamed John, and that she will have preferred this last poem to any of the earlier ones addressed to her. If she did not, it nevertheless served her right.

John amplified some of the more practical advice contained in this poem, in the set of rules that he drew up for household servants. 'Thy maids keep short', he had warned Isabella. 'Item, that none toy with the maids, on pain of 4d.' He listed more specifically in his rules.

Item, that none swear any oath, upon pain for every oath 1d.

Item, that none of the men be in bed, from our Ladyday to Michaelmas, after six of the clock in the morning; nor out of his bed after ten of the clock at night; nor, from Michaelmas till our Ladyday, in bed after seven in the morning; nor out after nine at night, without reasonable cause, on pain of 2d.

Item, that no man make water within either of the courts, upon pain of, every time it shall be proved, 1s.

Item, that no man teach any of the children any unhonest speech, or baudy word, or oath, on pain of 4d.

Item, that meat be ready at eleven or before at dinner, and six or before at supper, on pain of 6d.

Item, that the court gate be shut each meal, and not opened during dinner and supper without just cause, on pain the porter to forfeit for every time 1d.

It is sad to discover that despite Isabella's admirable influence, John yet ranked the punctuality of his meals twopence higher than the morals of his maids. Nor is his finance very sound in the matter of bawdy words, for everyone knows with what uncanny perspicacity small children pick up the words that adults try so properly to conceal from them. However, the fines for these, and a great many other offences, were to be paid out of wages to the relief of the poor.'¹

How one wishes that the descendants of John and Isabella had preserved a single letter from this time. The only one to have survived is a letter that their son wrote, when he was a boy of ten at Eton, to Mrs Penn in the household of Lord Burghley.

'Although, good Mistress Penn, my long silence may make you suppose that I am unmindful both of you and also of your benefits, yet truly it is nothing so. For I have often times since my coming to Eton purposed to write to you, and now at the length I have found leisure to write these letters, which though they be rude and unworthy of your sight, yet I trust you will accept them as coming from an humble and loving mind. Many things you have at many times bestowed on me, more I know than I can requite, but not more surely than I willingly bear in mind and intend always hereafter to show myself thankful for. You promised that you would send me a letter when I was with you last, and I would gladly see it, that I might have occasion to write to you again. I would very gladly hear that Master Penn were in good health. Thus, wishing you with Master Penn great health and long life, I take my leave of you this 19 day of May anno 1571. Yours to command John Harington.' ⁷⁴

There is nothing strange in the preservation of this letter. Burghley kept every scrap of his correspondence. But his connection with the Haringtons requires explanation.

Burghley's minute researches had revealed that his maternal grandmother was also the grandmother, by a subsequent marriage, of a Lincolnshire branch of the Haringtons. He made one of the Lincolnshire Haringtons a steward of one of his manors. The wife of Sir James Harington of Exton, Lady Lucy, wrote to Burghley about his gout in 1573, addressing him: 'My very good lord and dear uncle . . .' When John of Kelston's son went to Cambridge, Burghley wrote to him as an uncle might do, signing himself, 'your father's friend that loves you'. The founder of the house of Cecil was living midway between the time when Lord Harington was companion in arms to Edward I, and his own descendant Lord Salisbury served in the present Government. At one end of this period of time the Cecils are unknown, at the other the Haringtons. The situation in the middle of it is illuminated by Burghley's impartial attention to any Harington, whether of the Exton, Kelston, or Lincolnshire branch.' ⁷⁵

John wrote a poem for his son, less chilling than the instructions to his wife and servants. It is undated, but perhaps young John was given it to take away with him when he went to Eton.

> A boy that should content me wondrous well
> Should keep these rules set down for his behoof.
> In fearing God, all boys he should excel,
> And lead a life unworthy just reproof.
> An upright gait, a forehead smooth and plain;
> A countenance good, with feet even set on ground;
> A steady eye, still hands, and steady brain,
> An open ear to good instructions bound,

> A courteous tongue that talketh true and plain,
> An humble heart, of guile void evermore;
> A constant mind, that will refuse no pain
> To purchase still the fruit of virtuous lore,
> And learn to know, and know to do the best:
> And such a boy should worthy pass the rest.[75]

How well he was to obey those precepts, John did not live to see. Isabella died while her son was at Cambridge, and three years later John died also. His son, now reading law at the Inns of Court, was with him during his last days and left a note of what occupied his thoughts then. They took wing to that eventful period which had marked the turning point both of his career and of his character; when many had suffered for their convictions and many more had stifled their convictions, and John had done neither. 'And my father (I remember) but a week before he died, which was in the year 1582, wrote with his own hand the names of those were then living of the old Admiralty (so he called them that had been my Lord's men), and there were then 34 of them living, of which many were knights and men of more revenue than himself. And some were but mean men, as armourers, artificers, keepers, and farmers. And yet the memory of his service was such a bond among them all of kindness, as the best of them disdained not the poorest.'[77]

Perhaps Seymour really was a better man than the historians allow, or perhaps he is merely reflected in the rare qualities of his servant. The memory of these qualities were now left to John's son, with the unfinished house of Kelston, and the bed that his father had inscribed, with his taste for aphorisms:

> No state can be more sound, no life more sweet,
> Than is the happy yoke where good minds meet.
> Happy are they, can cut the wings
> Of their desires, to need less things.
> Fortune giveth too much to many,
> But never gives enough to any.
> He was friend never
> That is not friend ever.[78]

EIGHT

THE BYRON OF HIS AGE

IF John of Kelston's son possessed half the wit and a quarter of the literary skill with which he was credited by his contemporaries, he is surely the most unfairly neglected figure in English letters. It is partly a question of changing tastes. 'How my poetry will be relished in time to come, I will not hazard to say', he wrote modestly at the height of his fame. The Victorian bishop hazarded his judgment in the *Dictionary of National Biography* that Sir John's epigrams, disfigured by coarseness, were forgotten. In a century in which the *Decameron* has been suppressed on moral grounds by a public library, it is not for us to laugh at the squeamishness of our grandfathers. The same biographer declared that Sir John's translation of the *Orlando Furioso* had been superseded, though he did not divulge by what. As it has been out of print since 1634, few have the opportunity to judge whether it is not one of the outstanding translations of the English language.

We are not allowed to forget, however, that John invented the water-closet. It was the passing idea of an inventive mind. It was enshrined in a witty mock scholarly work that includes a sonnet explaining its use, and a blueprint which shows fish swimming in the tank. The publication was called *The Metamorphosis of Ajax*, or A Jakes: the Elizabethans thought such puns funny.

Posterity, censorious about the full-blooded candour of the Elizabethans, has sniggered long and often at the lavatory joke. One of the latest books in which John appears is Mr Pudney's *The Smallest Room*. A recent article, *Justice for Harington*, asks in its sub-title; 'why, in this age when culture and civilization are judged increasingly in terms of plumbing, should there be this continued neglect of the "Master Plumber" himself?' Television has already given John the recognition of an age which expresses its culture increasingly in terms of plumbing. And the only work of his that has been constantly reprinted from his century to ours is *The Metamorphosis of Ajax*.'¹

John would only have wagged a finger at us in amused reproof. He knew people were like that: they always had been and they always would be. With total absence of malice he lifted the lid under which hypocrisy and prurience lurk, until those who pretended to be outraged were forced to smile. And he can still make us smile, rather than merely titter, if we will forget his water-closet and look for the man who fascinated all who knew him.

He was handsome, as all his portraits show; he was charming, as his writings prove. From his earliest years he was pampered and spoiled, and yet he remained to the last simple, guileless, a little childlike. Above all, he was merry. He must not be judged from that ceremonious letter he wrote to Mrs Penn from Eton, to have been merely serious and precocious. In later years he remembered his teacher saying, ' "thou varay lazy fellow" (so he used to pro-nounce)' and his memory of the Provost was a profane one too. 'He brake his leg with a fall from a horse that started under him. Whereupon some waggish scholars, of which I think myself was in the quorum, would say it was a just punishment, because the horse was given him by a gentleman to place his son in Eton.' We can picture John setting off from the solemn atmosphere of the Prebend House to give vent to his high spirits at Eton, with one auspicious and one dropping eye.[80]

But the improving, admonitory influences pursued him like furies. It is not surprising that John should have learnt so young to disguise the fundamental seriousness of his thought, and his capacity for industry, under an appearance of frivolity and idle-ness. His seriousness is revealed in the tribute he paid later to Dr Still, his tutor at Cambridge, 'who, from that time to this hath given me some helps, more hopes, all encouragements in my best studies; to whom I never came, but I grew more religious; from whom I never went, but I parted better instructed'. But in his anxiety to conceal it, he referred to himself as a truantly scholar who had taken but little learning for his money.[81]

Encouragement dogged John's steps. His royal godmother sent him at Cambridge, when he was fourteen years old, a copy of the speech she had delivered on 15 March 1576, in Parliament. It was strange matter for a youth, being a determined defence of her decision to remain unmarried. 'Boy Jack,' she wrote, 'I have made a clerk write fair my poor words for thine use, as it cannot be such stripplings have entrance into Parliament assembly as yet. Ponder them in thy hours of leisure, and play with them till they enter thine understanding; so shalt thou hereafter, perchance, find some good fruits hereof when thy godmother is out of re-membrance; and I do this, because thy father was ready to serve and love us in trouble and thrall.'[82]

Three years later he was being offered yet stronger fare from 'your father's friend that loves you', Lord Treasurer Burghley. 'I thank you, my good Jack, for your letters, which I like not for the praise they give me, but for the promise they make me; that is, that you will continue your endeavour to get understanding, without the which a man is little accounted of, and indeed cannot tell truly how to account of himself. But, as the way to knowledge is not short, so the travellers therein must neither be idle nor weary; nor think a little enough of that whereof none can have too much. For that were like a man going home, that took the next inn for his own house, or the half way for his journey's end.'

The busy Burghley then proceeded to put his last remark to the test. 'For the Latin tongue, Tully chiefly, if not only; for the Roman story (which is exceeding fit for a gentleman to understand) Livy and Caesar; for logic and philosophy, Aristotle and Plato. And so in all tongues and sciences, the most notable and approved (as your tutor can best tell you), not dealing with over great variety of books, which young men delight in; and yet, in my opinion, they breed but a scattering of the mind.'

It was not Burghley's opinion that the invention of the printing press had rendered lectures obsolete. 'For at a good lecture you may learn in an hour that a good teacher, perhaps, hath been studying for a day, and yourself by reading shall not find out in a month. Again, you shall reach more discerning of truth in an hour's reasoning with others than a week's writing by yourself.' So the advice poured on, until it reached its peroration. 'Thus first fearing and praising God, and following your book and good company, you shall become a great comfort to your father and praise to your Master, an honour to the university that breeds you, a fit servant for the Queen and your country, for which you were born, and to which, next God, you are most bound; a good stay to your self, and no small joy to your friends; which I that loves you both wish and hope of. And so commend me to you, my good Jack, and us both to God's goodness. From the court, the 6th of June, 1578.'[11]

As a youth at Cambridge, the Queen and her chief minister among his correspondents, John committed perhaps the greatest act of superbity on record in his family. It was a letter to Sir Francis Walsingham, that he wrote in Latin on 2 November 1580, when he was nineteen years old. The composition is skilful, though there is not the grace which places him among the greatest of English letter writers. But it was a formal, ornamental letter which gave him little scope. First he paid Walsingham a compliment or two, and then he informed him that he proposed to take up the study of law. He concluded: 'et adolescens summa nobilitate . . .' or in translation: 'and a young man of the highest nobility, outstanding ability and remarkable virtue, the Earl of Essex, has treated me with great kindness. This he does, partly from the goodness of his nature, partly from consideration for my duties, but most of all because he regards me as numbered among those whose interests and welfare matter to you. Therefore it seems to me it will be most worthy of your honour, most acceptable to that accomplished young man, and most convenient to your very loving suppliant, if he may receive assurance that his kindness to me is acceptable to you'.[14]

The son of plain John Harington and grandson of the mysterious Alexander had written a letter to one of the Queen's ministers stating that a Devereux was treating him with kindness. He could only assume that a Devereux did this because it was a means of obtaining favour at court, to show kindness to a Harington at Cambridge. So began the association between these two proud young men, whose pride was to have such a strange and sorry ending.

Having delivered himself of this pompous recommendation, we can see John toss his pen aside at the approach of the stagekeepers, 'that for fear lest they should want company to see their comedies, go up and down with vizors and lights, puffing and thrusting, and keeping out all men so precisely, till all the town is drawn by this revel to the place; and at last, tag and rag, freshmen and subsizers and all be packed in together so thick, as now is scant left room for the Prologue to come upon the stage'. Or perhaps when there was no play to be seen he would seek that 'old school-fellow of mine in Cambridge, that having lost five shillings abroad at cards, would boast he had saved two candles at home by being out of his chamber'. Very certain it is that he did not entirely fill his time according to Burghley's advice, with his book and good company.[15]

The trouble was that his tutor observed as much, and indiscreetly informed John's father. He must have gone so far as to hint that there was a danger of John's contracting an unsuitable marriage. The news came full circle. At last John had the theme for the first of his memorable letters. It belongs to the same year as his Latin letter to Walsingham.

'There be two things,' began John vaguely, 'that if a man can attain in his doings he must needs prosper. The one is that it be well meant, the other that it be well taken. The one a man may provide for, the other he must pray for, or else if he want it, his good meaning may have ill success. And this plainly appeareth in my case at this present, which if others would take as well as I meant, they should rather have cause to commend my discretion than to rebuke my rashness.' Having established a prima facie case of victimization, he proceeded cautiously to explore the charge against him. 'As for my Tutor's letter, I know not what was in it, and it may be that he, for the good affection, great love, and special care he hath of me, would doubt the worst, fear the hardest, and write the most. But if you knew all the truth, and nothing but the truth, and would bring with you no prejudicial opinion of the matter, I think you would not be in such despair of my well-doing as you seem to be.'

He took back in one sentence what he offered in another. He would do nothing to earn displeasure, 'whether married or un-married'. He would certainly not plunge into an imprudent match as another 'whose doings I detest' had recently done, 'drawn by desire, led by lust, won by wantonness'. By curious chance, the name of this other youth was Byron.

But he had no sooner given this assurance than he relapsed again into evasions. 'Youth is slippery, flesh is frail, love is light, wedding is destiny . . .' His father was a widower now, his mind dwelling increasingly in the past, and perhaps this made him tolerant.[86]

> When I look back, and in myself behold
> The wandering ways that youth could not descry,
> And see the fearful course that youth did hold . . .

If it did not, there was little he could do about it any more. When John was only twenty-one years old, a student of law at the Inns of Court in London, his father died and was buried in the church of St Gregory by old St Paul's. The younger John's grandfather had died over twenty years before his birth, and now his father was dead, only just twenty years after it. This was to be a recurrent feature in the Kelston branch, helping to explain the vagueness and inaccuracy of family traditions among its early members.

SIR JOHN HARINGTON OF KELSTON AND HIS WIFE
1561-1612

John abruptly abandoned the study of law, and travelled down to supervise the completion of the unfinished house at Kelston; 'for, on forfeiture of twenty-five rich manors, it was time for our house to travel southward, where, if they brought no lands, they found some, from the goodness of Henry VIII'. He set out to learn about the people who lived upon these lands, and the secrets of their country crafts; laying the foundations of an affection for simple people and their ways which is one of his most lovable qualities.

He indulged his flair for invention on the great house that was sapping his revenues. Running water was a particular source of inspiration to him. There is a sketch among his papers of the fountain he designed out of a description in Ariosto, a square canopy set on four pillars, with a spire rising from its centre. On the pinnacle of the spire a hare sat on a tun, or barrel, holding a ring in its paws. (John also used this device representing his name on a seal, and on the title-page of one of his books.) At the base of the spire were the tap and other gadgets operating the fountain. The other use to which he put running water will appear presently.[87]

So the mansion of Kelston reached completion. The only record of its appearance is Bishop Pococke's description, who travelled from Bath to see it in 1764, as it was being demolished. 'There is a handsome Doric door-case to it, with niches in front, divided by Ionic pillars; and at the back of the house is a door-case, if I mistake not, with an Ionic entablature, and a broken pediment with a vase in the middle, which is not judged to be in good taste, but it is in other respects a fine door-case.' (The critics of the Georgian era did not often judge the work of the Elizabethans to be in good taste.)

'There are two grand chimney-pieces, one in the Corinthian order, the other a bad execution of a kind of Tuscan, with a bas-relief of a king and people about him, and a tower as with men on it. Under it is this inscription: Psalme CV.

'The windows are the large kind divided into several compartments. There is a grand room both below and above in which are these chimney-pieces; within them are two smaller rooms divided in two by cage-work, to which are closets in the one tower. The staircase is in the other tower, the floors of which are of solid timber. The room up two pair of stairs seems to have been designed for a gallery; so that the sleeping rooms seem to have been in the tower. The house is all hewn stone, but of the tower only the coigns and window frames. A wing joined on each side of it of stables and kitchen offices. They are pulling all down to build a house in a very fine situation on the hill over it.'

A survey, made in 1744, shows in rough outline how the wings were joined to the main building. It shows too the relation of these to other buildings that escaped the destruction of the manor house, the rectory, and a dovecote, the crumbling orchard wall and beside it, a little stone building that may have been the brewery. Apart from this, and Pococke's scrappy notes, only one other fragment of evidence can be added to show what kind of house it was that the first two John Harington's of Kelston spent fifteen years in building. It is four square feet of stone from the chimney-piece that Pococke described as a bad execution of a kind of Tuscan, and it shows the battered king with his people about him, and the tower with men on it. In 1857 a member of the family who owned Kelston Park found it lying out in the open. It was lithographed for reproduction in the *Memoranda of Kelston*, and removed to the schoolhouse, in which it is still preserved.[88]

Among the neighbours with whom John relaxed from the responsibilities of his house and estates were the Rogers of Cannington. These were a generation ahead of the Haringtons among the new landowners of Somerset. Henry VIII had granted the manor of Cannington to Edward Rogers on the suppression of the monastery, and his son had died, a belted knight, in the same year as John's father. The family with whom John exchanged civilities at Cannington consisted of the widowed Lady Jane Rogers and her three children, Edward, William, and Mary. They were rich, but Mary had two brothers.

John's first definite connection with the Rogers family occurred in July 1586, when he went with Edward to Ireland. John was now twenty-five years old, and he appears from his epigrams to have already visited the court at which Philip Sidney lingered until he was over thirty years old, before he was given employment. In choosing men for their proper vocations, Queen Elizabeth was as slow as she was infallible. She was too slow in the case of Philip Sidney. He died at Zutphen in the year in which John and Edward Rogers joined the undertaking to settle the ravaged province of Munster.

The project was a failure, and John returned to Kelston in a few months. Already Ireland was marked out as his fate: his en-

THE BYRON OF HIS AGE

thusiasm for Ireland remained with him all his life, though it brought gain neither to that country nor to himself. Already on this first visit he showed sensitiveness in his attempt to understand a different people, whether their superstitions, their religion, or their agriculture. If this quality of sympathy and understanding had been less rare in the Irish administration of the Tudors and Stewarts the story of Ireland might have been a happier one. So might the story of John Harington, who longed all his life for some cause to which he might dedicate himself. There was another, more suited to his genius than Ireland, but it did not occur to him until death was near.

We do not know exactly when he married Mary Rogers, but it may have been soon after he returned from Ireland. 'Sweet Mall', the first mistress of Kelston, remains altogether an elusive figure. Her private life with John was publicized in poems as no English wife's had ever been, yet she remains entirely silent. She looks out of the portrait of her beside her husband, demure, enigmatic, perhaps faintly amused. John himself paid tribute to her discretion: 'thy lips do not wanton out of discretion's path, like the many gossiping dames we could name'. John told all the world of his devotion.

He told the Queen. 'The Queen did once ask my wife in merry sort how she kept my good will and love, which I did always maintain to be truly good towards her and my children. My Mall in wise and discreet manner told her Highness, she had confidence in her husband's understanding and courage, well founded on her own steadfastness not to offend or thwart, but to cherish and obey. Hereby did she persuade her husband of her own affections, and in so doing did command his.'[39]

He told Lady Jane Rogers with a candour, astonishing for the age in which he lived:

When with your daughter, Madam, you be chatt'ring,
I find that oft against me you incense her.
And then forsooth, my kindness all in flatt'ring,
My love is all but lust — this is your censure.

He told Mall herself, repeatedly, in lines all the more moving for the gentle humour they contain.

Your little dog that barked as I came by
I struck by hap so hard, I made him cry;

And straight you put your finger in your eye
And lowering sat. I asked the reason why.
'Love me and love my dog', thou didst reply,
'Love as both should be loved.' 'I will', said I,
And sealed it with a kiss. Then by and by
Cleared were the clouds of thy fair frowning sky:
Thus small events great masteries may try.

His poems to her were never couched in the high romantic vein of those his father had addressed to Isabella.

Because I once in verse did hap to call
Thee by this loving name, my dearest Mall,
Thou think'st thyself assured by the same,
In future ages I have given thee fame.
But if thou merit not such name in verity,
I mean not so to misinform posterity.
For I can thus interpret if I will,
My dearest Mall, that is, my costliest ill.

Only two great masteries were ever tried between them, those that concerned the mother-in-law with whom John enjoyed such an extraordinarily frank relationship, and the occasions of John's visits to court. Mall did not care for the life of the court, neither did her mother, and they united in deploring John's absences there.

Your mother lays it to me as a crime
That I so long do stay from you sometime,
And by her fond surmise would make you fear
My love doth grow more cold, or less sincere.
But let no causeless doubts make you believe
That, being false, that being true would grieve.
I, when I am from thee the farthest distance,
Do in my soul, by my true love's assistance,
Instead of sweet embracements, dove-like kisses,
Send kindest thoughts and most endeared wishes;
Then letters, then kind tokens pass, and then
My busy Muse employs my idle pen.
Then memory in love's defence alleges
Nine organ-pipes, our love's assured pledges.

Alas, how many live still with their wives,
Yet in true kindness absent all their lives.
Absence is true love's sauce, and serves to whet it;
They never loved whom absence makes forget it. [90]

In the end John became a hearty convert to the prejudices of his wife and mother-in-law against the life of the court: but going there young, well connected, witty, and admired, it took disillusion many years to overtake him.

He liked, for one thing, to be within earshot of great affairs. 'I do remember', he noted later, 'what Burghley did once say in my hearing to Walsingham, who had been waiting to confer with him about many great matters, whereof I had borne some part,' and so he proceeds to an anecdote capped with a moral. Another day he recorded that the Queen seemed troubled, and that 'Hatton came out from her presence with ill countenance, and pulled me aside by the girdle, and said in secret way, "if you have any suit today, I pray you put it aside. The sun doth not shine". ' Lest posterity should be left in any doubt as to what his suit is likely to have been, John included this little plan of campaign among the notes that he left: 'I must turn my poor wits towards my suit for my lands in the north . . . I must go in an early hour, before her Highness hath special matters brought up to counsel on. I must go before the breakfast covers are placed, and stand uncovered as her Highness cometh forth her chamber; then kneel and say, "God save your Majesty. I crave your ear at what hour may suit for your servant to meet your blessed countenance." Thus will I gain her favour to follow to the auditory.' [91]

He liked to be at the centre of affairs, partly because there lay the path to fortune, and partly because he had a genuine taste for the life it involved. It amused him to act the courtier. 'The Queen stood up, and bade me reach forth my arm to rest her thereon. Oh! what sweet burden to my next song! Petrarch shall eke out good matter for this business.' His song, needless to say, was on the same subject as his suit; or at any rate, the only one addressed by him to Queen Elizabeth that has survived. 'I will attend tomorrow, and leave this little poesie behind her cushion at my departing from her presence:

For ever dear, for ever dreaded Prince,
You read a verse of mine a little since,

And so pronounced each word, and every letter,
Your gracious reading graced my verse the better.
Sith then your Highness doth, by gift exceeding,
Make what you read the better for your reading,
Let my poor Muse your pains thus far importune;
Like as you read my verse, so — *read my Fortune.*
From your Highness' saucy Godson.' [92]

There is a disarming childishness about his little stratagems.

Nor must John's attitude to his godmother be allowed to appear callous. She had been surrounded for years before he ever came to court by sycophantic men, who used a language of exaggerated gallantry for which Elizabeth herself must be held responsible. If certain letters from Hatton to Elizabeth had not survived, one could scarcely have believed the language of gallantry could fly so high. John does not seem to have received any benefits from the Queen (despite his generous acknowledgments at her death) except the gift of love. And as time passed he came to value this at its true worth, and to speak of the Queen with an ever-increasing devotion.

Of this trait of vanity in her he wrote after her death: 'there is almost none that waited in Queen Elizabeth's court and observed anything, but can tell that it pleased her much to seem, and to be thought, and to be told, that she looked young. The majesty and gravity of a sceptre, borne forty-four years, could not alter that nature of a woman in her'. No one who knew her has left a more penetrating picture of Elizabeth than that of her godson. But before he learned to understand her fully, he could raise a laugh at her expense, even though his earliest references to her are filled with affection. [93]

'I came home to Kelston, and found my Mall, my children, and my cattle all well fed, well taught, and well beloved. 'Tis not so at court; ill-breeding with ill-feeding, and no love but that of the lusty god of gallantry, Asmodeus. I am to send good store of news from the country, for her Highness' entertainment . . . Her Highness loveth merry tales.' [94]

He was already half way to the views Sweet Mall and her mother held on the life at court. But it was the easier half of what was to be a painful journey.

Mall, in my absence this is still your song:
Come home, sweetheart, you stay from home too long.

John's next return home, if tradition speaks true, was the first of a succession of increasingly censorious dismissals by his god-mother. It occurred in this way. John, with his father's imagina-tive sympathy for the constricted lives of young women in his day, had observed that the ladies of the court 'cannot always be prick-ing in clouts'. They wanted a little diversion sometimes. The entertainment he chose them was the twenty-eighth book of Ariosto's *Orlando Furioso*, and he translated this scurrilous tale of feminine frailty into fluent eight-line stanzas. These circulated among the delighted ladies-in-waiting until finally they fell into the hands of the Queen. Elizabeth may just possibly have been shocked, or she may have felt it necessary to affect indignation. But more probably the verses served to confirm her in a judgment that she had half formed already. The right vocation for her godson was that of poet. She dismissed him from court, with a show of indignation, until he should have translated the whole of Ariosto's enormous work.

The result is a forgotten masterpiece of English literature. It is a landmark in English book production alone, with its beautiful copper-plate illustrations, and fortunately there is evidence of the trouble John took over the appearance of his book. Even if there had not been, one might have suspected his enthusiasm for the mechanics of this (to him) new craft. But in the year following the book's appearance, on 31 May 1592, John received this curious message from the Privy Council: 'We are informed that by sinister and indirect means you have formerly withdrawn one Thomas Wells from his master, Augustine Rither, printer and graver of London, to serve you in that profession, being a matter contrary to your quality and calling, and having at last with much ado restored him to his master, you have of late gotten him again by like indirect means from his said master, detaining him still, to the utter impoverishing of the poor man whose living only consisteth on his master and manual occupation, wherein with much travail and charges he hath brought up and instructed his said apprentice, hoping to reap some benefit and relief thereby as were fit. We have thought good to let you know that we very much marvel at and mislike your uncharitable manner of dealing in this matter, not fitting a gentleman of your place and haviour, and do therefore strictly require you immediately upon sight hereof to redeliver him back to his said master, or to make your personal appearance before us without delay to answer your default therein.'[95]

Considering John had received no calling, in spite of all his efforts, except this calling from the Queen to produce an English *Orlando Furioso*, the strictures of the Privy Council appear rather unfair. But it had moved too late to injure the quality of John's first book, and as to its lesson on what was fitting to a gentleman, John prepared to show the Privy Council what activities he considered consistent with his place and haviour. The Privy Council's letter is the first evidence that John's contemporaries were beginning to learn the shocking truth about him. Fundamentally, he was a traitor to his class. The most royalist of all the Haringtons, he was yet the sort of man who might, and did, beget a Republican son.

This is what made Ariosto's epic such a congenial theme for him. The legend of Roland had been dressed in all the splendour of medieval pageantry, but Ariosto's treatment is half mocking, and the half-vanished world of chivalry is seen through disturbed, Renaissance eyes. John saw the life of Elizabeth's court through the same eyes, penetrating, sometimes mocking, sometimes deadly serious. So he understood Ariosto well. And he expanded, contracted, and added to the original until he had achieved a perfect freedom and flexibility in the most exacting of literary forms. Here is his introduction to Ariosto's twenty-eighth book, the cause of his punishment:

> You ladies, ye that ladies hold in prize,
> Give not (perdie) your ear to this same tale
> The which to tell mine host doth here devise,
> To make men think your virtues are but small.
> Though from so base a tongue there can arise
> To your sweet sex no just disgrace at all,
> Fools will find fault without the cause discerning,
> And argue most of that they have no learning.
>
> Turn o'er the leaf, and let this tale alone,
> If any think the sex by this disgraced.
> I write it for no spite, nor malice none,
> But in my Author's book I find it placed.
> My loyal love to ladies all is known,
> In whom I see such worth to be embraced
> That their's I am, and glad would be therefore
> To shew thereof a thousand proofs and more.

Peruse it not; or if you do it read,
Esteem it not, but as an idle babble.
Regard it not; or if you take some heed,
Believe it not, but as a foolish fable.
But to the matter . . .

Ben Jonson said that Harington's *Orlando Furioso* was, under all translations, the worst, and Professor Raleigh is among the modern scholars who have praised it highly, and it has not been reprinted since 1634.⁹⁶

But meanwhile, in his thirtieth year, it had made John Harington famous. He was created High Sheriff of Somerset, the office so many of his name had held in other counties. A family tradition tells that Queen Elizabeth visited Kelston during her progress to Bristol in the following year; that she dined beneath the Ariosto fountain; and that St Catharine's Court had to be sold to pay the expenses of her compliment. John was certainly present during her visit to Oxford the same year.

For the rest, he seems to have remained away from court now for several years, attending to his estates 'among clouted shoes, in his frieze jacket and galoshes', and mastering his new public duties. Of these he has left a charming anecdote that tells as much of his character as of the times in which he lived.

'There was a craftsman in Bath, a recusant puritan who, condemning our church, our bishops, our sacraments, our prayers, was condemned himself to die at the Assizes. At my request Judge Anderson reprieved him, and he was suffered to remain at Bath upon bail. The bishop conferred with him, in hope to convert him, and first my lord alleged for the authority of the church, St Augustine. The shoemaker answered:

' "Austin was but a man."

'He [Bishop Still] produced, for antiquity of bishops, the fathers of the Council of Nice. He answered:

' "they were also but men, and might err."

' "Why then," saith the bishop, "thou art but a man, and mayest and dost err."

' "No Sir," saith me, "the spirit bears witness to my spirit, I am a child of God."

' "Alas," saith the bishop, "thy blind spirit will lead thee to the gallows."

' "If I die," saith he, "in the Lord's cause, I shall be a martyr."

'The bishop turning to me, stirred as much to pity as impatience,
' "this man," said he, "is not a sheep strayed from the fold, for
such may be brought in again on the shepherd's shoulders. But
this is a wild buck broken out of a park whose pale is thrown down,
that flies the farther off, the more he is hunted."

'Yet this man, that stopped his ears like the adder to the charms
of the bishop, was after persuaded by a layman, and grew
conformable.'[97]

John possessed the tolerance of a very compassionate nature, and
he expressed it in memorable phrases. It was not as a lecher that
he wrote 'for that same sweet sin of lechery, I would say as the
friar said, a young man and a young woman in a green arbour
in a May morning; if God do not forgive it, I would. For as Sir
Thomas More saith of Edward IV: he was subject to a sin from
which health of body in great prosperity of fortune, without a
special grace, hardly refraineth. And to speak uprightly of him,
his lusts were not furious but friendly, able, with his goodly person,
his sweet behaviour, and his bountiful gifts, to have won Lucretia.
Besides, no doubt his sin was the less in that he ever loved his
wife most dearly, and used her most respectively. For I have
ever maintained this paradox; it is better to love two too many
than one too few'.[98]

He recognized in his own actions the interplay of good and evil
forces, and this made him generous in his interpretation of the
actions of others. 'We go brave in apparel that we may be taken
for better men than we be. We use much bumbastings and
quiltings to seem better formed, better shouldered, smaller waisted,
and fuller thighed than we are. We barb and shave oft, to seem
younger than we are. We use perfumes both inward and outward,
to seem sweeter than we be, corked shoes to seem taller than we be.
We use courteous salutations to seem kinder than we be, and
sometime grave and godly communication, to seem wiser and
devouter than we be. And infinite such things we may observe
in ourselves, which are some of them commendable in this respect,
that by good and true endeavour to seem to be, we may obtain at
last the habit and grace to become to be such indeed.'[99]

Such sensible observations had been circulating at court for
years, in John's epigrams, and were already pouring into his
wonderful letters. They had first found their way into print in
the bizarre notes to the *Orlando Furioso*. When he scribbled his
reflections on lechery during these idle years at Kelston, he was

toying with the most famous of his mechanical inventions. In recommending it to the world, he took occasion to publish the first and last anthology of his wit and wisdom.

On 14 August 1596 he wrote to the Dowager Lady Russell, explaining his intentions. 'I was the willinger to write such a toy as this, because I had lain methought almost buried in the country these three or four years, and I thought this would give some occasion to have me thought of and talked of: not as he that burned the temple of Diana to make him famous; nor as Absalom, that burned Joab's corn to make him come to speech with him; but rather as Sophocles, to save himself from a writ of dotage, showed the work he was presently in hand with.'[100]

The work was one of reform. 'We hear them say daily,' he observed, 'that there was never under so gracious a head so graceless members; after so sincere teaching, so sinful living; in so shining light, such works of darkness. When they cry out upon us, yea cry indeed, for I have seen them speak it with tears, that lust and hatred were never so hot, love and charity were never so cold; that there was never less devotion, never more division; that all impiety hath all impunity . . . these phrases (I say) being written and recorded, sounded and resounded in so many books and sermons in Cambridge, in Oxford, in the court, in the country, at Paul's Cross in Paul's Churchyard: may not I, as a sorry writer among the rest, in a merry matter, and in a harmless manner, professing purposely *Of vaults and privies, sinks and draughts to write,* prove according to my poor strength, to draw the readers by some pretty draught to sink into a deep and necessary consideration, how to mend some of their privy faults?'[101]

That was the question put by *The Metamorphosis of Ajax* when it was published in 1592. And the answer was No. If it was unfitting a gentleman of John's place and haviour to dabble in the trade of book production, it was still less fitting that he should make learning and letters the tools of sanitary engineering.

Once again the rebel reared his head; the underlying seriousness peeps through John's gentle scorn. 'If they cry "fie, for shame" when they hear the title read or such-like, do but you say (for company) that it is a mad fantastical book indeed. And when you have done, hide it away, but where they may find it, and by the next day they will be as cunning in it as you. For this is not the first time that I have said of such a kind of book:

"In Brutus' presence, Lucrece will refuse it;
But let him turn his back, and she'll peruse it." [102]

His apology has the spirit of the apology that his father sent from
the Tower to Bishop Gardiner. 'If I had entitled the book *A
Sermon shewing a sovereign salve for the sores of the soul; or, A wholesome
haven of health to harbour the heart in; or, A marvellous medecine for the
maladies of the mind*, would you ever have asked after such a book?
Would these grave and sober titles have won you to the view of
three or four tittles, much less three or four score periods? But
when you heard there was one that had written of A Jakes, straight
you had a great mind to see what strange discourse it would prove.
You made inquiry who wrote it, where it might be had, when it
would come forth. You prayed your friend to buy it, beg it,
borrow it, that you might see what good stuff was in it. And why
had you such a mind to it? I can tell you. You hoped for some
merriments, some toys, some scurrility; or, to speak plain English,
some knavery.' He often used that term 'in plain English', and
similar expressions, to emphasize the overriding importance of
honest thinking: 'I holding my purpose to speak frankly and truly,
as far as my understanding will serve me.' It does not always pay
to do this. [103]

John was threatened with the Star Chamber. It was not the
sauce he had mixed to tickle the public appetite for merriments
and toys that had exposed him to this danger. In *The Metamorphosis of Ajax*, as in his verse epigrams, he had made satirical
allusions to people whose identity is now generally obscure. But
one of his victims was identified as Leicester, who had died four
years earlier in the year of the great armada. The allusion is uncertain now, but we know of John's dislike of Leicester, because he
stated it in a later composition, *A Brief View of the State of the Church*.
Elizabeth's magnanimity and her affection for her godson emerge
pleasantly from the tradition that it was she who saved him from
legal process, and sent him packing to Kelston a second time.
At the end of 1598 he was still buried in cautious obscurity, but
by now his cousin Robert Markham could write: 'your book is
almost forgiven, and I may say forgotten; but not for its lack of
wit or satire ... and though her Highness signified displeasure in
outward sort, yet did she like the marrow of your book ...'. The
Queen is minded to take you to her favour, but she sweareth that
she believes you will make epigrams and write *misacmos* again on

her and all the court. She hath been heard to say, "that merry poet, her godson, must not come to Greenwich till he hath grown sober" '. Misacmos was the supposed author of the offending book, though it bore on the title-page John's device of a hare, a ring, and a tun.[104]

Back at Kelston, John was exposed to the rightness of his mother-in-law's, and his wife's, views on the unprofitable nature of the courtier's life. He encouraged Lady Rogers herself to help mend matters.

> If I but speak words of unpleasing sound,
> Yea, though the same be but in sport and play,
> You bid me peace, or else a thousand pound;
> Such words shall work out of my children's way.
> When you say thus, I have no word to say.
> Thus without obligation I stand bound,
> Thus wealth makes you command, hope me obey.
> But let me find this true another day,
> Else when your body shall be brought to ground,
> Your soul to blessed Abraham's bosom, I
> May with good manners give your soul the lie.[105]

One of Sweet Mall's brothers was now dead, leaving only Edward, with whom John had gone to Ireland over ten years before. It was John's object to ensure that Mall inherited at least half of her mother's wealth. The outcome of his efforts will appear later. The startling thing about his tactics at this stage is that they would seem to have been fatal to his success. So far from having no word to say, he addressed her with a candour that scarcely any son-in-law can have dared to use in any age or circumstances. Yet they were successful up to a point. Lady Rogers must have been a person with a sense of humour and great breadth of mind.

> My Mall, in your short absence from this place,
> Myself here dining at your mother's board,
> Your little son did thus begin his grace;
> 'The eyes of all things look on thee, O Lord,
> And thou their food dost give them in due season.'
> 'Peace boy,' quoth I, 'not more of this a word,
> For in this place, this Grace hath little reason:
> Whenas we speak to God, we must speak true,

And though the meat be good in taste and season,
This season for a dinner is not due.
Then peace, I say; to lie to God is treason.'
'Say on, my boy,' saith she, 'your father mocks.
Clowns, and not courtiers, use to go by clocks.'
'Courtiers by clocks,' said I, 'and clowns by cocks.'
Now if your mother chide with me for this,
Then you must reconcile us with a kiss.[106]

John had apparently inherited his father's concern for the punctuality of meals.

Life in this bantering, affectionate family was divided between Kelston, Cannington, and Bath; which 'hath, since her Highness' being there, wonderfully beautified itself in fine houses for victualling and lodging, but decays as fast in their ancient and honest trades of merchandise and clothing'. It was becoming a fashionable spa. John possessed a town house there, and in one of his epigrams he tells how he built another for the convenience of Lady Rogers. At Bath he met his metropolitan friends, as he remarked in a letter to Sir Hugh Portman in the spring of 1598:

'I have been to visit at the house which my Lord Treasurer [Burghley] doth occupy at the Bath, and found him and another cripple together, my cousin Sir John Harington of Exton; when it grieved me to see so much discretion, wisdom, and learning in peril of death.' John's cousin of Exton, the late Sir James and Lady Lucy's heir, was over twenty years older than himself. But he was destined to outlive the author of those words.[107]

It was during this period following his second dismissal from court that John of Kelston wrote *A Treatise on Play*. The man who had been censured by the Privy Council for supervising the printing of a book, and criticized at court for wasting his talents on sanitation, was moved to express his thoughts on one of the principal occupations considered seemly for a courtier. It was as well that this work was not published during his lifetime. It exposed a fashionable recreation as 'a spoiler of youth, a waster of wealth, yea, and of that which is not to be redeemed by wealth, our most precious time'. The idleness of court life is revealed in it, and the qualities of sloth and pride engendered there.

'And then, as though two shilling and sixpence had not as many syllables in it as one hundred pounds, you shall hear them still talking of hundreds and thousands. And wherefore is all this forsooth? Because the beholders may extoll their brave minds, and say one to another, "did you ever see gentlemen that cared so little for their money, so brave, so bountiful, etc." And perhaps even herein they are deceived, and that instead hereof, some of the standers by tell how they heard, but three days past, a mercer importuning some one of them for £10 matter, and could get no other answer but "God damn me, if I pay you not the next money I receive". And another had a poor widow following of him, suing to buy a copyhold in which she had a widow's estate, and offered in a year to pay fifty pound. And he protested "he had such present need of money he could not stay so long", and sold it to another for £30 in hand. And a third, perhaps, was hard chaffing with the bailey of his husbandry for giving 8d. a day this dear year to day labourers, saying "he might have had them for 7d." Lo, the bounty of these magnifical players!'[108]

It is hard to recognize, in the author of these words, the man who has been dismissed as a wag. *A Treatise on Play* does indeed contain the old humour, and the lightness which can be mistaken for levity: 'the persons being such with whom 5000 crowns is but a reward to a courtesan for a night's lodging, it cannot in them seem covetousness'. But that other quality, which John may have learnt to conceal first in the Prebend House at Stepney, his parents' high seriousness, peeps out of this treatise. 'O Christians! If you will not learn fair wars and fair play and honesty from heaven, learn it from the heathen.'

Early in 1599 John's contemplative life at Kelston was rudely interrupted by a letter containing an extraordinary postscript. 'Her Majesty's Grace appointeth me to go to Ireland, and hath specially commended yourself to my assistance and notice. Hence you are to learn mine affections for her commands. You must get forward and well accoutred in all haste for this undertaking. I shall provide you to a command of horsemen in consort and command of the Earl of Southampton. Your service shall not be ill reported or unrewarded for the love the queen beareth you. I will confer such honour and advantages as are in my breast and power, forasmuch as her Majesty maketh me to command peace or war, to truce, parley, or such matter as seemeth best for our enterprise and good of her realm. Be now assured of my love for her sake who bids it, and account your happiness in her favour, and his whom she favoureth, even myself, who wisheth your advancement, ESSEX. I have beaten Knollys and Mountjoy in

the council, and by God I will beat Tyronne in the field. For
nothing worthy her Majesty's honour hath yet been achieved.'[109]

So John was summoned to return to Ireland, and to meet Hugh
O'Neill, last of the kings of Ulster, whom the English compelled to
subscribe himself Earl of Tyrone. A surviving letter from his
cousin Robert Markham suggests that John was perfectly informed
of the politics of the situation. 'Sir William Knollys is not well
pleased, the queen is not well pleased, the Lord Deputy [Essex]
may be pleased now, but I sore fear what may happen hereafter.'
The great Lord Burghley had just died, and feeling ran high
between the younger Cecil and Essex. 'If my Lord Treasurer had
lived longer, matters would go on surer. He was our great pilot,
on whom all cast their eyes, and sought their safety. The Queen's
Highness doth often speak of him in tears, and turn aside when he
is discoursed of.'[110]

Why did Elizabeth think so belatedly of employing her godson
when Essex finally persuaded her to send him to Ireland? Perhaps
Robert Markham has the right answer, perhaps indeed the
nephew of her former lady-in-waiting Isabella had it in confidence
from her own lips. 'You are to take account of all that passes in
your expedition, and keep journal thereof, unknown to any in the
company; this will be expected of you. I have reasons to give for
this order.' One by one Elizabeth's confidential servants had died,
Hatton and Leicester, Walsingham, and now at last Burghley also.
Lonely on her pinnacle of power amongst a new generation of
wrangling and ambitious men, the Queen perhaps decided at last
how she could best use her godson, his outspoken honesty, and his
rare reporting skill. But John's own story of his expedition to
Ireland under Essex, and his interpretation of events there, would
fill a separate chapter.

He set off in such haste, 'I had scant time to put on my boots'.
But he found time to scribble to his wife from Chester, before he
crossed the Irish Sea:

> When I from thee, my dear, last day departed,
> Summoned by honour to this Irish action,
> Thy tender eyes shed tears; but I, hard-hearted,
> Took from those tears a joy and satisfaction.
> Such for her spouse (thought I) was Lucrece' sadness,
> Whom to his ruin tyrant Tarquin tempted.
> So mourned she, whose husband feigned madness,

Thereby from Trojan wars to stand exempted.
Thus then, I do rejoice in that thou grievest;
And yet, sweet fool, I love thee, thou believest.[111]

In due course John was busy composing apologetic verses, explaining what he meant by the term 'sweet fool'. But by then he was applying it, in a harsher sense, to himself.

From Ireland John wrote enthusiastically to his confidential servant Thomas Combe: 'I have informed myself reasonably well of the whole state of the country, by observation and conference; so that I count the knowledge I have gotten here worth more than half the three hundred pounds this journey hath cost me. And as to war, joining the practice to the theory, and reading the book you so praised, and other books of Sir Griffin Markham's, with his conference and instructions, I hope at my coming home to talk of counterscarps and casemates with any of our captains.'[112]

Sir Griffin Markham was John's first cousin, and the author of *The Souldier's Accidence*, *The Souldier's Grammar*, and *The Souldier's Exercise*, helpful handbooks in those days of amateur warfare. There were 'three Markhams more' in Ireland at the time, the sons of Robert, who had advised John to keep an Irish journal.

And there was Sir Henry Harington, the younger brother of Sir John Harington of Exton. He had received nothing out of his father's rich patrimony, and he has been designated 'of Elmsthorpe' after the property he obtained at his marriage. He is one of the younger sons, more often buried in oblivion, who possessed the pardonable itch to create a patrimony where they had inherited none, but who lacked the wits to achieve their ends. Sir Henry would perhaps have preferred oblivion to the publicity he has been accorded. His misfortunes have placed him in a historical novel, and have secured him the first mention among any of his name in Professor Trevor-Roper's thesis concerning the 'declining gentry' of 1540-1640. He is joined there by some of his family who declined later, and surprisingly enough, by some who did not.[113]

This is how John of Kelston described the fate of his cousin Henry, in the journal of his campaign. 'The next day following (July 1) his Lordship [Essex] viewed the place where (some weeks before) Phelim McPheogh, with 400 foot and 150 horse (on a plain of unspeakable advantage to our men) had overthrown Sir Hen. Harington, Knight, who had with him 450 foot and 60 horse. They which escaped by flight, or by base hiding of themselves from the force of the rebels' sword, were by a Court Martial condemned (on the 3rd) to be hanged on the gallows; which sentence was mitigated by his Lordship's mercy, by which every 10th man was sentenced only to die; the rest appointed to serve in the army for pioneers.'[114]

From Athlone John wrote to Sir Anthony Standen shortly afterwards: 'my cousin Sir H. Harington, in a treacherous parley with Rorie Ogie, a notable rebel, was taken and conveyed to his habitation a prisoner. His friends, not complying with the terms offered for his ransom, sent a large band to his rescue, which the rebel seeing to surround his house, rose in his shirt, and gave Sir Henry fourteen grievous wounds, then made his way through the whole band and escaped, notwithstanding his walls were only mud'.[115]

Poor Henry returned to England to be censured; and the magnanimous John began to revise his harsh opinion of him. At least there was one person in Ireland, he reported, who would not hear it said that Sir Henry lacked courage. John was present when Tyrone signed the treaty that sealed the fate of Essex, and he recalled how the great O'Neill 'asked of Sir Henry Harington and said he had much wrong to have an imputation of want of courage for the last defeat at Arkloo; protesting that himself had known Sir Henry serve as valiantly as ever any man did, naming the time, place, and persons'.

John and his cousin Markham fared better. 'My Lord gave Sir Griffin Markham great commendation, and made him colonel and commander of all the horse in Connaught; and gave me and some others the honour of knighthood in the field.' This knighthood being reported back to England in a manner designed to raise the familiar laugh across the Irish Sea, it has been entered with all seriousness in the Calender of State Papers as that of Sir Ajax Harington.

But alas, it proved to be no laughing matter. Elizabeth was sparing in her awards of honours, and had given Essex strict written instructions to follow her example. The number of knighthoods that Essex bestowed in Ireland became a public joke in England, and a matter of special fury to the Queen. John had one of them: he was present when Essex made a truce with the man he had been sent with a costly army to fight: the name of Harington had been disgraced by his cousin: and to crown all,

Essex ordered John to return with him to England when he made his fatal attempt to reconcile himself personally with his sovereign. He received the third, most painful, and least deserved of his dismissals. Since we shall have to consider later the bitter accusation of young Cecil that John had been disloyal to the memory of his godmother, let his conduct now be carefully noted. He had received no material benefits at any time from her. He had hurried to Ireland at considerable expense, on her command; and had returned on the order of her Lord Deputy. Yet in the face of her accusations and anger he displayed only an increasing affection, and a profound pity. Moved by these feelings, he wrote the finest descriptions of the Queen that anyone has ever written, and the best prose that ever flowed from his fluent pen.

Even his good nature did not forsake him. 'I came to court in the very heat and height of all displeasures. After I had been there but an hour I was threatened with the Fleet. I answered poetically that, coming so late from the land service, I hoped that I should not be pressed to serve in her Majesty's fleet in Fleet-street. After three days every man wondered to see me at liberty. But though in conscience there was neither rhyme nor reason to punish me for going to see Tyrone, yet if my rhyme had not been better liked of than my reason (I mean when I gave the young Baron of Dungannon an Ariosto), I think I had lain by the heels for it. But I had this good fortune, that, after four or five days, the queen had talked to me, and twice talked to me, though very briefly. At last she gave me a full and gracious audience in the withdrawing chamber at Whitehall, where herself being accuser, judge, and witness, I was cleared, and graciously dismissed. What should I say? I seemed to myself for the time, like St Paul, wrapped up in the third heaven, where he heard words not to be uttered by men. For neither must I utter what I then heard; until I come to heaven, I shall never come before a statelier judge again, nor one that can temper majesty, wisdom, learning, choler, and favour better than her Highness did at that time.' So he wrote to Sir Anthony Standen from Kelston on 20 February 1600, five days before Essex was executed. But another letter he wrote eighteen months later reveals that Elizabeth's forgiveness was not complete.[116]

His sympathy for her unhappiness was greater than his personal bitterness. 'I humbly thank you for that venison I did not eat, but my wife did it much commendation. For six weeks I left my oxen and sheep and ventured to court, where I find many lean-kinded beasts, and some not unhorned. Much was my comfort in being well received, notwithstanding it is an ill hour for seeing the Queen. The madcaps are all in riot, and much evil threatened. In good sooth I feared her Majesty more than the rebel Tyrone, and wished I had never received my Lord of Essex's honour of knighthood. She is quite disfavoured and unattired, and these troubles waste her much. She disregardeth every costly cover that cometh to the table, and taketh little but manchet and succory potage. Every new message from the city doth disturb her, and she frowns on all the ladies. I had a sharp message from her brought by my Lord Buckhurst, namely thus; "go tell that witty fellow, my godson, to get home; it is no season to fool it here." I liked this as little as she doth my knighthood, so took to my boots and returned to the plough in bad weather . . . and will not leave my poor castle of Kelston, for fear of finding a worse elsewhere, as others have done. I will eat Aldborne rabbits, and get fish (as you recommend) from the man at Curry-Rival; and get partridge and hares when I can, and my venison where I can; and leave all great matters to those that like them better than myself.'

By 'fooling it here', the queen referred to John's attempts to cheer her dreary court with his wit. He still did so from the country, and even tried to stimulate her appetite with sweet-meats, in spite of a warning he had given himself many years before. 'The Queen's Majesty tasted my wife's comfits, and did much praise her cunning in the making. Send no more; for other ladies' jealousy worketh against my Mall's comfits, and this will not comfort her.'

But amid the Queen's varying moods her godson's presents were now acceptable, and Sir Philip Sidney's brother Robert wrote to tell him so. 'Worthy Knight, Your present to the Queen was well accepted of. She did much commend your verse, nor did she less praise your prose. Your Irish business is less talked of at her Highness' palace, for all agree that you did go and do as you were bidden; and if the commanders went not where they ought, how should the captains do better withouten order? But mum, my worthy knight. I crave all pardon for touching your galled back.

'The Queen hath tasted your dainties, and saith you have marvellous skill in cooking of good fruits . . . Now you have left the sword in Ireland and taken to the plough in England, let me have proofs of your employ, and send me verses when you can. I do see the Queen often. She doth wax weak since the late troubles, and Burghley's death doth often draw tears from her goodly cheeks. She walketh out but little, meditates much alone, and sometimes writes in private to her best friends . . .'[11]

Lady Rogers lived to see the triumph of her views on the life of the court. Then she died, in the spring of 1601, leaving many manors to John and James, the sons of Kelston's worthy knight, and making provision also for his daughters. He had no excuse to give her soul the lie, when it lay in blessed Abraham's bosom. The family of Edward Rogers was also provided for. But like so many wills, that of Lady Rogers was not sufficiently explicit: it did not cover the personal effects of her house of Cannington. In a few years the Court of Star Chamber was to investigate what occurred as a result.

Meanwhile the minds of men were turned increasingly to the question of the succession. Sir John pictured this preoccupation with vivid strokes when he came to write of Bishop Hutton. 'I no sooner remember this famous and worthy prelate but I think I see him in the chapel at Whitehall, Queen Elizabeth at the window in the closet, all the lords of the Parliament, spiritual and temporal, about them, and then (after his three courses) that I hear him out of the pulpit thundering this text: "the kingdoms of the earth are mine, and I do give them to whom I will, and I have given them to Nebuchadnezzar and his son, and to his son's son." Which text when he had thus produced, taking the sense rather than the words of the prophet, there followed first so general a murmur of one friend whispering to another, then such an erected countenance in those that had none to speak to, lastly so quiet a silence and attention, in expectance of some strange doctrine, where text itself gave away kindgoms and sceptres, as I have never observed either before or since . . .

'He noted that Nero was specially hated for wishing to have no successor; that even Augustus was the worse beloved for appointing an ill man to his successor. And at last, insinuating as far as he durst the nearness of blood of our present sovereign, he said plainly that the expectations and presages of all writers went northward, naming without any circumlocution, Scotland! "Which," said he, "if it be an error, it will be found to be a learned error."

'When he had finished this sermon there was no man that knew

Queen Elizabeth's disposition, but imagined that such a speech was as welcome as salt to the eyes or, to use her own words, "to pin up her winding sheet before her face." '[118]

John paid his last visit to his godmother. He wrote back to Kelston on 27 December 1602: 'Sweet Mall, I herewith send thee what I would God none did know, some ill bodings of the realm and its welfare. Our dear Queen, my royal godmother, and this state's natural mother, doth now bear shew of human infirmity, too fast for that evil which we shall get by her death, and too slow for that good which she shall get by her releasement from pains and misery ... I find some less mindful of what they are soon to lose, than of what they may perchance hereafter get. Now, on my part, I cannot blot from my memory's table the goodness of our sovereign Lady to me, even (I will say) before born; her affection to my mother who waited in privy chamber, her bettering the state of my father's fortune (which I have, alas! so much worsted), her watchings over my youth, her liking to my free speech and admiration of my little learning and poesie, which I did so much cultivate on her command, have rooted such love, such dutiful remembrance of her princely virtues, that to turn askant from her condition with tearless eyes would stain and foul the spring and fount of gratitude.

'It was not many days since I was bidden to her presence. I blessed the happy moment; and found her in most pitiable state. She bade the archbishop ask me if I had seen Tyrone. I replied with reverence that I had seen him with the Lord Deputy. She looked up, with much choler and grief in her countenance, and said, "oh, now it mindeth me that you was *one* who saw this man *elsewhere*:" and hereat she dropped a tear, and smote her bosom. She held in her hand a golden cup, which she often put to her lips; but in sooth, her heart seemeth too full to lack more filling ... Her Majesty enquired of some matters which I had written. And as she was pleased to note my fanciful brain, I was not unheedful to feed her humour, and read some verses; whereat she smiled once, and was pleased to say; "when thou dost feel creeping time at thy gate, these fooleries will please thee less. I am past my relish for such matters. Thou seest my bodily meat doth not suit me well. I have eaten but one ill-tasted cake since yesternight." She rated most grievously at noon, at some who minded not to bring up certain matters of account. Several men have been sent to, and when ready at hand, her Highness hath dismissed in anger. But who, dearest Mall, shall say that *"your Highness hath forgotten"*? . . .

'Next month I will see thy sweet face, and kiss my boys and maids, which I pray thee not to omit on my account. Send me up, by my man Combe, my Petrarch. Adieu, sweet Mall. I am thine ever loving John Harington.'[119]

Less than three months later the great queen was dead. Did John remain in London until the end? This is how he wrote to Lord Thomas Howard a few days after. 'I am now setting forth for the country, where I will read Petrarch, Ariosto, Horace, and such wise ones. I will make verses on the maidens, and give my wine to the masters. But it shall be such as I do love, and do love me. I do much delight to meet my good friends, and discourse of getting rid of our foes. Each night do I spend, or much better part thereof, in council with the ancient examples of learning. I con over their histories, their poetry, their instructions, and thence glean my own proper conduct in matters both of merriment or discretion. Otherwise, my good Lord, I ne'er had overcome the rugged paths of Ariosto, nor won the high palm of glory which you brought unto me (venture to say it), namely our late Queen's approbation, esteem, and reward. How my poetry will be relished in time to come, I will not hazard to say. Thus much I have lived to see, and (in good sooth) feel too, that honest prose will never better a man's purse at court. And had not my fortune been in *terra firma*, I might, even for my verses, have danced barefoot with Clio and her schoolfellows until I did sweat, and then have gotten nothing to slake my thirst but a pitcher of Helicon's well.'[120]

In his mood of sadness and disillusion, John resolved never to write poetry again.

> Sweet wanton Muse that, in my greatest grief,
> Wast wont to bring me solace and relief,
> Wonted by sea and land to make me sport,
> Whether to camp or court I did resort:
> That at the plough hast been my welcome guest,
> Yea, to my wedlock bed hast boldly pressed:
> At Eton now (where first we met) I leave thee.
> Here shall my son and heir of me receive thee.[121]

But there was another reason for John's dejection, first expressed in this letter to Lord Thomas Howard: 'but I am a cripple, and not made for sports in new courts'. He was forty-two years old, and he was mortally ill.

NINE

PRISON

SIR JOHN HARINGTON had remarked on one occasion that men wondered to see him still at liberty, and it cannot have been the only occasion to give rise to such speculations.

His ancestor Sir James Harington (so the knight of Kelston called him) had been lodged in the Fleet in circumstances which the historian of South Yorkshire hailed as a wholesome triumph of the law. His father had twice enjoyed divers and many commodities in the Tower. Sir John enlarged this family tradition further, when he was confined in the Gate-House prison at Westminster.

Disaster overtook him very suddenly. In April 1603 he wrote to tell Lord Thomas Howard of his intention to retire to Kelston among his books and his friends. In the following month he was writing to Robert Cecil for help: 'it is ill soliciting business out of prison'.

The circumstances of the disaster are obscured by the fact that Sir John had become involved recently in three separate issues concerned with family property. His fortune had been, as he confessed, 'much worsted' by the expenses of court and camp, by the magnificence of Kelston, and by the luxury of his nine children, seven of whom had survived. But his prospects brightened when Lord Mounteagle of Hornby Castle died without a male heir, and soon after Sir John's return from Ireland, he had set out to take possession of the lands whose reversion had been granted to his father in 1570.

'Of a tedious and chargeable journey I have yet made this use. I have entered into the Haringtons' lands, and by help of those gracious letters you procured me in her Majesty's name, I did it with less peril, though in one place I had like to have been beaten. If I make anything at all of the title, I must acknowledge it only of her Majesty's goodness that first gave it my father, and now by this her favour continues it to me ... but for my stirring in it, it had been perpetually concealed from the Crown, as well as it is detained from the right heir. Yet I will adventure to give her Majesty £500 in money and some pretty jewel or garment, as you shall advise, only praying her Majesty will be pleased to refer the consideration of this my offer to some one or two of her Majesty's Council for expedition . . .' The letter that Nichols attributed to Sir John's father falls into context in the stratagems of the son.[122]

They were unsuccessful. The Stanleys had barred the claims of the Haringtons to the reversion of their lands by the legal device of fine and recovery, and Elizabeth presumably declined to intervene to make her grant effective. It was left to a Stewart sovereign to compensate them for their heavy loss.

Then in the following year, 1601, Lady Rogers died. The details of what really occurred at Cannington at her death may be buried among the Star Chamber records. For her son Edward deposed in the Star Chamber three years later 'that Sir John Harington in the 44th Elizabeth, foreknowing that the Lady Rogers, his wife's mother lying then at Bath, could not live above four days, did take the keys of her house at Cannington thirty miles distant, against her will, and there in riotous manner rifled the said house, and carried thence in plate and money £5000 which belonged of right to Edward Rogers Esquire, and to son Francis. That after the decease of the said Lady Rogers, the same Sir John Harington came in like riotous manner to the same house, and there burned and razed the evidences of the said Edward Rogers'.

Sir John's reply to this charge was as follows: 'That Lady Rogers ever purposed that Edward Rogers should have neither lands nor goods of hers. That on the 13th of January 1601 Sir John had the keys delivered to him by Lady Rogers, and her man Backway appointed to attend him to Cannington. That the Lady Rogers did not dislike with his going there, but her disquiet arose the next day, from the arrival of Middleton, her son's man. That Sir John behaved himself quietly on his second visit, and sustained much wrong by Mr Edward Rogers (the plaintiff), of which he had complained in the court of Star-Chamber, where he had a bill depending: neither was there anything proved of defacing evidences, etc.'

Lady Rogers's will benefited neither of her children, whom she presumably considered sufficiently well provided for already. She left her property to her grandchildren, the children both of Edward and Mary. There is no evidence as to what Lady Rogers's feelings were towards her son Edward. The nearest thing to evidence is that Sweet Mall, usually so silent, spoke up on this subject. Whether she did so from her knowledge, or from loyalty

137

to her husband, we cannot tell. He wrote to Cecil on the 17th
June 1604: 'my cause in the Star-Chamber hath had a very
honourable and full hearing, between my wife's brother and me,
and by the general consent of the whole court upon the special
motion of my Lord Chancellor, seconded most honourably by
my Lord of Northampton and other of my Lords, the sentence is
respited for a time, and the matter referred to [and here follow
five learned names]. My wife is an earnest suitor to his Majesty,
to allow and authorize this course of arbitrament by his most
gracious letter, and beseecheth your Lordship to recommend the
procuring thereof'. It may appear that Edward Rogers was at a
disadvantage in the arbitration with his influential brother-in-
law. But between the Harington case of 1600 and the Rogers case
of 1604, Sir John had become involved in a third and far more
serious family quarrel, involving not only property but high
treason. It is at least as likely that Sir John was being victimized
by Edward Rogers, exploiting his other misfortunes with this tale
of rapine so long after Lady Rogers's death.[123]

The third case that Sir John managed to cram into this brief
period of misfortune concerned the Markhams. More particularly,
it concerned Sir Griffin Markham, the eldest of the twelve sons of
Thomas Markham of Ollerton, whose sister Isabella's cheeks had
shamed the rose. Sir Griffin had already beaten his cousin of
Kelston to the Gate-House prison in 1596, before they went
campaigning in Ireland together. What his offence was remains
unknown. In July 1603 he was arrested with Ralegh, Grey, and
Cobham for his part in the conspiracy to place Arabella Stewart
on the throne.

Sir John showed in his writings from Ireland that he admired
his cousin; 'a man with a large broad face, of a bleak complexion,
a big nose, and one of his hands maimed by a shot of a bullet',
as the proclamation for his arrest described him. Sir Griffin was
a man of action and a man of letters; but the first was predominant,
as Sir John would have wished in his own case. Sir Griffin was
condemned at Winchester and brought out to a scaffold before
the castle for execution on December 9. As he was about to lay
his head on the block he was ordered by the sheriff to rise.
Together with Grey and Cobham he had been spared, under
sentence of banishment and confiscation of his estates. A week
later he entered the Tower, of which his grandfather Sir John
Markham had once been governor. Then he left England for

ever. Forty years later he wrote to Lord Newcastle, apologizing that he was too old to return and fight for Charles I in the civil war.

Sir John's capacity for getting into scrapes is better illustrated by the Markham story than by almost any of the other accidents in his life of misfortunes. He was in no way involved in the Bye Plot, as it came to be called. But he had engaged to stand surety for his cousin, and in the month between his letter to Lord Thomas Howard saying he proposed to retire to Kelston, and Sir Griffin's arrest for treason, he was imprisoned for his cousin's debts.

On 21 May 1603 he wrote, 'a prisoner in body and fortune', to Robert Cecil, now Lord Cecil of Essingdon. 'My very good Lord, I hope your Lordship never had cause to have ill opinion of me, and of late you seemed to interpret kindly and as I meant it my just dealing with you in an accident that happened. I am now in distress, in an honest cause. I look for no relief, but from the King. Your Lordship's good word may hasten it. It will cost you little, it may avail me much. If the world would, God would not forsake me in so just a matter. Yet expedition doubles both the justice and benefit. Briefly it is thus.

'I that never committed crime in my life (let all my enemies object what they can) am betrayed by my kin into a debt of £4000, and thinking to prop up a house not contemptible, and allied to you, being a prop too weak it is all fallen on me, and so must lie here.'

Cecil's father Burghley had been a sincere friend both to Sir John and his father. Cecil himself was godfather to Sir John's eldest son. By chance he wrote Sir John a letter on May 29, before he had received this message of distress. It was addressed to 'My noble knight', and subscribed 'Your true friend, R. Cecil'. It was a letter of gratitude for the household rules of the first John Harington of Kelston, that great exponent of the arts of friendship. 'My thanks come with your papers and wholesome statutes for your father's household. I shall, as far as in me lieth, pattern the same, and give good heed for due observance thereof in my own state. Your father did much affect such prudence; nor doth his son less follow his fair sample of worth, learning and honour. I shall not fail to keep your grace and favour quick and lively in the King's breast, as far as good discretion guideth me.' Sir John was to discover how far discretion guided the younger Cecil along the paths of friendship.

There can be no doubt that Cecil delayed cautiously while Sir John lay in the Gate-House. 'Right honourable, I would have been glad to have heard some comfortable answer either by letter or message in this my distress', he next wrote. Meanwhile things were immeasurably complicated by Sir Griffin Markham's arrest for treason, and the contingency that the estates which could pay his debts would be forfeited.

But Sir John had always attracted friends in his not infrequent need, and a new one now appeared from a quite unexpected quarter. King James brought with him from Scotland a young man called Erskine, whom he later created Earl of Kellie. Erskine had written Sir John an impulsively friendly letter earlier in the year, perhaps before they had ever met. 'I entreat your favourable censure as one that shall ever love you, and do his best for the accomplishment of your desire. In short time I hope to see (?when and where) I am not certain, but then shall you know more of our master's love to yourself, and my devotion to do you service, who shall constantly remain Your assured friend T. Erskine.' He spelt it Areskyne, and meant what he said. Sir John was able to write to Cecil on 27 June, 'Sir Thomas Erskine and other my honourable friends send me word his Majesty's gracious favour to me is such, that to the relief of my distress by the Markhams, he hath said in his princely word I shall have their forfeiture.' The king was as good as his word too, and Sir John was granted the forfeited lands of Sir Griffin Markham exactly a year later.

A year is a long time to spend in prison, however, and there Sir John should have remained until either he obtained the Markham property, or sold his own to discharge the debt. By October he decided that he was satisfied with neither of the two alternatives open to him. So he escaped from prison. It appears that Lady Mary had moved to London to be near him, and resided at a house in Cannon Row. It appears further that Dobbinson, the bailiff of Westminster, entered this house with a warrant from Cecil. The rest must be guessed from the letter of expostulation that Sir John wrote him.

'Right honourable and I hope, still my special good Lord: My wife sent me your Lordship's letter written to her from Kensington, which at first sight did trouble me, both fearing she had given your Lordship some just offence, and finding some phrases in it tasting of some passion in behalf of your officer. And I wish men in your Lordship's place void of all passion but compassion, and so I beseech you be in reading mine answer.

'First my wife, who in all kind of truth I dare swear is truer than Dobbinson, affirms she said nothing but this, that she thought your Lordship nor no Lord of the Council would condemn my escape considering the danger, and much less offer her that indignity to break open her doors as Dobbinson did. And though your Lordship's warrant as a Councillor and principal secretary of the State is above any privilege and indisputable: yet her neighbours tell her that but for treasons no officer can enter a house in Cannon Row. And I am sure it was wont to be far from your honour's course to lend the countenance of state to such a wrangle of debt . . .

'If all this my adversity and cross and affliction (for good my Lord, call it not misery) have fallen on me merely by their [the Markhams'] debt, I do not unconscionably to beg their land, the King doth most graciously to grant it, and your Lordship shall do justly and honourably to further it, as you have promised favourably in your former letters.' It is unfortunate that none of these former letters have survived, while Cecil's answer to this one has done so. For it is one of the most unpleasant letters ever written.

Allowances must be made for Cecil. He was steering the ship of state through troubled waters. He had had Essex to destroy, and now he had Ralegh, with many powerful supporters even among Cecil's own relatives. He was five feet two inches tall and hunchbacked, and his deformity was the subject of cruel lampoons. He possessed little enthusiasm for literature and learning. Amidst all his preoccupations he was being bothered by a man of letters, handsome and popular, impatient of the processes of law for which Cecil stood, utterly irresponsible by his standards, and apparently of rather doubtful scruples. In the letter just quoted, Sir John had lectured Cecil on the exercise of his powers, and had gone on to criticize his law officers in detail. The reply is dated 26 October 1603.

'Although I have not so good leisure as you have to write, nor have so well studied other men's humours as you, yet I conceive I have that knowledge which is most necessary, which is to know God and myself. And therefore, although I love counsel, and have been taught patience by undergoing the sharp censures of busy brains, yet your advice at this time to me, to banish all passion but compassion, was as superfluous as many other labours of yours, which I could never con without book, and therefore cannot so particularly remember you of them as you can do me of the faults of my letter. I will therefore only answer you now in truth and plainness with what mind I wrote my letter. First I assure you I had both compassion of your imprisonment and your escape. For in the first I knew you had suffered misery, or rather affliction (for so you prescribe me to call it) which I always pitied, when it falls upon gentlemen that have any good parts in them. Secondly I was grieved in your behalf, because the reasons said to be used by you for your escape, especially concerning myself, proclaimed you to the world to have neither honesty nor conscience, both which should always be found in those whom I respect, as I have done you . . . Thus have you the motive of my letter and my passions, which if it hath wrought any other effects than it deserves in your mind to one of my place, or shall become your pen (which men say is always so full of ink as in many of your writings many blots drop upon the paper) I shall be sensible of it, howsoever other men have swallowed your censorious writings . . . And therefore, Sir John Harington, trust no more thereby to make me your solicitor than to purchase grace of the time present the sooner by railing (as you are accused to do) of the late Queen of famous memory at your dinners. For if you knew my sovereign lord as I do, you would quickly find that such works are to him unacceptable sacrifices . . .' Cecil concluded his letter by remaining 'as I have been, Your loving friend'.

To have quoted the two letters in full would not have helped to illuminate the scene. They contain too many details whose significance is lost. All that stands out clearly across the centuries is the silhouette of the two men; John Harington, pursuing family property mischievously, incompetently, and probably a good deal more innocently than the lurid evidence of these years suggests; and the future Earl of Salisbury, conscientious but mean — mean in his style, mean in his attempts at wit, meanest of all in his friendship.

BRIEF ZENITH

Sir James Harington of Exton, died 1592

- John, first Lord Harington of Exton, *c.* 1540-1613 Marr. Anne, dau. of Robert Kelway of Combe Abbey
- Sir Henry Harington, died 1613
- Sir James Harington, first Baronet, of Ridlington, died 1614

- John, second Lord Harington of Exton, died 1614
- Lucy, Countess of Bedford, died 1627
- Frances, Lady Chichester, died 1615
- Sir John Harington, died 1615
- Sir William Harington, died 1613
- Henry Harington

- Anne, Lady Bruce, died 1627

BRIEF ZENITH

SIR JOHN had written to Sweet Mall of those who showed less concern over the Queen's death than for what they might gain from her successor. But at the same time as he wrote this he sent to the King of Scots the last of his mechanical devices of which record remains, as a New Year gift.

It was a lantern made of gold, silver, brass, and iron. On its top was a crown of gold containing a perfume pan, and within it a silver reflector in the shape of a shield. On one side of the shield were engraved a sun, moon, and seven stars: on the other the story of the birth and passion of Christ had been engraved as David II, King of Scots, had scratched the scenes on the wall of his prison in Nottingham Castle. 'Lord remember me when thou comest into thy kingdom' was added by way of explanation, and the details of the allegory were further explained in poems both in Latin and English.[124]

For the time being King James only replied: 'To our trusty and well-beloved Sir John Harington Knight. Right trusty and well-beloved friend, we greet you heartily well. We have received your *lantern*, with the *poesie* you sent us by our servant William Hunter, giving you hearty thanks; as likewise for your last letter, wherein we perceive the continuance of your loyal affection to us and your service. We shall not be unmindful to extend our princely favour hereafter to you and your particulars at all good occasions. We commit you to God. James R. From our court at Holyrood House, April the Third, 1603.'[125]

Neither did he forget his promise. He created Sir John a Knight of the Bath in the year of his succession, granted him the forfeited Markham properties, added the advowson of the rectory to the manor of Kelston, and confirmed all the properties his father had obtained through his Tudor marriage to the family for ever.

But the favours shown to the knight of Kelston were nothing to what his tenth cousin of Exton might expect. Sir John Harington of Exton was the twelfth cousin of the King of Scots through their common descent from the family of Bruce. Indeed Sir John was enjoying the English patrimony of the Bruces while James was

JOHN, FIRST LORD HARINGTON OF EXTON
Died 1613

LUCY HARINGTON, COUNTESS OF BEDFORD
Died 1627

heir to their Scottish patrimony. It is sad that the correspondence in which the two cousins discussed their relationship has not survived: but it clearly ended on a note of the greatest amity.

Sir John of Exton travelled north with his younger brother James of Ridlington to meet the King on his way south, and at Grimstone in Yorkshire James knighted James, together with ten others. The King loved to transform ordinary mortal men into knights, as though in so doing he were scattering 'some sparkles of the Divinity' with which he felt himself to be endowed. As he approached London, he knighted a hundred and thirty-three more at the Charter-House alone, two more Haringtons among them. In 1611 Sir James of Ridlington was created a baronet.

Sir John of Exton was singled out for greater honours. When the King reached Rutland he halted at the home of the Earl of Rutland, and then travelled on to dine with his cousin, not at the ancestral home of Exton, but at near-by Burley. The King hunted hares on Empingham Heath, and was diverted by the appearance of 'a hundred high men that seemed like the Patagones, huge long fellows of twelve or fourteen feet high'. The King wondered what they were until, coming nearer, they proved to be a company of poor suitors on high stilts, preferring a petition against Lady Hatton.[126]

In the June of 1603 the King's daughter Elizabeth came to stay for a few days at the third family mansion of Combe Abbey and on the twenty-first, at the coronation, John was created Baron Harington of Exton. The title that had left the male line in 1458, and been extinguished altogether by the attainder of Lady Jane Grey's father in 1553, was revived.

It is not without significance to the story of the Haringtons that it had been revived solely on grounds of blood relationship to the reigning dynasty. As was remarked in more recent times of the honour of the Garter, there had been 'no damned merit about it'. Lord John of Exton had sat in the Parliaments of 1593 and 1601 as the senior representative of Rutland, without making any contribution of which evidence survives. He had been Sheriff of Rutland also, since 1592 when his father died. It is doubtful whether these evidences of virtue would have sufficed to translate him to the peerage without the blood of the Bruces.[127]

He drew closer and closer into the royal family circle. On October 19 the Princess Elizabeth was placed in his charge by an order under the privy seal, and an annual pension of £1,500

K   145

was granted to him for her maintenance. His son and heir John began · what might have become one of the most significant friendships in English history, with the heir to the throne, Prince Henry. Young John was created a knight of the Bath on January 5, when he was just thirteen years old. The four John Haringtons at the zenith of the family's fortunes are thus distinguished as follows. There is Lord John of Exton, and his son Sir John, K.B.: at Kelston there is Sir John, K.B., and his son, plain John.

Sir John of Kelston had described Lord John (in company with Burghley) as a man of discretion, wisdom, and learning. To these qualities were added an exemplary piety and a fretful, fussy nature. Lord John might have been happier had he remained a silent Member of Parliament, and the respected Sheriff of his county. Instead he was plunged into the ferment of high affairs.

On 7 November 1605 the plunge was very sudden indeed. The conspirators of the Gunpowder Plot had planned to abduct the Princess Elizabeth from her guardian and place her on the throne as soon as they had blown up her father. Lord John escaped with her from Combe Abbey a bare two hours before the rebels arrived there. He took Elizabeth to Coventry, left her under a guard of citizens there, and set off with Sir Fulke Greville to besiege Catesby at Holbeach. Surely his cousin of Kelston must have smiled as he read this worried, self-important account of what had occurred.

'Much respected Cousin, Our great care and honourable charge, entrusted to us by the King's Majesty, hath been matter of so much concern that it almost effaced the attention to kin or friend. With God's assistance we hope to do our Lady Elizabeth such service as is due to her princely endowments and natural abilities; both which appear the sweet dawning of future comfort to her royal father. The late devilish conspiracy did much disturb this part. The King hath got at much truth from the mouths of the crew themselves; for guilt hath no peace, nor can there be guilt like theirs. One hath confessed that he had many meetings at Bath about this hellish design. You will do his Majesty unspeakable kindness to watch in your neighbourhood, and give such intelligence as may furnish enquiry. We know of some evil-minded catholics in the west, whom the prince of darkness hath in alliance. God ward them from such evil, or seeking it in others . . .

'I am not yet recovered from the fever occasioned by these

disturbances. I went with Sir Fulke Greville to alarm the neighbourhood, and surprise the villains who came to Holbeach; was out five days in peril of death, in fear for the great charge I left at home. Winter hath confessed their design to surprise the Princess at my house, if their wickedness had taken place at London. Some of them say she would have been proclaimed Queen. Her Highness doth often say, "what a Queen should I have been by this means? I had rather have been with my royal father in the Parliament-house, than wear his crown on such condition." This poor lady hath not yet recovered the surprise, and is very ill and troubled . . .

'My being created Baron of Exton did give much offence to some of the catholics; and his Majesty's honouring my wife and self with the care of the Lady Elizabeth stirred up much discontent on every side. I only pray God to assist our poor endeavours, and accept our good will to do right herein, maugre all malice and envious calumny. If I can do you any service with the king, you may command my friendship in this and every other matter I can. He hath no little affection for your poetry and good learning, of which he himself is so great a judge and master. My Lady Sidney desires her remembrance to you, as do all friends from Warwickshire. I hope your disorder is much better. May you feel as much benefit from the Baths as I did aforetime.

'Thus dear cousin I have given my thoughts in large of our sad affright, as you desired by your son's letter, which is notably worded for his age. My son is now with Prince Henry, from whom I hope he will gain great advantage, from such towardly genius as he hath, even at these years. May Heaven guard this realm from all such future designs, and keep us in peace and safety! My hearty love waits on Lady Mary and everyone belonging to her household. Pray remember what I desire as to noticing evil-minded men in your parts, as it is for the King's sake and all our sakes. Adieu, dear cousin, Harington.'[128]

The knight of Kelston received that kindly, busy letter in January of 1607. By now he no longer craved the limelight and the advantages that his relatives and friends offered him at court. After so many buffetings of fortune he had arrived at last at the haven of which, as a young man, he had written in his *Orlando Furioso*:

There are (said he) some better lessons taught
Than dancings, dallyings, or dainty diet.
There shall you learn to frame your mind and thought
From will to wit, to temperence from riot.
There is the path by which you may be brought
Into the perfect paradise of quiet.[12]

And another thought returned to him from the notes he had
scattered in that work: 'I might take occasion to magnify the
felicity of our realm of England, for the gracious and mild
government of our sovereign, save that so high and plentiful a
matter requires an entire treatise, and not so broken a discourse
as I use in these brief notes. And therefore I reserve it wholly for
another work of mine own, if God give me ability to perform it.'
So in 1607, when he was already so paralysed that his son wrote
some of his letters for him, he composed the *Brief View of the State
of the Church*. It is the largest fragment that remains of the history
he never wrote, and he sent it to Prince Henry.

He also issued a slim work in verse this year, despite his eternal
farewell to the Muse of poetry. It is called *The Englishman's
Doctor*, and it presents the precepts of the Salerne school of
medicine in ten-line stanzas. The introduction is all his own:

The Gods upon a time in counsel sitting,
To rule the world what creature was most fitting,
At length from God to God this sentence ran,
To form a creature like themselves (called Man).
Being made, the world was given him, built so rarely,
No workman can come near it; hung so fairly
That the Gods, viewing it, were overjoyed:
Yet grieved that it should one day be destroyed.
Gardens had Man to walk in, set with trees
That still were bearing: but (neglecting these)
He longed for fruits unlawful, fell to riots,
Wasted his god-like body by ill diets . . .

Sir John had paid what appears to have been his last visit to
court in the summer of 1606, when the King of Denmark, brother
of James's queen, visited England. He described the drunkenness
and disorder of the celebrations in a memorable letter. In another
he drew his scathing portrait of the King, after his first interview
with him.

'Soon upon this, the Prince his Highness did enter, and in much good humour asked if I was cousin to Lord Harington of Exton. I humbly replied, his Majesty did me some honour in enquiring my kin to one whom he had so late honoured and made a baron, and moreover did add, we were both branches of the same tree. Then he enquired much of learning, and showed me his own in such sort as made me remember my examiner at Cambridge aforetime. He sought much to know my advances in philosophy, and uttered profound sentences of Aristotle and such like writers, which I had never read, and which some are bold enough to say, others do not understand. But this I must pass by. The Prince did now press my reading to him part of a canto in Ariosto; praised my utterance, and said he had been informed of many as to my learning in the time of the queen. He asked me what I thought pure wit was made of, and whom it did best become? Whether a King should not be the best clerk in his own country; and if this land did not entertain good opinion of his learning and good wisdom? His Majesty did much press for my opinion touching the power of Satan in matter of witchcraft, and asked me with much gravity if I did not understand why the devil did work more with ancient women than others? I did not refrain from a scurvy jest, and even said (notwithstanding to whom it was said) that we were taught hereof in scripture, where it is told that the devil walketh in dry places. His Majesty, moreover, was pleased to say much, and favourably, of my good report for mirth and good conceit: to which I did covertly answer, as not willing a subject should be wiser than his Prince, nor even appear so.

'More serious discourse did next ensue, wherein I wanted room to continue, and sometime room to escape. For the Queen his mother was not forgotten, nor Davidson neither. His Highness told me her death was visible in Scotland before it did really happen, being, as he said, "spoken of in secret by those whose power of sight presented to them a bloody head dancing in the air." He then did remark much on this gift, and said he had sought out of certain books a sure way to attain knowledge of future chances. Hereat he named many books, which I did not know, nor by whom written; but advised me not to consult some authors which would lead me to evil consultations. I told his Majesty the power of Satan had, I much feared, damaged my bodily frame. But I had not farther will to court his friendship, for my soul's hurt. We next discoursed somewhat on religion,

149

when at length he said: "Now, Sir, you have seen my wisdom in some sort, and I have pried into yours. I pray you, do me justice in your report, and in good season I will not fail to add to your understanding, in such points as I may find you lack amendment." I made courtesy hereat, and withdrew down the passage and out at the gate, amidst the many varlets and lordly servants who stood around.

'Thus you have the history of your neighbour's high chance and entertainment at court; more of which matter, when I come home to my own dwelling, and talk these affairs in a corner. I must press *silence* hereon, as otherwise all is undone. I did forget to tell that his Majesty much asked concerning my opinion on the new weed tobacco, and said it would, by its use, infuse ill qualities on the brain, and that no learned man ought to taste it, and wished it forbidden.'[130]

The searching scrutiny of scholars over a period of three hundred years has confirmed the accuracy of this portrait of King James.

The knight of Kelston had always been a religious man, with a consistent interest in comparative Christian doctrine. His analysis of the religious position of Bishop Gardiner in the *Brief View* is masterly. But orthodox Anglican that he was, he could not resist free thought even in religious matters, nor expressing those thoughts. His cousin Robert Markham had warned him at the time of the Irish affair: 'that damned uncovered honesty will mar your fortunes ... The heart of man lieth close hid oft time; men do not carry it in their hand, nor should they do so that wish to thrive in these times and in these places'.

That damned uncovered honesty had already expressed itself, in the *Metamorphosis of Ajax*, on a subject not unknown to trouble Christians. 'I have always had a Bible in my parlour these many years, and oft-times when the weather hath been foul, and that I had no other book to read on, and have wanted company to play at cards or at tables with me, I have read in those books of the Old Testament, at least half an hour by the clock ... Nay, further, I have heard a preacher that hath kept an exercise a year together upon the books of Moses, and hath told of Genesis and genealogies, of the ark and propitiatory, of pollutions, of washings, of leprosies ...' But such views were powerless to harm their author's friendship with Dr Still, once his instructor at Cambridge, and now Bishop of Bath and Wells.[131]

When Dr Still was appointed to this bishopric, the abbey church at Bath was still falling into ruin from the removal of lead from its roof at the Reformation. The restoration of the church was to Sir John a matter of deep concern. His descendant Henry Harington related in the *Nugae Antiquae* how he took Bishop Montague into it one rainy day. When the Bishop found it gave him no shelter, Sir John said to him, 'if it keep not us safe from the waters above, how shall it ever save others from the fire beneath?' Between 1607 and 1610 he wrote letters to Thomas Sutton, begging him to spend some of his ill-earned wealth on the church. He urged him one 'foul Friday morning' in November 1607: 'I only wish you not to undervalue yourself, pluck up your spirits, linger not in good purposes, reject not friendly advices.'[132]

It was three months after Sir John of Kelston wrote this earnest appeal that Lord John of Exton's daughter Frances took part in Ben Jonson's Masque of Beauty, 'the only thing thought upon at court', especially staged for Lord Harington's marriage. Frances was received on land by the River God with sixteen other young ladies. Sir John of Kelston, the erstwhile courtier, scoffed in his rustic detachment: 'my cousin Lord Harington of Exton doth much fatigue himself with the royal charge of the Princess Elizabeth; and midst all the foolery of these times, hath much labour to preserve his own wisdom and sobriety'.[133]

The ways of life of the two cousins were indeed quite reversed. The time had been when Sir John of Kelston was much fatiguing himself with the charges of another Elizabeth, and it is worth recalling that at the height of the *Ajax* scandal Lord John was the one who had been given over to good works. Here is an example of his fussy helpfulness in those days. It is a letter he wrote to Dr Neville of Trinity College, Cambridge, in 1595, concerning the sale of the Gray Friars in connection with the foundation of Sidney-Sussex College.

'Good Mr Doctor Neville, I have stayed to send to you longer than I purposed for that, to satisfy your Council, I have been enforced to send to all the Executors severally; whereof some were at Oxford, others beyond London and in other places distant far from me. But now having procured them all to seal, I have sent the Assurance unto you ...' Now Lord John was becoming enmeshed in the ruinous expenses of court life, while Sir John of Kelston turned to good works.[134]

The limelight in which Lord John of Exton's daughter Frances moved at court was faint beside the lustre that surrounded her sister. Lucy was the eldest of Lord John's three surviving children, and she had been married to the third Earl of Bedford in the Queen's reign. Lucy was a patroness of a most refined sort. '*Musis dilecta*', Wake called her, beloved of the muses.[13]

She was childless, and became a prominent patroness of the arts. Sir John Harington sent her in 1600 some of the psalms translated by the Countess of Pembroke that, he once prophesied, would outlast Wilton walls. 'I have presumed to fill up the empty paper with some shallow meditations of mine own,' he told her, 'not to conjoin these with them; for that were to piece satin with sack-cloth, or patch lead upon gold. Much less to compare them, that are but as foil to a diamond; but as it were to attend them. So as, being both of meaner matter and lighter manner, yet may serve as a wanton page is admitted to bear a torch to a chaste matron. But as your clear-sighted judgment shall accept or praise them, I shall hereafter be emboldened to present more of them, and to entitle some of them to your honourable name, unto which I vow to rest an ever much devoted servant.' Sir John had had considerable experience in this style by 1600, and Lucy was to receive a great deal more in similar vein, though far more extravagant in its conceits, from the pens of Drayton and Donne. She did much to secure herself the reputation of a cultured and estimable person.[14]

But someone in her time preserved, in a commonplace book, a rather different kind of application to Lucy to exercise her taste and good nature. It is a poem written by Henry Harington, son of Sir Henry of ill fame and fortune in Ireland. It cannot be called a distinguished poem, and it sheds a mysterious twilight on the relations between Henry and his first cousin Lucy.

> Read and pity as you go
> These my unhappy rhymes
> Who expect; if you say no,
> No pity from the times.

> Sublunary things do move
> As the celestial do,
> And if you'd begin to love
> The world would do so too.

But if you should once begin
To frown upon my state,
The world would then account it sin
To cherish what you hate.

Then let it not accounted be
My fault, if I do call
To save that which is yours in me,
For then you should save all.

Which, though you should refuse to do,
When sorrow strikes me dead,
How much I served and honoured you
Shall in my death be read.[137]

This poem would have indicated no more than that the unlucky son of an unlucky father was the favourite neither of Lucy nor the muses, had not someone scribbled a helpful explanation above it: 'Mr H. Harington to the Countess of Bedford, he being her kinsman and in prison for debt; his friends neglecting him for fear of displeasing her in regard of her distasting and being angry at some of his unthrifty courses.' It is one thing to sit in judgment on the weaknesses of others, another to refuse to assist in relieving them. Lucy, however, was a person of influence. She had only to express distaste, to dissuade others from assisting either. It is ill soliciting business out of prison, as the Knight of Kelston had recently had cause to remark, and nothing could have made iller soliciting than the wretched poem the unthrifty Henry addressed to the patroness of the arts. Indeed, he is never heard of again. It is as though Lucy's distaste had extinguished him altogether.

Lucy is the first female in the Harington family whose features are preserved for posterity. There is the Woburn portrait, Number 74, and the line engraving described in A. M. Hind's *Engraving in England*, volume II. The likeness is almost identical in them, and in only one significant detail do the portraits differ. Lucy is wearing a high tiara in one of them, not unlike the coronet of an earl in design, and in the other a large feathered jewel in her hair.

Anyone might wonder to see both of these splendid accessories worn together in the portrait of Queen Elizabeth in the royal Swedish collection, at Stockholm. Behind them is painted the legend 'Konigin Elisabet von Engelant': legend indeed, for on a cushion beside the full-length figure is an escutcheon empaling the arms of Harington and Kelway. The portrait represents Lucy's mother Anne, Lady Harington, and it was painted by the same unidentified artist whose revealing portrait of the favourite Buckingham now hangs in the National Portrait Gallery. Lady Harington and Buckingham both stand on a carpet of the same elaborate pattern, and they even wear identical shoes. Both appear to have attended their sittings wearing every jewel and decoration they possessed; Lady Harington sports both the feathered jewel and the tiara, which her daughter kept for two separate portraits.[138]

No one could have been more unlike the two daughters of Lord John of Exton than their brother John. He was a saint. How soon he cast his spell over Prince Henry it is difficult to say. There was a portrait of them painted together, out hunting the stag, when John was twelve and Henry was nine, and King James had only just succeeded to the throne. But was it really painted in 1603, and of these two?

The painting now hangs in the Metropolitan Museum, New York: and there is another, almost identical in the British royal collection. The only important difference is that in the royal picture it is not John Harington kneeling over the stag, with the Harington arms in the background behind him, but the young Earl of Essex in an identical pose, with the arms of Devereux behind him. One of these pictures is a faithful copy of the other, except that the friend of Prince Henry has been changed and (with more skill than the improvers of Anne's portrait used) the coat of arms has been altered to match.

Neither is it very easy to judge how early the friendship of the two youths ripened from their correspondence. John's earliest surviving letters to Henry are in Latin, written perhaps when he was thirteen years old, and travelling in the company of his tutor. Can we see into the heart of this extraordinary youth, as he addresses his future sovereign in competent Latin under the watchful eye of his instructor?

He had been invested a Knight of the Bath in January 1604, and the same September he set out for Europe with his tutor Tovey. His eighth account to Prince Henry reads in translation: 'The greater part of Belgium and of lower Germany, most illustrious Prince and Lord, has been described in these seven; three

ANNE KELWAY, D. 1620, WIFE OF JOHN,
LORD HARINGTON OF EXTON

royal palaces and as many colleges I have seen, together with some great cities, walled towns, strong camps and fortresses. And I have written down in Latin to the best of my ability what I was able to observe of the politics, the councils, the men outstanding in authority, prudence and learning; of military matters, of the present state of affairs, of the situation of cities and customs of the people, in order that an account of all my days may be punctually rendered to Your Clemency (as is right) since I and my studies are in your debt for every kind of merit. For whatever my own weakness, which I know well, I do not wish to be numbered with those who are wont to visit and explore distant lands, basely to indulge their pleasure, or from a desire to feed their eyes on novelty. Certainly, Most Illustrious Prince and Lord, I spare no pains that by gaining some prudence from experience I may be able to conduct my life more wisely and more worthily of Your Clemency's intention. This alone is both the summit of my hope and the sufficient inducement to carry on all my work. I cannot write any more, Illustrious Prince; this letter-carrier is in such a hurry and interrupts me. Your Clemency has a letter put together in haste. Please forgive me and my [words] as you are wont to do. Such is always your supreme gentleness towards me. And I pray that every day you may deign to enrich me more and more with your favour.'[139]

How young John of Exton protected himself in early adolescence from the world's delights appears in another letter he wrote to Prince Henry during this tour. 'O decus nostrum,' it begins, after the manner of Virgil to Maecenas in the *Georgics*. Translated from the Latin, it continues: 'what thanks can I speak, what return can I make? For what in the whole world could please me more than to receive from Your Clemency these letters and indictments of affection? So far has your kindness exceeded my deserving that it is altogether beyond me to discover what I am to write, or how I am to write it, or what not to write.

'My love grows inwardly. [This is a quotation in Greek] I am silent. To Your Clemency I owe and shall owe the deepest gratitude in every way, ever and without remission pouring out prayers to the good and great God that good fortune may attend you on whatever road you travel. Indeed Your Clemency has already begun and, as it were, almost accomplished the journey which leads to honour, to virtue, to immortality. And so, since I desire nothing more than to explore your wisdom, to reverence your genius, to be instructed and corrected by your censure, and to accept your judgment, may I as a suppliant beg from Your Clemency the solution of a certain problem I have encountered.'

The problem concerns a passage in which Tacitus was writing about Agricola, and it is hard to believe that it really presented any difficulties to John. Supposing it had done, he could always have consulted Tovey. No, it looks as though John were giving his friend an easy chance 'to throw light on this passage where otherwise I might perhaps wander in darkness for ever. I pray God that Your Clemency may keep his mind where it may enjoy the best in men and things'. The disclosure is sudden, perhaps inadvertent. John was not only exploring the straight and narrow path to sanctity for himself; he was planning to lead Prince Henry along it with him.[140]

John was well placed to observe the follies and vanities of court life, from which he wished to protect Prince Henry. His father's allowance as guardian of the Princess Elizabeth was increased by £1,000, but such was her extravagance that the debts of the house of Exton still continued to soar. In 1608 Elizabeth was given her own establishment at Kew, with Haringtons in the first places of her household. But still Lord John could not bring himself to relinquish his ruinous charge. He continued to govern the princess's movements and expenditure. In the year 1612-13 alone she involved him in debts of £3,500.

And what might young John of Exton have thought of the lives his own sisters led, the sumptuous Lucy, and Frances, one of the lovely ladies of the court taking part in the Masque of Beauty? 'He spent not his time in courting of ladies', Pastor Stock assures us, 'and amourously contemplating the beauty of women; but he preferred his books before their beauty; and for his society chose men of parts and learning for arts and arms.'[141]

And what of the men of parts by whom he would find Prince Henry surrounded at his father's court? His observant cousin of Kelston had remarked on the many varlets and lordly servants he noticed in the antechambers of King James, as he came out from his first royal audience. Lord Thomas Howard sent a more detailed description of one of them in a letter to Kelston in 1611. 'Robert Carr is now most likely to win the Prince's affection, and doth it wondrously in a little time. The Prince leaneth on his arm, pinches his cheek, smooths his ruffled garment, and when he looketh at Carr, directeth discourse to divers others. This young

man doth much study all art and device; he hath changed his
tailors and tiremen many times, and all to please the Prince . . .'
And then he echoed the sentiment that must have been in the
mind of Kelston's 'Good and Trusty Knight' already as he read
this letter. 'You have lived to see the trim of old times, and what
passed in the Queen's days. These things are no more the same.'¹⁴¹

But young John of Exton looked, not to the past, but the future.
His sole object from the time of his first return from abroad was
to capture and protect the heir to the throne from the vicious
young men who decked themselves out like prostitutes to attract
the eye of the king. He would achieve his object by unremitting
industry, ceaseless prayer, and complete personal devotion. 'After
his return from his travels,' preached Pastor Stock, 'by way of
thankfulness to God, he gave yearly, by the hand of a private
friend, twenty pounds to the poor. And the second sabboth after
his landing in England, (having spent the day before with his
tutor Mr Tovey in prayer, fasting, and thanksgiving) he heard the
Word, received the sacrament, and gave to the poor of that parish
five pounds. And besides, he gave forty pounds to be bestowed
upon poor ministers, and other Christians, for the relief of their
necessities. Yea, such were his bowels of tender mercy, that he
gave a tenth part of his yearly allowance, which was a thousand
pounds, to pious and charitable uses.'

The preacher has left a minute description of the manner in
which John, at least from the year 1609 when he was eighteen
years old, spent his day. 'He usually rose every morning about
four or five o'clock, seldom sleeping above five or six hours at a
time. When he first waked, his constant care was to set his heart
in order, and fit it for holiness all the day after, offering the first
fruits of the day and of his thoughts unto God. Being up, he read
a chapter out of the holy scriptures. Then, with his servants in his
chamber, he went to prayer. Then did he spend about an hour
reading some holy treatise to enliven his affections and increase
his knowledge. He read over Calvin's *Institutions* and Rogers'
Treatise, which were his two last books. Before dinner and supper
he had a psalm, chapter and prayer in his family, and prayer after
supper. And besides those public duties, he prayed privately
every morning in his closet, after which he betook himself to some
serious study for three or four hours together, except he was
interrupted by some special business. The residue of the morning
he spent in converse with his friends, riding the great horse, or

some such other honest and noble recreation, till dinner-time. Thus avoided he idleness, and prevented temptations which commonly ensue thereon. Presently after dinner, he retired into his study, to meditate on sermons he had lately heard. Or if he was disappointed of that opportunity, he neglected not to take the first that was offered to him. Yea, many times in his travels by land or by water he thus busied himself. The rest of the afternoon he spent in business, study of histories, the art of war, mathematics, and navigation; wherein he attained to a great measure of perfection. After supper he prayed with his servants; then he withdrew himself into his study, where he kept a diary or day-book, wherein he recorded what he had done that day; how he had offended, or what good he had done; what temptations he met with, and how he had resisted them. And surveying his failings, he humbled himself to God for them; and for such failings as were fit to be known only to God and his own soul, he wrote them down in a private character which none could read but himself, and then betook him to his rest. And to prevent evil thoughts before sleep, one that waited on him in his chamber read a chapter or two out of the holy scripture, and this practice he continued for four years together before his death.'[143]

Lord John of Exton had complained to his cousin of Kelston at the time of the Gunpowder Plot that the Catholics regarded his house with particular dislike. And no wonder. Not only was he a Puritan and his daughter Lucy married to the Puritan Earl of Bedford, but the heir to the throne was falling under the influence of his Calvinist son. Pastor Stock in his funeral oration openly accused the Catholics of taking preventive action again, at the time when John and his tutor went abroad.

'How dangerous a thing it is for religious gentlemen to travel into these popish countries may appear by the example of this nobleman and his tutor, whose sound religion and heavenly zeal for the truth, being taken notice of by the Jesuits, they took their opportunity to administer a slow-working poison to them; that, seeing they had no hopes of corrupting their minds, they might destroy their bodies, and bring them to their graves.

'Of this poison Mr Tovey, being aged, and so less able to encounter with the strength of it, died presently after his return to England. But the Lord Harington, being of a strong and able body, and in the prime of his age, bore it better and conflicted with it longer. Yet the violence of it appeared in his face presently after his return.' It may have been these evidences of Jesuit devilry that John's father the first Lord of Exton mistook in the letter he wrote to Lord Salisbury on 5 March 1611, when he remarked that his son had contracted measles.[144]

The younger John certainly courted the hatred of the Catholics. He made his second journey abroad in 1609, to Italy this time. From Venice he wrote in the month of May to Prince Henry's tutor, Sir Adam Newton: 'I thought of sending Your Worship a letter with my rough remarks on the absurdities and trifles of false religions, either practised or at least tolerated in these parts. I thought of sending them to Your Worship as to a person who (I know) will look at my efforts with benevolent eye, knowing it is the work of his beloved friend: while I hope that these efforts will not be altogether unwelcome to Your Worship, but rather that they will cause you some pleasure by showing you the poltrooneries of the Roman and the Greek churches, as well as of the Jews.' Later in the same letter he remarked, 'a wall of paper seems to me too frail to guard important secrets'. The observation reads oddly in its context.[145]

By this time John had mastered most of the European languages, and was now writing in Italian. 'Most illustrious and revered master and friend,' he wrote to Newton again from Venice, 'although I have not yet received an answer to my first letter written in this tongue, to tell me how it pleased Your Worship, nevertheless I feel sure that my letters will not displease Your Worship, but on the contrary will cause you some pleasure, knowing the love and favour that, by special kindness, Your Worship shows me. And furthermore it increases the hope I have already mentioned that these letters of mine, though of little value, may help Your Worship to exercise yourself in this noble language, which, after the language of the learned, is the one I love and esteem most.'[146]

It was only that the posts were slow. On June 1 John was able to write to Newton from Venice, 'I congratulate Your Worship on your mastery of the Italian language, in which, without having been in Italy, you are so perfect a master in the writing of it that the Academy of Crusca itself would hardly find the least mistake, while Your Worship furthermore adorns it with high ideas and marvellous ways of expressing them.'

In the next sentence John makes it clear that all this is for the Prince's eyes. It is a device with which all who have loved are familiar. 'What can give me, besides, so much joy and happiness as to be assured of the continuance and stability of his Serene Highness's favour, his Highness being, as he knows with his all-revealing eye, my sovereign good in this world . . . The undiminished extent of his Serene Highness's favour towards me I attribute only to the benevolence, goodness and constancy of his Highness, and to the faithful and constant love towards me of Your Worship, in whom is placed my sole confidence . . .'[147]

But John was not only pouring his affection for Prince Henry into letters to the Prince's tutor. In that same month of June 1609 Salisbury wrote to his son: 'I find every week, in the Prince's hand, a letter from Sir John Harington, full of news of the place where he is, and the countries as he passeth, and all occurrents; which is an argument that he doth read and observe such things as are remarkable.' Prince Henry must have been proudly showing his friend's letters at court, and Salisbury perhaps thought to stimulate his own son by his example.[148]

For Henry did return the love and admiration of John Harington. When Sir Henry Wotton, the English ambassador to Venice, was telling the Doge of the visitor who had just reached his republic, he said: 'I must add this story to show your Serenity how prudent he is. When the Prince, with tears in his eyes, took him to the King to ask leave of absence, his Majesty said to him, "what hast thou done, John" (that is his name) "that thou art so master of the Prince's favour? Tell me what art hast thou used? Not flattery; that belongeth not to thy age." To which he replied, "Holy Majesty, not with flattery, which I know not how to use, have I won his Highness's love, but by truth, of which as your Majesty's true son, his Highness is the lover." '[149]

On 23 November 1609 the ambassador reported to the Venetian cabinet: 'Harington has been recalled by the Prince, who is very fond of him.' And the Doge was sufficiently moved by this tale of youthful friendship to reply, 'we seem to see him now before us as he was that day when he showed us the beautiful portrait of the Prince, and told us that he was fairer within than without. We do not wonder the Prince loves him.'[150]

In his letters to John, Prince Henry shows a diffident eagerness to follow in his footsteps. He answered the Tacitus inquiry: 'do you believe me to be a person capable of untying knots, explaining riddles, and illustrating the obscurities of difficult authors? . . . I who am, in all kinds of polite learning, a mere novice and have made scarce any advances from the depths of ignorance, finding that I am not able to comprehend anything but what is low and contracted, never dared to look into Tacitus . . . Since you challenge me into the field, I am determined to follow you, though with a slow pace. For I have begun, but a few days ago, to read with attention the Life of Agricola'.

This is Birch's translation from Henry's Latin, published in his life of the Prince, in 1760. But fortunately a letter survived among the Kelston Papers which shows how these youths might have expressed themselves, had they not been so constantly practising their erudition in foreign tongues.

'My good fellow,' wrote the Prince, 'I here send you certain matters of ancient sort, which I gained by search in a musty vellum book in my father's closet, and as it hath great mention of your ancestry, I hope it will not meet your displeasure. It gave me some pains to read, and some to write also; but I have a pleasure in over-reaching difficult matters. When I see you (and let that be shortly) you will find me your better at tennis and pike. Good fellow, I rest your friend, Henry. Note. Your Latin epistle I much esteem, and will at leisure give answer to.'[151]

Perhaps it was in that musty vellum book that King James had discovered his kinship with the Exton branch of the Haringtons, before he came to England.

During these years Prince Henry also received letters, very different in quality, from Sir John Harington of Kelston. In 1606 'for your pleasure's sake and my promise I present your Highness this collection, or rather confusion, of all my idle epigrams'. On 14 June 1608 he sent Henry from Kelston a long and delightful letter in praise of his dog Bungay. Sir John had already immortalized his dog in an epigram, and on the title-page of the *Orlando Furioso*, where he lies beneath the portrait of his master. The painting of Bungay remained in the possession of Sir John's descendants until it was sold in 1942.

The *Brief View of the State of the Church* which Sir John wrote for Prince Henry has been mentioned already. In 1609 he wrote the last of his letters of entertainment and advice that has survived. It is a review of some of the earlier Henrys who had sat on the English throne, Henry VI, whom 'my ancestor Sir James Harington did once take prisoner'; Henry VII, from whom his family suffered 'forfeiture of twenty-five rich manors'; Henry VIII, who wrote a sonnet that he quotes, according to his father, 'who was in his household'. It is curious that Sir John did not begin

L   161

this account of the long and close connection between his family and the kings of England with Henry V, whose standard a Harington had carried at Agincourt. It would have been less questionable than his assertion that he descended from Sir James, or that his father (rather than Sir John Harington of Exton) had been in Henry VIII's household. But the substance of his tale is perfectly clear, even if he could not expect to live long enough to complete it. Under Henry IX the Haringtons, he confidently believed, would come into their own again — indeed, they would reach the pinnacle of power on whose lower slopes they had so often stumbled in the past.

It was not merely a dream of the Haringtons; it was the subject of ambassadorial reports. The Venetian ambassador in London wrote to the Doge and Senate 'any show of regard for them will be well invested'. In Venice itself the English ambassador treated the Doge to a lengthy panegyric on young John, on his arrival there:

'He is a youth but little over sixteen, son of Lord Harington, a gentleman of the highest quality in our country and of great weight on account of the vast barony which he holds in England, where it is not the custom for the sons to bear their father's title during his lifetime. The sister of this young gentleman, the Countess of Bedford, is the Queen's favourite maid-of-honour; and the Princess her Majesty's only daughter, is brought up at the house of Lord Harington, father of the youth, whose mother is governess to the Princess. Add to this that it is thought certain that the young man will marry Lord Salisbury's only daughter, and being the right eye of the Prince of Wales, the world holds that he will one day govern the kingdom.'[152]

It was not to be. In a period of mere months from the May of 1612, God answered the prayers of his saint, John Harington, with one of the most sweeping acts of intervention in the whole course of English history. On May 18, Sir John Harington of Kelston was carried, 'sick of a dead palsy', to see Lord Salisbury at Bath. A mutual acquaintance had restored their friendship, the angel of death. Salisbury died on the twenty-fourth, on the way back from Bath to his home.

Sir John returned to Kelston. His last surviving letters are to the King, recommending his metrical translations of the psalms to his notice.

O Sion! When on thee we think,
Our harps hanged up do silence keep
On trees along the river's brink.[153]

He lived to hear of the death of Prince Henry on November 6, which was instantly attributed to poison, though the wiser noticed the epidemic of fever that was raging at the time. On 20 November 1612 the worthy knight of Kelston was also dead.

It would take royal responsibilities to kill Lord John of Exton. On February 13 following, he preceded the Princess Elizabeth in her wedding procession to Whitehall. There he received from the Prince Palatine, her bridegroom, a gift of plate valued at £2,000. With debts rising to £40,000, he begged, a few weeks later, for the royal patent to coin brass farthings of which the Venetian ambassador reported home: 'after it had been granted and confirmed by the Council it was suspended on account of the immense profit. His share was limited to 20,000 crowns'. Even this proved to be a complete exaggeration, and Lord Harington did not even see the printed proclamation that gave his name to farthings for a time.[154]

It was issued in May. On April 19 the Elector and his princess went with the King and Queen to Greenwich for three days. Then they all went to Rochester, where the young pair embarked, and the Haringtons with them. Isaac Wake had remarked in February that Lord Harington would be going at his own expense to Germany to see the princess happily settled there. This time gossip was accurate, though it omitted to mention that his lordship was invested with the honorary rank of Ambassador.[155]

After spending four months at Heidelberg he embarked on the journey home, but like Lord Salisbury he died on the way. Fever and exhaustion overtook him on August 23, as he passed through Worms.

His saintly son died in the same year according to the old calendar, 27 February 1614 in the new. He was twenty-two years old. 'From the first day of his last sickness he strongly apprehended the approach of his death, and therefore accordingly prepared himself for it. Besides his private meditations, he called often others to pray for him, and often prayed himself . . . He uttered many heavenly speeches, desiring to be dissolved, and to be at home with God his father, professing, not two hours before his death, that he felt the assured comforts and joys of his salvation

by Christ. And when death itself approached, he breathed forth
these longing expressions: "O thou my joy! O my God! When
shall I be with thee!" And in the midst of such desires, sweetly
and quietly resigned up his spirit unto God.'[156]

The death of John, last Lord Harington, took place at Kew, and
it was mourned like the death of Germanicus. Donne composed
an elegy of two hundred and fifty-eight lines. They are not easy
to read today.

> Now I grow sure, that if a man would have
> Good company, his entry is a grave.
> Methinks all cities now but anthills be,
> Where, when the several labourers I see,
> For children, house, provision, taking pain,
> They're all but ants, carrying eggs, straw, and grain;
> And churchyards are our cities, unto which
> The most repair, that are in goodness rich.
> There is the best concourse and confluence,
> There are the holy suburbs, and from thence
> Begins God's city, new Jerusalem,
> Which doth extend her utmost gates to them.
> At that gate then, triumphant soul, dost thou
> Begin thy triumph. But since laws allow
> That at the triumph day the people may
> All that they will 'gainst the triumpher say,
> Let me here use that freedom, and express
> My grief, though not to make thy triumph less.

While Donne was trying to decide who had triumphed by the
second Lord Harington's untimely death, his patroness Lucy
became co-heir to her brother's fortune. In Exton church she
commissioned Nicholas Stone to build a second memorial, rather
similar to the one her uncle Sir James Harington, Bt., had raised
there to the memory of her grandparents, but larger. For this
monument Stone received £1020, the largest fee he ever obtained.
Lucy outbid Verneys, Villiers, and Pastons, even the fabulous
Suttons, in the magnificence of her last monument to her extinguished house. And now, having 'distasted' the unthrifty
courses of her cousin Henry, she prepared to exhibit her own
standards of tasteful and thrifty living.

164

ELEVEN

THAT FANTASTIC LADY

JOHN, second Lord Harington of Exton, had already sold
Exton before his death, but he left to his sisters Lucy and
Frances the remainder of his property, together with the
remainder of his father's debts. He had intended to pay all of
these but they remained £40,000 at his death — the sum must be
multiplied by ten to equate it to its present value. But the great
properties of Burley and Combe Abbey with their attendant
manors would have been well able to discharge these debts, and it
was Lucy who annihilated the fortunes of her house, as she might
easily have done those of the house of Russell also, if she had lived
long enough.

The Haringtons of Exton died in bewildering succession. In
addition to Lucy's father and brother, there died in 1613 her uncle
Sir Henry and his younger son Sir William. His eldest son Sir
John (a fifth of this name, unmentioned hitherto) became the
senior male representative of the family. Sir John made a rapid
attempt to save a part of what remained of the family property
from Lucy's clutches, 'whereby he will get nothing but lost
labour, nor will it cost me more than some few lawyers' fees, and
a little trouble', as she correctly prophesied. In 1615 this other
Sir John died also; and so did Lucy's sister Frances. The previous
year Sir James, first Baronet of Ridlington had died and been
buried in Ridlington church, where his kneeling figure in alabaster
is still to be seen.[157]

Nothing now stood between Lucy and the remainder of her
family's fortune save the legal claims of Frances's daughter Anne,
and the moral claims of her own mother.

In these circumstances Lucy, Countess of Bedford, proceeded
with piety, with self-pity, and with the utmost extravagance. She
lived the self-indulgent life of a victim of cruel circumstances whom
it was estimable to aid, rewarding to praise. Lady Bacon lent her
money and received long devout letters from her. Donne celebrated her in atrocious verse, and was able to report that 'she
rained upon him her sweet showers of gold'. In Ben Jonson's case
it was haunches of venison. Others she was able to reward through

her influence at the venal court of King James, where her flair for intrigue and aptitude in making rich friends had ample scope.

In all ages there are people who acquire a reputation for being clever, and witty, and infinitely desirable to meet, although the foundations for such a reputation do not always stand the test of time. Lucy was one of these, and she therefore possesses a cautionary interest in addition to her interest as the first woman of the Harington family who still lives in the pages of history.

Her character has been the subject of some controversy. 'That fantastic lady', Pennant called her in the eighteenth century, gazing at one of her portraits with distaste. But in the nineteenth century the editor of the Cornwallis papers rhapsodized: 'the Countess Lucy, full of grace and animation, was born to shine in courts, where her high station and a felicitous combination of wit and beauty enabled her to exercise so much influence'. If this claim is true, it will be edifying to inspect her wit and her influence and particularly the 'tone of meek and unaffected piety' which the Victorian editor noted in Lucy's letters with such satisfaction.[158]

Lucy's mother, the heiress of Combe Abbey, was left penniless. Her daughter might have provided her with one of the many houses amongst which she divided her time during the years ahead, but she did not. The Electress Elizabeth, however, invited Lady Harington to enter her service as a lady-in-waiting. Lady Harington made a number of charitable bequests in the parishes where her properties had lain, small ones such as her purse could afford. There is one such commemorated on a board in the vestry of Oakham church, where there are also two presses filled with religious books, her gift, still to be seen by the worshippers there. Then, in 1614, the aged Lady Harington departed for the country near which her husband had died.

'My mother goes presently into Germany', was the way Lucy explained it, 'by my Lady Elizabeth's extreme earnest desire, and the King's commandment; which, the season of the year considered, is so cruel a journey I much fear how she will pass it. But her affection to her Highness keeps her from being frighted with any difficulty; and her spirit carries her body beyond what almost could be hoped at her years, which I trust will not fail her in this no more than in other labours.' Her mother's departure added to her mood of self-pity, and she wrote to her friend Jane, Lady Bacon in the same letter: 'other than sad news I cannot send you'.[159]

Lady Harington returned to England for the last time nearly

five years later, and Lucy travelled to Dover to meet her. So did Sir Edward Harwood, who wrote, 'I have been out of town at Dover to meet my Lady Harington, where my Lady Bedford attended for some time. Soon after our return my Lady Harington fell very sick, and is now recovered.'[160]

But it was only the appearance of recovery. Within the year Lucy was writing to the Lady Jane Bacon, 'as full of sorrow as my heart can bear, I return you affectionate thanks for your kind sending. What a mother I have lost I need not tell you, that know what she was in herself, and to me. Yet God, that sees no affliction to work sufficiently upon me, hath this night added another heavy one to my former woe, having taken my Lord Chamberlain's son. Yet with this mercy to him, that he hath given him the hope of another, my Lady being, as we think, with child again'.[161]

Writing to her friend Lady Jane in the country, it seems to have occurred to Lucy that her mother's death would not suffice to secure all the sympathy she craved. So she threw in the dead child of a courtier for good measure, and then some gossip, which she always found irresistible, all in the first few sentences. But as her letter grew longer, she seems to have recollected the main subject, contained in its opening sentence. She wove her mother into the tale of her afflictions once more. 'My loss of a dear mother came not so unexpectedly as My Lord Chamberlain's did at this time, for to outward appearance his child mended, but my mother so manifestly decayed daily as I could not flatter myself with hope she could continue long: though I looked not her end would have been so sudden, yet the disease she was subject to threatened no less.'

Lucy's eloquence on the subject of death and decay is as remarkable as her complete silence on many subjects more often associated with wit and culture. When her friend Lord Hamilton died in 1625 she told Lady Jane, 'being at first, by the testimony of all the surgeons, physicians and his own servants, as fair a corpse as ever their eyes beheld, in the space of three hours his whole body, head, and every part swelled so strangely and gangrened so generally as it astonished them all; though the physicians affirm to have seen the like in pestilential fevers, when the spots break out afore death, and impute part of the cause to the expedient of chafing his body at least for the space of an hour before he departed, with hot cloths, and keeping it too close in the bed after'.[162]

Hamilton and her mother were people in whose decay Lucy may be said to have had a particular interest, and Lady Jane was a close friend, to whom she imparted it. But her taste in these things was quite catholic, and she assumed it to be widely shared. For instance she wrote to Sir Dudley Carleton in 1621, 'I have inquired after the manner of my Lord Chandos's death; which . it is said was hastened by the violent operation of the Spa waters; which though they passed not by urine, yet wrought so forcibly on his inward parts as his formerly decayed body was not able to bear. Yet he never kept his bed, though many days before he was assured his end was at hand, which happened as he was on his way homeward in his coach; but in a place where, because they would not allow burial to his bowels, he was not opened. So I am not able to give your Lordship any further account of the state of his body.' The disappointment is unconcealed.[163]

Lucy's principal headquarters in that year of her brother's death and her mother's departure was Bedford House. The 'Palais de Bedford' a Frenchman described it; and Strype has left a record of the 'large but old built house, having a great yard before it for the reception of coaches; with a spacious garden, having a terrace walk'. It faced Covent Garden among other mansions of the nobility, and its gardens sloped down to the river.[164]

But Lucy did not indulge herself for long periods with the pleasures of those terraced walks. She was writing from 'Bedford House, in haste, this Saturday morning, 30th July 1614', to describe how 'the King of Denmark's unexpected coming hath constrained me to defer my setting forward towards Rutland from the 8th of August to the tenth'. She was back in 'Bedford House, from whence I shall remove as I am able to Harington House, and there winter', on September 9. In the interval she had been to Rutland, 'where within eight days the King overtook me; against whose coming, and during whose stay at my house, all my time and little wit was so taken up about the business of house-keeping as it made me leave all else aside'. Lucy's time and little wit were constantly absorbed by her many houses, by attentions to royalty, and even by interest in ordinary noblemen, provided they were sufficiently rich or influential.[165]

The year 1616 will serve as an introduction to more of her houses. Lucy had written in December 1615 from Bedford House, that she was 'like to be a Londoner the most of this winter, to air my house at Twickenham against the spring'. But on Good Friday

1616 she was at Whitehall Palace, where 'the Queen's leg is whole; to prevent a relapse, as soon as the King is gone, she returns to Greenwich and enters into a diet this spring'. Lucy went to Greenwich too, from where she wrote to her friend Jane, Lady Bacon, 'in extreme haste'. She next wrote to her from Moor Lodge 'in haste' only this time. 'In haste' again she wrote to Jane from Bedford House. She apparently had no time to write any more to her friend until 1617, when she was at Harington House.[166]

In London, then, Lucy possessed Bedford House, Harington House (whose whereabouts remain a mystery), and a house at Twickenham. In the country there were Combe Abbey in War-wickshire and Burley in Rutland. No wonder she was able to add to an invitation to Jane the reassurance that it would 'no whit straiten me, for I can well spare your wonted lodgings'.

But in that year 1617 Lucy's husband obtained another house which seems to have exerted a strong and soothing influence on her. It was the lodge of Moor Park in Hertfordshire. In May she was speaking of 'some little building I have in hand at the Moor', and in the autumn of 'my works at the Moor, where I have been a patcher this summer, and I am still adding some trifles of pleasure to that place I am so much in love with as, if I were so fond of any man, I were in hard case'.[167]

After her restless wanderings with the court, and among the mansions of her mother's, her husband's, and her father's families, Lucy had found a home that she could create for herself, and which she loved because it was all her own. 'This month puts me in mind to entreat the performance of your promise for some of the little white single rose roots', she was writing to Jane the following October. They must have arrived promptly, for in a matter of weeks she sent thanks for 'furnishing me with such helps for my garden'. It has vanished now, and the only monument to Lucy's care is the praise of Sir William Temple.[168]

At the same time that she fell in love with Moor Park, Lucy parted with her house at Twickenham to her cousin Sir William Harington of Bagworth. She opened negotiations with the Duke of Buckingham over Combe Abbey. But Sir William Craven, a principal creditor of the family, secured this prize for £37,000 and the Duke of Buckingham had to be content with Burley instead.

In the negotiations over Combe Abbey, Lucy was hampered by the legal interest of her niece Anne, 'my niece, her father and I

169

having bargained, she with him for the present possession of her land, and I with her for her possibility in the lease of Combe . . . I intend to turn Combe wholly into money'.[169]

Anne's father was protecting her against Lucy. It is not difficult to understand the childless Lucy's bitterness, 'having now none but myself to provide for; those designs I had for my neice being crossed by her father's untowardness'. At the same time, Anne's father could judge Lucy better than the Victorian editor who praised her piety and wit, and there can be little doubt that he acted wisely. How much more wisely he acted than Sir William Harington of Bagworth, who placed his daughter Sarah in Lucy's household, will appear presently.[170]

Lucy's first attempt to act as a mother to the motherless Anne occurred in 1618. She planned a match with the Earl of Arran, 'if I can compose things according to my wishes; an offer being made for her pleases me well, and I doubt not will take effect if her unreasonable father can be brought to do what he ought, which, if love will not make him, I hope fear will prevail'. Anne, the object of these threats, was thirteen years old. She married Lord Bruce in the end and died at the age of twenty-two. On her tomb in Exton church it is written that she was 'a lady endowed with a natural disposition to virtue, a true understanding of honour, most noble behaviour, perpetual cheerfulness, most elegant conversation, and a more than ordinary conjugal affection'. Perhaps this is as much as to say that in the end she was allowed to marry for love.[171]

The tragedy of Lucy is that she had no one to love. The Earl of Bedford, to whom she had been married in childhood, was an invalid who took no part in Lucy's hectic and extravagant life. Her longest reference to him in a letter is this, written to Jane in 1614. 'Out of a very great and almost hopeless danger my Lord of Bedford hath recovered so much health and strength as we are out of all fear of him, and do conceive that the violent fever he hath had hath done him some good for his palsy, his speech being better than it was before he fell sick, though his lameness be nothing amended.' This was the husband whose wife wrote of a garden; 'if I were so fond of any man, I were in hard case'.[172]

She had little to do with her closest Harington relatives. The first cousins who were the senior representatives of her house occur only in her reference to Sir John's case against her in chancery, and in the poem Henry wrote in prison. Her other first cousins, sons of her uncle James, first baronet, are never mentioned. Only Frances, one of the baronet's grand-daughters, played her short part in Lucy's life. It ended in 1614 in her death, 'the news whereof came to me yesterday and brought me a great deal of sorrow, having ever had cause to hope, if God had spared her life, she would have repaid my care of her with honour and comfort'.[173]

Lucy had many other, more eligible cousins with whom to associate. Among her first cousins were men from whom descended the Kings of Portugal, the Dukes of Manchester, Montagu, and Ancaster, the Earls of Sandwich, Chichester, Southampton, Northampton, and Leicester. The Haringtons were still allied, as they had been for centuries, to half the nobility of England. But Lucy's surviving letters only speak of a visit to Lord Huntingdon, Aunt Sarah's son, and of a cousin Kelway, who lived not far from Harington House.[174]

She cultivated friends more than relatives. She cultivated the King, and was able to write in 1618: 'after many difficulties I have made an end, according to my wishes, of my business with the king, and received his grant with many excuses for the delays it hath had, and so much compliment as hath made amends'. This was a grant of £2,000 a year, and it was supplemented the same year. 'The Lady of Bedford hath gotten an imposition of two-pence a cauldron upon sea-coal', wrote Chamberlain to Sir Dudley Carleton at the Hague, 'and yet all will not serve. For she is upon selling all the land that descended to her from her father or her brother, being (they say) £50,000 in debt, so that the overplus will hardly amount to £20,000.'[175]

She cultivated Jane, Lady Bacon, a rich woman who lived quietly in the country and lent Lucy money. It appears that Jane released her from the debt, for Lucy once wrote to her (from Harington House): 'if I durst at this time say I would refuse what you so press, which your kindness only and the knowledge of your disposition takes off the shame I have so long detained, yet I will now keep it in my hands as you will have me; though I must still as your treasurer, not as a legacy . . .'[176]

Jane's generosity might have had a more deserving object. It was not long since Lucy had written to her: 'I was told last night that your father-in-law was like to die, and that he had some pieces of painting of Holbein's, which I am sure as soon as Arundel hears he will try all means to get. But I beseech you to entreat Mr

Bacon, if they will be parted with to any, to lay hold of them afore-hand for me . . . I do not care at what rate I have them for price.' A strange way, surely, to have spoken to someone to whom she owed money, at a parent's deathbed, even if it displays good taste in art.[177]

Lucy's concern for Holbeins and roses is more attractive than some of her other interests. She flung herself into the petty quarrels of the court: 'tomorrow my Lady of Roxburgh's business, whom I must not forsake, will pass a trial, so I can neither go my journey nor hope to see you'. The trial was the Queen's anger when Lady Roxburgh told her that her husband had been prom-ised the office of Chamberlain to Prince Charles, without consulta-tion with the Queen.[178]

Lucy loved to use her influence over appointments. 'Doctor Burgess coming to me yesterday,' she wrote to Carleton, the Ambassador at the Hague, 'told me that he was making all the happy preparation he could to send over the youth he brought with him to the Hague and whom it seems the King of Bohemia was resolved should have gone to Duke Charles, whereof his friends make full reckoning. But I willed Doctor Burgess to make stay of his journey till I heard from your Lordship, by reason of what you said to me of the King's desire concerning Will. Gomble-ton. For it were too much for the other friends not only to lose the cost they have been at, but to have the youth receive the disgrace of being refused when he came there. And that they might the sooner know what to expect, I spake yesterday with my boy's father, who leaves him to me to dispose as I please, that am very willing to present him to the King if he will command his service, but otherwise will make it no request of mine. For I neither covet to be rid of him, nor for his advancement to prefer him as a burden to the King. Wherefore I beseech your Lordship order this according to your discretion; and believe, I had rather keep than part with the boy, if you do not find in the King himself the con-tinuance of such a will to have him as he may be very acceptable. Whereof when you have informed yourself, I beseech you let me as soon as may be hear what he, and the other shall do, and I will see your directions obeyed . . .' and a great deal more in the same vein.[179]

Lucy had established an ascendancy over both King James and his queen. She maintained her influence with the Winter Queen, who had been brought up from childhood in her father's home.

But Prince Charles, the heir to the throne since Henry's death, remained in Lucy's eyes a doubtful asset. Not until 1623 was she confident enough to say: 'I will give you my testimony that the Prince is the most improved man that ever I saw, and that my Lord of Buckingham recovers much of what he had lost, so as you may see that the only Wise, who brings light out of darkness, can favour us by ways we could not imagine could have produced such happy effects.' Her confidence increased in the following year: 'we have much hope that the Prince will show himself of such a temper as will be his own glory and the good of these kingdoms'.[180]

But she was more doubtful of the dispositions of the only Wise when, in 1625, Charles ascended the throne. 'I have written as effectually as I could to my Lord Chamberlain, who I think, if it be in his power, will do what you desire. What the King's resolution is yet for his own and his father's servants, he hath not declared farther than the white staves, which are to remain as they were. But for the green cloth, and other inferior officers both of the household and chamber, it is thought he will employ his own and dismiss his father's . . . and for aught anybody yet can discover, he makes his own determinations, and is very stiff in them; having already changed the whole face of the court very near to the same form it had in Queen Elizabeth's time . . . After the funeral it is expected that he will make some alterations among the great officers, and the common voice is, change my Lord Chamberlain's staff into that I shall never but with sorrow see in other hand than that that held it last . . .'[181]

Lucy's fears for the Lord Chamberlain, and her hurried attempt to make use of him for the last time, were aggravated by the fact that death had just deprived her of another strong source of influence at court, Lord Hamilton, Steward of the Household. 'I acknowledge that I feel so to the quick', she had confessed piously, three weeks earlier, 'this last affliction God hath pleased to lay upon me as no worldly comfort will ever be able to prevail against it. For I have lost the best and worthiest friend that ever breathed, whom I could not love enough for what he was to me, nor sufficiently admire for what he was in himself and to all the world . . . For myself I must truly say I am a maimed body and worse, and so is my Lord Chamberlain, the last person left of power that I can rely on.'[182]

Lucy lived at the centre of events, and she commented copiously in letters on all she saw and heard. And her comments reflect the mind of an observer almost wholly concerned with scandal and petty intrigue; utterly incapable of embracing anything that was noble or creative in the life that surrounded her. Much of her comment would be impossible to unravel now, even if it were worth attempting to do so. 'I sent to Whitehall presently after you went from hence on Friday', she wrote to Jane in 1624, 'but my Lady of Lennox was not returned from Littleton so I could not get her second letter to the Keeper. But I hope I shall hear her first had the effect you desired.' She had written to Carleton at the Hague more mysteriously than this: 'were I an hour with you, I should give some reasons for divers things I have done, and may do, which perhaps you will not apprehend good grounds for. But at this distance preserve me in your opinion by an implicit faith; since letters must pass more hands than yours, and be confident that whatsoever I write seriously to the Queen [the Winter Queen] is not without cause'.[183]

She once sent an admonition to the Winter Queen through the ambassador at the Hague. 'I beseech you do me the favour to deliver or send the Queen this letter as soon as you can, with the contents whereof it is like she will acquaint you; which if she do, believe so well of me as that if I had not found much cause, I would not have done what I confess against myself. And for God's sake preach more warning to the Queen, whom she uses freedom to, else she will undo herself and make others afraid how they interest themselves in her service.'[184]

It is obscure, but it hardly arouses curiosity. And it is possible to read these words to the ambassador with little sense of loss: 'I have now written her [the Winter Queen] such a volume of such things as fill our ears, as I protest my hand will scarce hold a pen any longer at the present. Therefore of news I will refer you for your part to her.'[185]

Lucy's rare felicitous passages are usually concerned with the subjects nearest her heart. 'I dare neither advise you to persist nor desist in the same suit, being I protest grown so very a fool in the ways of the time as I can make no judgment of anything, all wonted grounds failing. And I assure your Lordship even those that are nearest the well-head know not with what bucket to draw for themselves or their friends.' She never described anyone more incisively than the man 'grown so in love with a plentiful fortune and a private enjoying thereof, as he shuns all other conversation'.[186]

Lucy was no more born to shine in courts than any other Harington girl who possessed brothers; she shone there because her brothers died, leaving her an heiress; and she shone without lustre.

But she is profoundly to be pitied. People who enjoy health and a happy outlet for their affections sometimes feel jealousy for those who possess riches. For such, Lucy is an object lesson. She possessed only riches, and these added poignancy to the emptiness she herself described as 'having no belongings'. As for her health, she did understand that she lived in 'the danger or canker of this sickly time, wherein my people everywhere have been visited with much sickness'. But her own she was quick to recognize as a special martyrdom, and it appears that she had exceptional cause.[187]

In 1614 she was at Woodstock, where she became so ill that 'I had much ado to get hither to use the help of some physic. Yet I thank God he strengthened me to bear out the extreme distempers I was in till I came to this house of mine'. Two years later she was ill all summer, and 'I was forced to settle here and break all my purposes to recover myself out of a very ill state of body'.[188]

Sir Edward Harwood wrote to Carleton in 1619: 'my Lady Bedford fell dangerously sick, and made us all afraid until yesterday, when our doctor assured us it was only the measles'. But the doctor was wrong. 'Since my last by the post my Lady Bedford her measles then are turned all into small-pox . . . but she is not sick and we hope she is in no great danger now.' But Chamberlain told Carleton differently. 'I was sorry I had nothing to send by Dieston, for having written so lately (as not above three or four days before) here was little left, but only that the small-pox had seized on the Lady of Bedford, and so seasoned her all over that they say she is more full and foul than could be expected in so thin and lean a body.' She was in fact very ill indeed. 'The Countess of Bedford was lately at the last cast and no hope of life left, insomuch that receiving the communion . . . she gave over the world and took her leave. But the worst is, they say, the master-pox hath settled in one of her eyes whereby she is like to lose it.'[189]

Lucy recovered. But Chamberlain's description of her, thin and lean and foul with pock-marks, makes a pathetic contrast with her face in her splendid portraits.

Her lameness is first mentioned in 1621. 'I have myself had an unhealthful spring of this, which I hope will not end in a lame leg, and that of that too I shall not long have cause to complain.' It was not her leg only that was affected when she next mentioned the complaint. 'I have had so much ill health and pain as made me for a good part of the time unable to write, and yet hath left me but a lame woman.' This long record of ill-health lends added charm to Lucy's lightly despairing comments on one of the most celebrated physicians of her time. The year is 1626.[190]

'My fear of relapsing makes me content to punish myself this spring by following a course of physic Sir Theodore Mayerne hath put me into, though I am very incredulous that it can prevent my having more fits of the gout. Howsoever, when I am troubled with any, they are accompanied with such accidents of sickness as shows they proceed from such humours as physic uses to correct, against which I have too rebellious a spleen I doubt to be brought into such obedience as not faster to pour out the sourness thereof into my stomach, and distil it into other parts, than all the pothecary's drugs will be able to correct. What I do therefore is rather because it shall not be laid to my charge that I neglect the means of health, than out of any great hope of cure by it; which, whether I have or no, God, I trust, will give me thankfulness to Him and patience till His appointed time of releasing me from all misery.' This was Lucy's last letter to Jane, and the most endearing. The second postscript contained a request to her friend to send her a dog: 'thus, you see, I cannot leave my custom of robbing you'.[191]

In the following year, a few days after her husband, Lucy died, 'having no belongings'. She was about forty-five years old.

THE CHANGE OF HEART

Sir James Harington
of Exton, died 1592

Sir James Harington,
first Baronet, of
Ridlington, died 1614
Marr. (1) Frances, dau.
of Robert Sapcote
(2) Anne, widow of
John Doyley

Sir Edward Harington,
second Baronet, of
Ridlington, died 1653
Marr. Margery, dau. of
John Doyley

Sir Sapcote Harington
of Sapcote, died 1630
Marr. Jane, dau. of
Sir William Samuel

Sir James Harington,
third Baronet, of
Ridlington, died 1680
Marr. Catharine, dau.
of Sir Edmund Wright

James Harington
of Sapcote, 1611-77

M

TWELVE

THE CHANGE OF HEART

PRINCE CHARLES had celebrated his twelfth birthday a fortnight after his brother Henry's death left him heir to the thrones
of England and Scotland. It is questionable how much he
may have remembered in later years of the far off days when Prince
Henry and John Harington had filled the limelight at his father's
court. Henry is reported to have said that his brother would make
an excellent archbishop; and he must surely have shown him the
Brief View of the State of the Church that the Knight of Kelston sent
him. Charles certainly spent some of his time with his sister
Elizabeth and her guardian: Lord Harington, who loved to tell
Lord Salisbury about his royal duties, once wrote to describe
a visit Elizabeth and Charles had paid to Nonsuch in his company.

But however close may have been Charles's association with his
Harington cousins, it belonged to an early period of his life that
not even the purposeful reminiscences of Lucy could have prevented from fading in his memory long before he looked up to see
one of them sitting in judgment on him, or handed a last memento
to another on the scaffold.

He did not escape from being informed of the claims of the
house of Kelston to the twenty-five manors in the north, a matter
in which the family had preserved the fullest documentation.

John, the third of Kelston, has already appeared elusively,
dining unpunctually with his grandmother; at Eton, where he
was made heir to his father's muse of poetry; next in the commendation of Lord Harington on a letter, notably worded for
his age. By a strange choice he was now at the new college of
Trinity, Oxford, and not at his father's university. From there he
proceeded to Lincoln's Inn to study law as his father had done,
and he was twenty-four years old, little older than his father had
been, when he inherited Kelston.

He had lost his powerful godparent Lord Salisbury, and he had
already married. His wife was Dioness, daughter of James Ley
of Ley in Devon, Lord Chief Justice. Ley was created a baronet

in 1619, and when Charles I succeeded to the throne he advanced Ley to be Lord Treasurer of England, and created him Earl of Marlborough.

It is evident that Marlborough did his best to advance John's fortunes along the road by which he had prospered himself. In 1626 he desired that his 'son-in-law Mr Harington might serve as Deputy and give the charge at the Sessions at Bridgewater'. His efforts were without success. Sir John Poulett wrote to Edward Nicholas on September 24, 'many of the principal gentlemen of the country being assembled and expecting Mr Harington, he neither came to the place himself, nor sent to request any other to supply the place for him; which we had all good reason to take ill at his hands'. The ink from the angry strokes of Poulett's pen passes right through the paper as he construes John's behaviour 'as a thing done of purpose to beget disorder in your Sessions'.[191]

John drew up a complete list of his properties, in his meticulous way, probably at the time when he inherited them. The list of manors and lands in Somerset, Cornwall, Wiltshire, and Dorset is long and impressive. He was able to pay a dowry of £1,500 at the marriage of one of his daughters, and £1,700 at the wedding of another. He lived in the great house of Kelston on the profits of his lands, as his ancestors had done since the Tudor marriage of 1547, and he showed no inclination to use his father-in-law as a means to obtaining office at court.[192]

Only the twenty-five manors, forfeited by attainder in 1485, exercised him as they had done his fathers before him ever since the last Harington of Brierley died fighting for the last of the Plantagenets. And where his fathers failed, he at last succeeded. In 1635 King Charles put his signature to the following document. 'Whereas John Harington of Kelston in the County of Somerset Esquire hath surrendered up into our hands all the estate, right, title and interest of him the said John Harington, in and unto the Manor of Brierley in the County of York, Farleton in Lonsdale in the County of Lancaster and the Manor of Farleton in Kendal in the County of Westmorland, and all other the Lordships, Manors, and Tenements and other Hereditaments which late were the lands or possessions of Sir James Harington Knight, attainted of treason in the first year of the late King Henry the Seventh, by Act of Parliament . . .' Perhaps King Charles hardly noticed the name of Sir James Harington, attainted of treason, before he read

179

on: 'which said surrender of his we graciously accept, and of our Princely grace, free bounty, and mere motion, do hereby grant unto the said John Harington . . . one full fifth part of all such profits and advantages whatsoever,' the remaining four-fifths to be used in beautifying the cathedral church of St Paul, London. After over a hundred and fifty years the dispute over the manors in the north was laid to rest at last, and John could devote himself to the earnest studies that produced his *Essays and Dialogues in Favour of the Presbyterian Doctrine*.[194]

On his shelves were the notebooks of his grandfather, containing the manuscript originals of the poems of Wyatt and Surrey. Dr Nott has described the use to which John put these priceless manuscripts. 'Mr Harington was a pious man and a biblical scholar: he had moreover a turn for mathematics. Unfortunately he was likewise a lawyer, a justice of the peace, and a rigid economist. To make room therefore for his diagrams and family receipts; his abstracts of sermons heard, his notices of justice meetings attended, and his "heads of charges to be delivered at Sessions", he has not only written unmercifully over whole pages of Wyatt's poetry, without the least regard to rhyme or reason, but he has in many instances studiously crossed out the lines, that they might not obtrude themselves upon his profounder speculations. Luckily Wyatt's ink was better than Mr Harington's, and therefore the original writing may yet be traced through the dim veil thrown over it by the laborious and thrifty justice.'

It is reassuring to learn that John became, in the end, conscientious in his judicial duties. And it should be mentioned in his favour that while he committed this act of vandalism against the Tudor poets, he preserved with care certain resolutions of the House of Commons sent to him by William Prynne from 1628 onwards.[195]

Unlike his father or his grandfather, John the third of Kelston was brought up from childhood in Somerset. He never lived the life of a courtier, and Eton, Oxford, and Lincoln's Inn only added a veneer to the descent and estates that raised him to the highest ranks of the west country gentry.

The climate of opinion in Somerset at the accession of Charles I is reflected in the lives of the two men with whom John associated in the years that followed. Sir John Poulett, who complained of his derelictions at the Bridgewater sessions of 1626, belonged to a family with longer puritan associations than John of Kelston could boast. He was even suspected of treason a little while before he earned the King's gratitude and a peerage in 1627, for his entertainment of the Huguenot Admiral Soubise. When the choice faced him, Poulett turned Cavalier, but his decision was by no means a foregone conclusion.

William Prynne was younger than either of these men, born at Swanswick in Somerset, and educated at Bath Grammar School before he went to Oxford. When he reached Lincoln's Inn, the preacher was Dr John Preston, a politician at heart, seeking to impose the Calvinist theology. Preston died in 1628, and so did Buckingham, whom he was trying to use as his tool, and the way was left open to Laud and the high churchmen. In that year Prynne was called to the Bar, strengthened in his militant puritanism. While Prynne was lying under sentence of life imprisonment and a fine of £5,000 for *Histriomastix*, his attack on stage plays in 1633, John of Kelston was reflecting the puritan thought of Somerset about such things. In that same year he, and the other Justices of the Peace of Somerset, petitioned the king for suppression of 'church ales, clerk ales, bid-ales, and revels, by reason of disorders inseparably accompanying the same'. They recommended that no more heady entertainment should be allowed than 'civil feasting between neighbour and neighbour in their houses, and the orderly use of manly exercises'. It is hard to recognize the son of Elizabeth's saucy poet behind this proposal to impose godliness by force. But it is not hard to recognize a child of the times, reared in one of the largest houses in Somerset in the van of a new surge of religious opinion, able now to give it expression by destroying the beautiful poems of Wyatt.[195]

John was one of the prosperous puritan gentry of the west country, opposed to the new high church policy of Laud. But Laud's authoritarian rule in the sphere of religion was only one aspect of the new absolute government, by divine right, and without parliament. In the surge of political opinion which this engendered, John was also involved. For the west country squirachy nurtured the bitterest and ablest opponent to absolute government in all England — John Pym. Pym's sister Jane was married to Robert Rous, one of whose brothers was Speaker of the Barebones Parliament, one of his sons a Member of Parliament during the Commonwealth, and the other, Robert, the husband of John's daughter Phoebe. This marriage did not take place until 1657, but it may not be fanciful to picture the new lord of

Kelston, discussing the resolutions that Prynne sent to him with such men as Pym and Rous.

Sweet Mall was still alive. She survived until 1634, never wandering out of discretion's path, and bequeathing to posterity a perfect silence. And her we must be allowed to picture too, observing the piety and talent of her son, which her husband had combined with such humanity.

The high church policy of Charles I alienated the puritans, and his theory and practice of absolute government roused the parliamentarians. Some of the ablest members of these two groups belonged to the class of society which had been largely responsible for local government since the days of the Tudors, the ancient or the risen gentry. The majority of these might be indifferent to doctrine or constitutional theory, but they could become incensed by inefficient administrations. Such was the Sheriff of Rutland, the sixth generation of Sheriffs of Rutland in unbroken descent since Henry VII assumed the Crown, Sir Edward Harington, second baronet.

Sir Edward had inherited his baronetcy in 1614 on the death of his father Sir James Harington of Ridlington, first baronet. When the last son of his father's elder brother, the unfortunate Sir Henry, died two years later, he became the senior representative of the Harington family. Until his cousin Lucy's death he watched her restlessly dissipating the huge fortunes of his house. There was nothing he could do under the laws of inheritance. Sir Henry's eldest surviving son had tried litigation and, in Lucy's smug words, had got 'nothing but lost labour'.

But the new senior branch had set about remedying this misfortune with the old family skill. The first baronet had added the property of Sapcote by his first marriage, to the manor of Ridlington which his father had conveyed to him. He next married a widow, Anne Doyley of Merton. This was unprofitable in itself, because Anne possessed daughters by her own first marriage. But it was brought to a happy issue when Sir Edward his heir married one of the daughters and co-heiresses of his stepmother. Sir Edward might not be living like the best barons in England as his grandfather had done when he was the head of the Haringtons, but his position was sufficiently secure to enable his younger brother Sir Sapcote to inherit the property after which he was named, to man the flank, as it were, in case the main body should once again be stricken. Sir Edward Harington

of Ridlington, second baronet, became High Sheriff of Rutland
in 1621, and again in 1636 when King Charles decided to raise
ship-money, not only in the ports, but inland as well.

Sir Edward was a simple, kindly man, conscientious in the
discharge of his duties, and thoughtful of the poor. He was
aggravated by disorder, whether it was provoked by religious
dissidence, or by inefficiency in the royal administration. 'Sir,' he
reported from Ridlington on 15 February 1637, 'I have made my
assessment for the raising of £800 in the County of Rutland for
the providing and furnishing of one ship of war for his Majesty's
service. And I have governed myself therein in making of the
assessment by such public payments as are approved of by all to
be most equal, and accordingly I have rated (with the advice of
the high Constables) every town within their several hundreds,
further charging the said high Constables that if any difference
do arise amongst the . . . of any the several towns in the subdividing
of the said sums . . . that they speedily repair to the said towns,
to reconcile and settle the said differences, and to bring the
assessment to me that I may further examine and sign them. This
I do daily as often as occasion requires . . .'[187]

He addressed this letter 'To my much honoured and very kind
friend Mr Edward Nicholas', which indicated that he enjoyed a
personal friendship with the able and disinterested servant of King
Charles's corrupt and inefficient Government. It contained no
comment on the legality of raising ship-money inland, or taxes
without the consent of Parliament. It was only concerned, and
concerned at detailed length, that the central administration should
be properly informed about this new function of local government.

The very next letter contains the first hint of exasperation as
Sir Edward detected the lack of similar efficiency at the centre.
'Sir. I hope you have received my answer of the 15th of February
to yours . . . and now I know to whom and where to direct my
letters I shall not fail from time to time (as occasion requireth) to
certify you of my proceedings according to their Lordships'
command. I acquainted you in my former letter, that the way I
take in this important business is such as I hope will expedite his
Majesty's service and give good content to his people, which I
find to succeed well. Some opposition I have now and then, but
I spare them not, neither will I till I have perfected the work.
And as soon as I have signed the assessments set on the persons
of every particular parish (which I do daily as they are brought

me, according to their Lordships' directions) I shall not fail to
send an exact and true certificate thereof to the Board, according
to their Lordships' command.'[198]

Writing again on March 15 'to his very loving friend Mr Edward
Nicholas', Sir Edward described his manner of dealing with
opposition.

'Sir, in my last letter of the 1st of this month I certified you that
I had £400 of his Majesty's money in my hands, which I would
endeavour to remit to Sir William Russell with all speed. But
in this time of Lent I find it very difficult to get any remitted, and
to bring it up, or send it up by any other is full of hazard and
danger. I have now received the greater part of his Majesty's
money charged upon this county except some few towns, wherein
some particular persons do obstinately refuse to pay anything (as
they pretend, out of matter of conscience) and so by their ill
example they do not only hinder the towns wherein they live, but
encourage other towns to do the like, which doth put me to much
trouble. I have distrained some of them, and am resolved to take
the same course with the rest, if they still persist to stand out.
And I punish the choicest of them that have good personal estates
by raising their assessment to a greater proportion than they were
before. I am now busy in sending money to all the towns that
have paid, for the easing of the poorer sort that have contributed
to this assessment (as I signified to you in my former letter of the
15th of February last) which gives the poor great comfort, and
so I purpose to do with the rest, as soon as the monies of those
towns (that stand out) come in . . .'[199]

Later in the same month Sir Edward surmised that he would be
able to hand in the whole £800 a little after Easter. But he added
a warning: 'the trouble I have been put to has been such that
were it not his Majesty's command, no profit or reward could
draw me to adventure upon the like business again'.[200]

The arrangements allowed for one final muddle and expostulation. 'Sir, I did write to you in my last letter of the 29th of March
that my endeavour should be to return his Majesty's Ship money
with all convenient speed, and accordingly I agreed with a man
to remit a good part of the said money to Sir William Russell as
you directed me, and upon his return he told me that he had been
at the said Sir William Russell's house with his money, who was
gone out of town 2 or 3 days before and (as he heard) would not
return in a week after. So there being none to receive his money

or that could give him a sufficient discharge for the same, he was fain to carry his money back again, and to bring it down with him into the country, to his great trouble and hazard.'[201]

A month later Sir William Russell signed a receipt for the full amount of ship-money due from Rutland: but King Charles little knew what he had bartered for that £800. He hardly guessed when, at the end of the following year, 1638, it fell to men like Sir Edward of Ridlington to raise troops for the first Scots war. Only when they faced him in Parliament, assembled under the relentless leadership of John Pym, did Charles begin to realize how he had antagonized the gentlemen of England. Neville and Cary, Devereux and Digby, Harington and Colepeper who shared with Stewarts the royal blood of Bruce, these and many other names from an earlier age joined the roll of Pym's opposition. They had always governed England, and the Tudors had made their government peaceful, systematic, efficient. The sovereign was merely the greatest among equals; and now a Stewart claimed to rule by divine right alone, and made a mess of it.

John the third of Kelston was a puritan, narrow and intense, the acquaintance of Prynne. Sir Edward of Ridlington was suspicious of religious fervour, straightforward, scrupulously honest, the friend of that selfless drudge of the royal cause, Edward Nicholas. The characters of these remote cousins were not alike. But they resembled one another in the size of their estates, their local offices of justice and sheriff, and in the influence of a family tradition as ancient as it was distinctive.

In this tradition their sons were now growing up, the children of the new puritan age. The first of these was Sir Edward's heir James, born a month before his time in 1607. 'The first thing I did then was to weep and cry', he later explained, as if from memory, though he concedes that it was a lapse 'as by a natural instinct with all other infants'.[202]

To his father's integrity James added a remarkable diffidence. He was a sickly child, who spent a great deal of time meditating on death when most children are absorbed in the excitements of living. After each illness he became more surprised to find himself still alive, and when his health improved in later life he retained this capacity for surprise in comparatively trivial predicaments like falling into a river while he was fishing, or discovering a fire in his house. He regarded these illnesses, not as a martyrdom as his cousin Lucy had done, but as a very special favour. 'By this correction, Heavenly Father, thou dist most wisely bridle, order, and allay the strong and indomitable lusts of my youth; that beholding daily Death, thy Sergeant, at the door, I might fear to act wickedness.'

Indeed his protection was of a most violent sort. His third illness he described as 'a pleurisy, the consequent and usual effect of a long and violent cough, which by a terrible pain and stitch made my breathing (the necessary servant and bellows of life) painful; which after divers months' suffering, and fruitless use of many remedies, Thou O Lord, that hearest and answerest prayer, heard mine, and by thy blessing upon a plaster laid to my stomach, and a purge, didst in one night and a day free me from all pains, coughs, and distempers, to the admiration of myself and relations'. He appears to have suffered from tuberculosis, for he mentioned that he coughed blood; and it seems that he recovered completely. In his thanks to God for each fresh deliverance from death he sometimes made an oblique, unflattering reference to his physicians. 'Praised be thy Name, O Lord, that in much loving kindness and faithfulness hath always afflicted me; and didst then also, after a few weeks, give me a perfect recovery, by thy blessing upon the medicine of a poor widow, even after that the utmost endeavours of a skilful doctor proved uneffectual.'[202]

But James was able to record one occasion in early youth when he was exempted entirely from affliction, which left him more surprised and grateful than ever. 'Charitable visits to our neighbours many times prove uncharitable to ourselves. Such proved this of myself, nurse, and others to the sick bed of the Vicar of the town; by which the inhabitants were infected and many of his parishioners followed him, not only to, but into the grave.' If this last macabre remark is a conscious joke, it is almost the only trace of humour in James's writings.[202]

That was the plague. He had an even more remarkable deliverance 'when, being a child, and alone in my father's coach, the horses running down a steep hill, the boot flew open by a jolt on the way, and I was cast out of the coach upon the ground, and taken up without any the least hurt or maim'.

So James grew up to invest the family piety, and the piety of the age, with a particular flavour, all his own. In the year of King Charles's succession, while Lucy was complaining that the new court appointments would injure her influence, James set off for London, protected by his piety 'from the vices of the times, when I was left by my parents to my liberty, and alone in the cities of Westminster and London, young, and about seventeen years of age'.[101]

The vices of the times never stood a chance with James, but they were sporting in their persistence. 'Seventy miles as to my labour seemed but a short stage, but as to my longing desires, five hundred; until I got a sight of the southern constellation of the English Gemini, Peter and Paul's churches, and the united cities of London and Westminster, where I was no sooner settled but I found myself unsettled through the multitude of temptations, and incitements to sin and vanity.' James found temptations in some places that ought not to have surprised him.

'After some time I adventured, at the instance of some of my acquaintance, not therein my friends, to go into a tavern. I stopped, and thought the fair structure, rich sign-bush and basin, had some resemblance to the Roman triumphal arches. But my admiration was soon changed into a detestation. For the roaring and singing, bawling and swearing of their tenants at will, the knocking of pots, the scraping of fiddlers, the gaping of tapsters at the bar (not of truth and justice, but too often of the contrary) made me think it to be a Bedlam, a place full of madness.'[102]

Another of his harsh judgments is a familiar complaint: 'the shopkeepers and their feminines being like the company of players I saw lately, that know how to act all parts . . . especially those of lying, equivocation, dissimulation, and overreaching, when they meet with country ignoramuses.'

The recreations for which people select the public parks were another source of pained surprise to James. 'Being almost suffocated with ill scent of pride and vanity, I rode out for recreation to a park near it [the city], to find out sweeter air. But there methought the proverb was verified, "the world runs upon wheels", which raised up clouds of dust, as though the earth against Nature would take place of the element of air . . . wherefore to avoid this throng, through some solitary meadows and winding paths, I sought in the centre of the wood for some place of privacy; and found some little hermitages, where I hoped to have discoursed with some sober or devout persons. But I found them to be chapels of ease, dedicated to Bacchus, Ceres, and Venus.'

Then there were the plays and the poets. 'Having heard extolled the wit and language of our English poets, and that their plays (a fit name for such airy poems) were much visited, and by the youth of our nation preferred above the best sermons, as also that they were acted to the life in the public theatres, I went thither.' The result of this particular piece of research, and of the meditations that followed, was an indictment that deserves a high place in the rhetoric of those times. 'So many precious hours lost, such high strains and veins of wit run waste, such excellent language defiled and abused, and such a happy Muse ravished and debauched: in the compiling and publishing so many false and unhallowed legions, to stir up and inflame your lusts, and the sleeping passions, and corruptions of the youth of both sexes in these nations: so many stage-plays, the scoffers of goodness and holiness of conversation, the consumers of useful time and of the innate virtue, modesty, and estates of all kinds of persons as also so many frothy and airy amorous verses, ditties, and songs, the nurses and panders of all manner of looseness and uncleanness, in all sorts of people.'[202]

The interesting thing about James's reflections on London in 1625 is that they do not mention the life of the court where his father's first cousin Lucy still blazed and his connection, Lord Treasurer Marlborough ruled. His comments were about courting couples in the park, surprised by the devout young man in search of sober discourse, the brawling in the taverns, the popular theatre and the songs and ditties. It was a great pity he did not describe the life in London before the rule of the saints more fully, because he could be vivid and, beneath his severity, humane. Indeed it was a secret act of humanity that saved him later from being dragged on a hurdle through the streets of London.

James returned, disillusioned, to his home. Journeys in those days provided more frequent occasions for the 'deliverances' which nourished his astonishment at remaining alive. One of them that he recorded was 'a great snow, and God's deliverance of me and my servant from being smothered and lost, when many others perished therein, in our travel and return home'. Another occurred during a different journey, in the month of May. The episode makes Sir Edward's anger easier to understand, when his ship-money was carried to London, and had to be brought back again with much hazard, because there was no one there to receive it.

James was returning home with a servant 'having a great charge of money' through the forest of Rockingham. 'My way led me into a most pleasant plain, a second temple or Arcadia, for delight and pleasure; to guard which from the hot invasion of the sun or the sudden eruption of storms, stood round in rank and deep files armies of sturdy oaks.' Into this peaceful solitude 'the careering of four horsemen, issuing out of several quarters of the woods, alarmed me to prepare for an onset and to alight with my servant, that drawing our swords and cocking our pistols, and backed by our horses, we might not be surprised, but secure ourselves and a considerable sum of money. This our prepared vigilency (as I conjecture) being at a near distance perceived by our adversaries, they stopped, united, and wheeled about, retreating into the woods again, thereby encouraging us to remount and to return that night with safety home'.

In 1628, on attaining the age of twenty-one, James was knighted, and the following year, 'having expended above the third part of my life in a single condition', he married Catharine Wright. London was not, after all, absolutely without merit, for Catharine was 'the eldest daughter and co-heir of a worthy person that was a knight, alderman, and Lord Mayor of London; a wife not only fruitful in children, but in many other blessings: as being a builder up of my family, by a large portion; one of nature's best pieces for beauty and proportion; the psalmist's olive and vine for fruitfulness; and which is above all, and the rarest perfection of that sex, a person chaste, faithful, and religious'. Sir James of Swakeleys (as he came to be known after his marriage) was not exaggerating in his tribute to his wife. And he deserved the blessings he described, for he had that loveliest of virtues, the gift of gratitude. He found gratitude for misfortune, and gratitude for prosperity. He could not take for granted the privilege of remaining alive, and he hastened to return thanks where they were due while he remained alive to do so.

'Most honoured and best beloved parents,' he wrote when he reached his majority, 'lest Death should proclaim me bankrupt before I had paid the due debt of gratefulness which I owe you next to my Heavenly Father, for my life, education, and preservation, I here presume to present you with these disordered and weak Meditations ... as a testimonial of my thankfulness for those your numberless merits, which are as far beyond requital as expression.'[202]

Such was the heir of the Exton branch, fashioned in this new puritan age, but wearing the new garb with something of the old elegance.

His uncle Sir Sapcote's heir, also called James, was four years younger than his first cousin. This other James was a robust precocious youth, whose parents confessed 'that he rather kept them in awe than needed their correction'. He was sent to the same new college of Trinity, Oxford, that John of Kelston had attended twenty-five years earlier where he became a pupil of that persuasive anti-papist, Doctor Chillingworth. But somehow his spells failed to ensnare James. While young Lucius Cary, the future Lord Falkland, was affected by them for life, James of Sapcote was left only with a hatred of interference in freedom of conscience. Perhaps it was Chillingworth who had succeded in working such contrary results.[203]

James inherited Sapcote when he was only eighteen years old, and before he had taken his degree. His mother had died eleven years earlier, leaving him with a younger brother and three sisters. But these were not his only responsibility when, in 1630, he found himself the head of his family. His father had remarried, and left him with a stepmother, two stepbrothers, and two stepsisters. If only his family papers had survived, we should be able to read how this generous and affectionate youth handled a situation of such complexity. For somehow he did arrange matters to everyone's satisfaction. His own brother William he set up as a merchant in London, and lived to see him a Fellow of the Royal Society. One of his stepbrothers went to sea, where he was killed, and the other obtained a captaincy in the army. Only one of the five sisters and half-sisters was unprovided with a husband. Not many Harington parents, with larger resources, had done better than that for their children.

For it must be remembered that the history of the Haringtons, as of any other family in England, has been predominantly the history of the eldest son. Occasionally the heir has been a daughter, and sometimes a younger son has succeeded in establishing a separate dynasty, as Sir Nicholas did under John of Gaunt, and the Haringtons of Exton, and John the first of Kelston. The ruthless law under which all property passed to the eldest son made easy the slippery descent from the position of younger son of the highest in the land, down through his younger children to a rank in society of which history preserves no record.

James was the son of a younger son (Sir Sapcote) of a younger son (Sir James, first baronet) of an Elizabethan knight. The fact that he was descended from a medieval baron, or that the peerage had been revived in the senior branch by recent letters patent, are not indications that he belonged to a family of fallen fortunes. For such a junior branch, James of Sapcote found himself exceptionally well provided, so well provided that with sense and generosity he was able to solve the very complicated family problems that suddenly faced him in his nineteenth year. But the situation had not always been so satisfactory in his family. James was already a child when his cousin Henry lay in a debtor's prison because his father had been a second son; and Lucy (of all people) expressed distaste at this unthrifty state of affairs. It was to suggest a solution which James made a corner-stone in his later political thought: 'that every one holding above two thousand pounds a year in land, lying within the proper territory of the Commonwealth, leave the said land equally divided among his sons'.

James of Sapcote obtained admission to the Middle Temple in 1631, and immediately went abroad. He wished to see Venice, where the sixteen-year-old John Harington had made such an impression two decades before: and the Netherlands, where the Winter Queen was not too busy trying to help her husband recover his throne to remember the family with whom she had passed her youth. But particularly, James was curious to discover how the governments of these countries functioned. His father's death had called him suddenly out of a world of growing political and religious controversy. The religious questions left him unmoved. But the problems of government fascinated him, as one day they were to fascinate everyone who heard him discuss them. For the student of institutions the study of history was important, but not enough. 'If he has no knowledge in Story, he cannot tell what has been; and if he has not been a traveller, he cannot tell what is. But he that neither knows what has been, nor what is, can never tell what must be, nor what may be.' In wide travel and deep reading, James sought the gift of prophecy.

It was fortunate that he went to the Netherlands first, because it enabled him to see the Elector Frederick before his death. For the last time a royal court was enlivened by the wit and charm of a Harington, and there is a poignancy in the thought that as the Winter Queen listened to James's talk, 'very friendly and facetious', neither of them could have suspected the imminent doom of both their houses.[204]

To James's charm an early portrait bears witness, which descended through his mother's family and now hangs in the National Portrait Gallery. And his friend Aubrey described him in his notes: 'of a middling stature, a well trussed man, strong and thick, well set, sanguine, quick — hot — fiery hazel eye, thick moist curled hair'. Aubrey was not always charitable in his descriptions of people, and in his picture of James it is as though he had been won to emulation by the 'very liberal and compassionate nature' of his friend.

Besides the court of the ex-King and Queen of Bohemia at the Hague, James visited the court of the Prince of Orange. Frederick also took him to Denmark, where his wife's uncle Christian IV, last of the sea-kings, ruled with a splendour that lingers still in his vast empty palaces. So James had seen monarchy in three very different forms, elected, rejected, and triumphant, by the time he set off to visit the Serene Republic of Venice. For good measure he stopped on the way to see the Pope.

This meeting with the Pope is the subject of an anecdote which proves incidentally that James of Sapcote met King Charles before he was of age, or had travelled abroad. He attended the English court on his return, no doubt to pursue his comparisons, and to bring Charles news of his sister at the Hague. The King had already heard that when James had met the Pope, he had refused to kiss his toe, and he taxed James with lack of respect for a temporal prince. 'He presently replied, that since he had the honour to kiss his Majesty's hand, he thought it beneath him to kiss any other prince's foot. The King was pleased with his answer, and did afterwards admit him to be one of his Privy Chamber extraordinary.' So began the last and saddest and strangest friendship between a Harington and an English sovereign. For James, in the words of his friend Aubrey, grew to love King Charles 'passionately'; and this affection was inconsistent with the views on government and kingship that he had been evolving on his travels abroad.

Meanwhile, in the solemn halls of Kelston that had once resounded to the laughter of an already vanished age, the third heir to new times was growing up. John of Kelston's eldest son was much younger than his twelfth cousin James. Although John was already married to the Lady Dioness in 1613, she did not bear him his first child — a son — until over ten years later. This son must have died in early infancy for the next child, born in 1627, was given the same name of John. There was one other surviving son and two daughters, the younger of whom was born in 1637 and married John Pym's nephew.[198]

SIR JAMES HARINGTON, 3RD BARONET
1607-80

LADY HARINGTON (WIFE OF
SIR JAMES HARINGTON)

THE CHANGE OF HEART

The long intervals between these children of the devout John of Kelston seem to confirm the sincerity of his stern principles. If we are conceived in sin and shapen in wickedness, it is estimable to leave a decent interval for contrition. But the result of this reluctance (if such it was) to relapse into parenthood was that the fourth John of Kelston was barely in his teens when the storm broke in King Charles's northern kingdom.

John Harington of Stepney
and Kelston, died 1582

|

Sir John Harington of Kelston,
1561-1612

|

John Harington of Kelston,
1589-1654
Marr. Dioness,
dau. of James Ley, first
Earl of Marlborough

John Harington of Kelston,
1627-1700

Phoebe, born 1637
Marr. Robert Rous
of Wotton

THIRTEEN

THE REPUBLICANS

THE history of England, like that of other nations, is interpreted by historians in a hundred different ways. Some recognize past events as the moves in a game of chess between giants. How differently the game would have gone, according to this view, if Prince Henry had lived longer, or Oliver Cromwell had died earlier. Others see the great actors of the past as puppets, dancing to the tune of an economic trend, rising (or declining) gentry moving inexorably into conflict with the crown, nations forced into war by their conflicting commercial interests. Others again discover history to be a key to the inscrutable purposes of God, a record of the triumphs and defeats of true and false doctrines. All these interpretations have helped to uncover the many faces of truth.

There is a theme of English history that recurs constantly to puzzle and fascinate later ages. A mood of scepticism and doubt spreads among thoughtful people. Ancient beliefs are questioned. New patterns of behaviour are adopted, untrammelled by the old rules of rigid doctrine. And all the while, beneath the surface, a new religious movement will be gathering strength, until it gains the power to impose upon emancipated (or licentious) man moral rules more exacting than those they had abandoned.

Something like this occurred when the Age of Reason gave place to the Victorian age. Something like it may be happening, for all we know, at this present. Something very like it indeed occurred between the time when the first John of Kelston composed his 'Monk's Hymn to Satan', and the fourth John of Kelston listened to his father's discourse on Presbyterian doctrine.

Many studies have been made of this eternal problem that sways the human race. And the difficulty of all such studies is to find exactly corresponding people, whose opinions and behaviour can be compared before and after the change of heart. To compare the views and behaviour of one set of people with that of a quite different social group whose beliefs triumphed over theirs is not to reach the roots of the matter. For this is the record merely of a victory and a defeat, not a change of heart at all.

It is hard to find eloquent apologists, belonging to the same family or social group, for an age of enlightenment and a Victorian age, for the age of Elizabeth and that of the saints. It is this, even more than their links with the Middle Ages and its thought, that gives the Haringtons such a particular interest. They left little discernible mark upon the course of events. But in their words and actions they left illuminating evidence of the kind of change that was taking place in the minds of men as Charles rode north to subdue his rebellious Scots.

Hitherto words had served; it was now the time for acts.

The King's problem was to raise an army without parliamentary aid. It was his failure to do this that compelled him to come to ignominious terms with the Scots, and to summon Parliament once more. Sir Edward of Ridlington had helped to raise ship-money for him, with gradually increasing distaste. His son and heir, Sir James of Swakeleys, now made the first gesture of defiance. He refused to take part in a war against co-religionists who were in arms for conscience' sake. On 28 February 1639 a warrant was issued by the Council at Whitehall to take him and many others into custody as defaulters at musters, unless they should submit, and conform in future. But his cousin James of Sapcote rode north with the King when he left London on March 27, as one of his Privy Chamber extraordinary. He did not often fail to be present where great issues were to be tried, and he never concealed his own attitude to them. From now on his relationship with Charles was to be extraordinary indeed, for 'the king loved his company; only he would not endure to hear of a commonwealth'.[205]

In a matter of months the war was over, and the King driven to the expedient of summoning Parliament. It was the new year of 1640. Back in London Charles argued coldly with the delegations of the Scottish Covenanters while he longed for the arrival of Strafford from Ireland. The country was in a ferment over the ship-money tax and the unaccustomed elections.

No one could have felt a keener curiosity in this revival of parliamentary government in England than James of Sapcote. The baffling question is whether he tried to take part in it himself. The Haringtons had been returned to Parliament as knights of the shires in which their lands lay since the fourteenth century. But even if James had not disposed of his property by this time to provide for his brothers and sisters, he did not reside upon it.

Nevertheless Anthony Wood, who was informed by James's friend Aubrey, says that James did once try to stand for Parliament. He does not name the constituency, and he says the date was 1642, for which there is no other evidence.

These are the blank circumstances that surround the letter of 27 February 1640, written by a Mr Harington to the Alderman and his brethren of Stamford, proposing himself as their representative. Who this Harington is cannot be known for certain, because the signature has been torn off. One solitary letter that James wrote to Aubrey survives, of all his correspondence, but it does not help to identify the Stamford letter, which appears to have been written fair by a clerk. The nearest approach to evidence is that Stamford is in Lincolnshire, the county of the Sapcote Haringtons. It was written by an untitled Harington of about thirty years. Its author referred to the King as a Solomon, and to his country as a republic. It is very tempting to believe that this is James's one surviving letter (the other to Aubrey is a mere note); but its author may have been a cousin of the Wolphege branch, also in Lincolnshire. Nevertheless it remains the most significant comment of a Harington at the dividing-place of political loyalties.

'My near habitation and three years' education within your liberties has made such a powerful and affectionate impression that I should seem infinitely ungrateful did I not labour after a thankful return. A fit opportunity I have long waited for, which is now effected in his Majesty's summons to a Parliament, wherein, if you shall think me worthy, I declare myself cheerfully willing to do you service. To adapt me for this I desire the favour, though absent by reason of urgent occasions, to be presently registered a member of your corporation, and I shall shortly attend you to take my oath, and to express both to you and the town my real thankfulness. This my request, though unusual, is not illegal as I am informed. But I refer myself therein to you and to your learned counsel. I should here conclude but that my duty to the republic, whereof we are all fellow members, commands me to put you in mind of the weight of the business which God and the King have entrusted you with. Our Solomon has, by virtue of his writ, made you principal architectors to choose fit materials for the building of a royal and living house for the safest peace and glory of his kingdom. Let it be your care then that it may prove a Bethel, a house of God, not a Babel, a tower of confusion.

This, like the first temple, must be built with stones ready squared; no hewing, no putting to school. Their thirty winters are scarce sufficient to warrant them from mouldering to dust under the pressure of that employment. To you is committed both the sword, and the balance to divide and distinguish. These corner-stones must neither recline, decline, nor incline, but stand upright and perpendicular to heaven, as being immovably fixed upon the basis and foundation of naked truth. The eye of wisdom and the hand respecting public good, not private and by-ends, must hold the plumb-line of judgment to each stone; from whose voluntary, not wracked or limited motion, will necessarily follow a right censure and happy election. I need write no more nor this, as being assured your piety abhors to betray his Majesty's trust and your country's good. If by these formal remembrances I have excluded myself, I am well contented with that reverend bishop, rather to want a place, than that the place should want a man.'[204]

It is of uncertain relevance to compare the style of this letter with the prose of James Harington of Sapcote. James's prose style was inclined to be turgid, but it was scattered with the unforgettable phrases of the brilliant conversationalist. As he grew older it became more incisive, with occasional effective lapses into biblical language. He was to write of the model republic he described in such detail: 'my dear Lords, Oceana is as the rose of Sharon, and the lily of the valley. As the lily among thorns, such is my love among the daughters. She is comely as the tents of Kedar, and terrible as an army with banners.'

But Stamford did not respond to the blandishments of Mr Harington. Once again it was left to the eldest cousin Sir James, defaulter at the musters, to take the first active part in the ensuing struggle.

A distaste for fighting had played no part in his decision to default. His resourcefulness when he was faced by the robbers in Rockingham forest is sufficient evidence of that. But when or why he took up arms remains uncertain. He himself described the loss he suffered in his property, with characteristic generosity. The royalists, desperate for funds to pay their armies, seized the estates of their enemies where they could, and Sir James's among them. Looking back on those violent years, Sir James praised his 'God of tender mercies, who didst not only give me a large paternal estate, but when that was all taken from me for five years in the late wars, didst in that time of my want and necessity relieve me, and my numerous family, by the gift of a good revenue (the legacy of my wife's father) who did not only, after the end of the late troubles in the year 1646, restore to me my confiscated estate, but greatly increased it'.[207]

It was nearly three weeks after Prince Rupert's defeat at Marston Moor in the July of 1644 that Sir James was first mentioned in the reports to the Committee of both Kingdoms as holding a command. King Charles had made his headquarters at Oxford, from which it was his recurrent objective to advance along the Thames to capture London. Sir William Waller had the problem of keeping sufficient forces between King Charles and his goal. At this distance of time it is easy to see that the King's cause was lost. But in 1644, when communications were slow, and so many separate forces throughout the country were pursuing separate random objectives, this was not so obvious.

One of the most difficult problems for both King and Parliament during this war was to prevent their forces from straying back to their homes, and this difficulty was in Waller's mind when he advised the Committee about the regiments at Abingdon. 'I am of opinion the City regiments with Sir James Harington might be persuaded to stay with Browne for a while here.'[208]

Major-General Browne expressed himself more strongly to the Committee from Reading. 'The forces that Sir William intends to leave behind him, I understand, are very few, if any, besides the remaining part of Sir James Harington's brigade, who are to go home within three or four days upon Sir William's late promise to them, which has retained them here till now.'[209]

Parliament had the enormous advantage over the King that it controlled the machinery of taxation and the resources of the city of London. Charles was dependent on the plate of Oxford and Cambridge, the wealth of his rich supporters, and what he could capture. The golden font which Queen Elizabeth had given her godson at his baptism had almost certainly been melted down for this purpose at Bristol by now. The Committee of both Kingdoms responded to the warnings of Waller and Browne by arranging that fresh forces should relieve Sir James, and entered the decision that he and other commanders of City forces must stay a fortnight longer while £2,000 was sent speedily 'for their better encouragement'. Sir James received a letter from the Committee dated July 24:

'In respect of the present posture of the west we have appointed

Sir William Waller to march that way with a strong party, and to leave the rest of his forces and ordnance at Abindgon with Major-General Browne. We desire you, with your forces, to tarry there for twenty days, until your absence shall be supplied with some of the new levied forces . . . We know your willingness to serve the public, notwithstanding the many difficulties your forces are under, which we shall endeavour to have supplied.' Five days later Sir James was in London, perhaps reporting on the situation, and the Committee saw fit to add a little flattery for his better encouragement. 'We have taken into consideration your long stay abroad with your brigade, which we are very sensible of, and give you thanks for your good service therein . . .'[208]

By such prompt attention to its task, efficient payment of troops, and orders that were half coaxing flattery, did the Committee set up by Parliament keep its army in the field. Before the fortnight's extension was over, Sir James heard again: 'notwithstanding a former order from this Committee for your forces to come away from Abingdon upon Monday next, the 12th inst., upon a very pressing occasion we have found it necessary to desire you to stay for a fortnight longer . . . We doubt not but by your endeavours they will continue in a service so necessary for so short a time, and return with honour and credit'.[208]

The anxieties of the Committee were well founded. Waller's forces mutinied for their pay and were defeated by the royalists that summer, and in the autumn Charles left Oxford for the south. Sir James received an order dated October 11, to march immediately to Colnbrook upon extraordinary service. To encourage him to march with all expedition, this order was followed by fuller information of the King's advance. On the nineteenth Sir James wrote to the Earl of Northumberland, at the Committee of both Kingdoms:

'I am and shall be punctual in the observance of your Lordship's commands. Since your order for quartering at Colnbrook, and moving towards the west, some part of the brigade has been every day, notwithstanding the unseasonableness of the weather, in motion. Neither have I been less obedient to the directions of the Earl of Manchester, by whose appointment the whole brigade is quartered at Reading, attending yours and his further commands. The first meeting and concentration of the regiments into a brigade was on Thursday last in Maidenhead thicket. Our numbers I then judged to be 3,000, from whence that night we marched to

Reading, where we hope in a day or two our companies, which are yet thin, will be 4,000 complete, if our Committee in London force out our defaulters.'[207]

The Earl of Manchester that day was writing in more urgent terms that there was a 'very hot alarm', 'that the King, with all his army, was come to Andover', and concluded: 'upon this sudden occasion I took upon me to write to Sir James Harington to desire him to bring up four of the City regiments hither to me. I thought it necessary for the safety of Reading to leave one regiment there'.[208]

This was a war conducted by men who prized saintliness, and there can be little doubt that it shone in the character of Sir James for all to see. But it was also being conducted by men who looked for military efficiency, and it seems that they found this in Sir James also. The delicate diffident youth had turned into a worthy successor to that other Sir James Harington who had held the bridge at Fisherton on the eve of Agincourt, and the boisterous Sir James who remained loyal to Richard III at Bosworth.

This third Sir James seemed to be on the winning side. The Committee was just in time to order ammunition to be sent to him before Charles's second defeat at Newbury on October 27. Manchester reported, 'I have written to Sir James Harington to signifiy your pleasure to him.'[208]

The Committee signified less pleasure in Manchester himself. The general was becoming worried as to where these victories over the King would lead. 'If we beat the King ninety and nine times, yet he is King still.' He was particularly concerned about the activities of the levellers and other radical movements, that were beginning to voice proposals for social change very far beyond anything the King's opponents had in mind.

Cromwell brought forward a specific charge against Manchester, of a 'desire not to prosecute the war to a full victory', and in the examinations that brought this year to an end Sir James testified 'that he heard the Earl of Manchester say that he did not believe this war would be ended by the success of either side, but rather desired it should be concluded by a proposition'. Cromwell ensured the failure of this prophecy by creating the new model army, and staffing it with new officers under the Self-Denying Ordinance.[209]

Sir James was unaffected by the purge. Immediately after the second battle of Newbury he was appointed to fortify and hold

Henley-on-Thames, in case the King should ever renew his plan to advance on London. He began the task without enthusiasm, reporting on November 25: 'I shall crave leave to offer to your wisdoms that this town is untenable by reason of the hills near about it, even for a winter quarter, unless manned with numbers of men; the line being large, and the old work scarcely visible. . . Were our horse quartered betwixt us and Oxford, and about Abingdon, the very eating up of the enemy's provisions, without fighting, would be a great service. P.S. I have stayed some wines and groceries here, which the owners had bills of excise and passes for to carry within five miles of, and probably to, Wallingford and Oxford. I desire to know the pleasure of the House of Commons and your Lordships, whether such a trade be permitted to those places.'[208]

He continued to press for the cavalry. 'It is my duty to represent to your Lordships,' he wrote on December 4, 'that these City forces think they are much neglected in that after many solicitations, though placed in a frontier garrison as yet unfortified, they have not assigned unto them the 200 horse promised . . . If you please to quarter 1,500 horse about Thame and 1,000 about Bicester and Banbury, and 1,000 about Abingdon, without which that garrison cannot long subsist or be useful, Oxford by the spring will be brought into great straits. And if the residue of our horse be active in Hampshire and the west . . . the enemy's designs of recruiting will be much hindered, and the war will, I hope, receive a happy and short conclusion. I am confident you will pardon my presumption, because of your love of plain dealing and sincerity . . .'[209]

Meanwhile he busied himself with the fortification of Henley, for he was convinced of its strategic importance. 'This town is of considerable importance,' he reported in mid-December, 'in respect of the river and pass, and for hindering the great trade and correspondence between Oxford and London, as also for the well-being of Reading and Abingdon, the great supplies of corn and wood for London, and its offensiveness by reason of its nearness to the enemy. Besides, our unwearied labours have made it within a week's work defensible . . .'[209]

It does not sound as though Sir James allowed himself time for the recreation that suited his reflective temperament so well; fishing. In his list of deliverances there are included 'three great dangers of drowning, twice upon the river Thames, and a third time in Rutland, when being a-fishing alone, I slipped from off a tree into a river'. But 'in the two distresses upon the Thames, when the water-men were all at a *non-plus*, thy only powerful providence preserved, steered, and rowed me into safety', and it sounds as though rather more space would have been necessary for this feat of divine seamanship than the Thames has to offer at Henley.[107]

While Sir James was using his growing experience of the arts of war to form new plans of offence and defence, the need for them was passing. As the hopes of the Parliament men rose, a gathering gloom was descending upon the court at Oxford. It was the time and place for hopeless loyalty and profitable perfidy. In this sad setting the fantastic Lucy's influence was exerted for the last time.

The circumstances were set down by Sir Gervase Holles, writing of his nephew John Frescheville. 'After he had buried his first wife ... he married Sarah, the daughter (and heir, if there had been any inheritance) of Sir William Harington of Bagworth. She had been bred up an attendant of Lucy, Countess of Bedford, her kinswoman, who preferred her to be one of the Maids of Honour to the Queen. From court he married her, whence she brought him no portion but court legacies: pride, passion, and prodigalities. He hath told me (and she hath owned it) that she has lost him five hundred pounds in cards in one night. But now they say she gains by it, having got the knack of the game (as gamesters call it) but others call it cheating. She had quickly got a great power over her husband, which she exercised at the beginning in two foul acts, making him force in all the leases his good father had granted his tenants at easy rates, and to take new of him at a rack rent ... Yet her last carriage was the worst of all, which I shall here give a short account of. She had long nourished a most violent ambition to have her husband created a Baron, and he (inclinable enough to comply with her pride), probably enough imagining that the time of this rebellion (in which he had done the King some services not inconsiderable) was the properest time for such request, petitioned the King to that effect.'

For Charles those days at Oxford must have been filled with the memories of happier times. The Haringtons cannot have filled a prominent place in those memories; neither can they have been wholly absent. There had been the fussy old Lord Harington, custodian of his sister, and the saintly John, his brother's friend. The ailing Knight of Kelston had been described as the greatest wit of his time, and Lucy had been a byword for magnificence. More recently Charles had kept in his company young James of Sapcote, with his scintillating talk and outrageous opinions. And now, in these twilight days at Oxford, the only Harington who attended the King was the despicable Sarah, pestering him for a title.

'And the King was graciously pleased to grant a warrant dated at Oxford the sixth day of April in the twentieth year of his reign, to prepare a patent for his creation. Which warrant the Lord Jermyn delivered her in my presence, only told her the patent could not presently pass, because the King was obliged to seal another first. At such words she falls into intemperate expressions both of the King and Queen (which are not without crime to be mentioned). Away she flies into the country to her husband, prevails with him to desert the King's service, so sacrificing both her ambition and his reputation to her malice and virulent humours.'[210]

In the new year of 1646, while the net was closing round King Charles at Oxford, and Sir James lay at Henley, fortifying, fishing, and writing sensible dispatches, John Harington of Kelston joined the forces of revolt. He was fifty-seven years old now, and did not enjoy good health. But he sympathized with the aims of the Parliamentarians as he understood them at his seat in Somerset, and he was moved by the pleas which reached him from the city of Bath.

'Worthy Sir. Out of the long experience we have had of your approved worth and sincerity, our City of Bath have determined and settled their resolutions to elect you for Burgess of the House of Commons in this present Parliament, for our said City, and do hope you will accept the trouble thereof.'[211]

John of Kelston's elder son, furthermore, had already joined the parliamentary army of the west country, although he was not nineteen years old. In February 1646 his father received a different kind of application from Bath.

'We, the Mayor, Aldermen, and Citizens of Bath, in fear and trouble, beseech you to give advices to your son, touching our city's distress at this present time, that he may in such wise get favour from the Commander to spare further levies, as we hear the troops are coming onward for our city, and our houses are emptied of all useful furniture, and much broken and disfigured. Our poor suffer for want of victuals, and rich we have none. God assist your love and friendship to us, and favour your goodwill herein. Your son hath good interest in the army, and we doubt not will use his endeavours to succour and save his poor neighbours . . . God protect us from pillage.'[212]

This was the mood of war weariness and fear in which the good fathers of Bath sent their urgent messengers up the Avon valley to Kelston for help. And both John and his son did as they were asked. Young Captain Harington must have been especially pleased with his letter of thanks from the city of Bath, because although he received it at quarters in Taunton he kept it carefully till his return to Kelston.

'Good Sir, It is commanded me to give the thanks of our City of Bath and all its inhabitants to you for your good care and concern in providing your own company to come hither, and thereby preventing such disorder as doth often happen, too oft, under soldier-like quarterings. The troop behaved well, as it was expected your good direction did so endeavour they should . . . The Town-house was filled with troops that came from Marlborough in their march westward. I have sent out five men and three horses, but have no orders for more yet. God preserve our kingdom from these sad troubles much longer! I hear the Parliament have taken into consideration the Scots business. Pray, good Sir, as far as your power goeth, do us all the service you can in these afflictions. I know your heart is ready to help us, and you stand fair with the General.

'Our meal was taken by the Marlborough troop, but they restored it again to many of the poorer sort. Our beds they occupied entirely, but no greater mischief has happened as yet. God direct your good ordering for our safety in future; and come to us when you can, as your presence will do us good. Your father went to London on Sunday. We have no Divine Service as yet; the churches are full of the troops' furniture and bedding. Pardon my haste, as I have sent this by a poor man who may suffer if he is found out, and I dare not send a man on purpose on horse-back, as the horse would be taken . . .'[213]

In this letter no trace of idealism remains over the issues of the war, only a deep desire for peace and security. It was the mood in which the bands of Somersetshire club-men were formed, to repel the armies of either side. Young Captain John pleaded at the Restoration, when Clarendon singled him out for persecution, that he had taken up arms solely to preserve order in his county. There is still sufficient surviving evidence to prove that he was speaking the truth.

Meanwhile his father, as he was informed, had gone to London a Burgess for the city of Bath. He noted punctiliously in his diary:[214]

'31 March 1646. I first sat in the House of Commons. Danger apprehended if his Majesty should come. Directions given to have guards to apprehend those that should come with him and to secure his person from danger (some would have had the words "from danger" omitted) if his Majesty should come within the line of communication that is, as I think, the fortifications about London and Westminster.'

John's diary makes sad reading after the vivid pages of his father. Only occasionally there is an arresting comment, as when he transfixed one of the scramblers of the new order in a succinct sentence. 'One Dr Corbet resigned a parsonage to the intent to be settled in another; he was disliked by divers, and he is in hazard to lose both.' John's principal interest was the religious revolution, the growing cause of discord between Presbyterians in Parliament and Independents in the army. On this subject he stuffed his diary with the minutiae of complicated bickerings.

'Wednesday. 1 April. The Parliament turned into a committee concerning the petition of the synod against the commissioners appointed by Parliament of the elders, many holding they had greatly broken the privileges of Parliament by charging their ordinance to be a hindrance to reformation and to the national covenant; against the word of God, by conscience void. They were called to advise in other things, not in this. That in pulpits they have eagerly against the ordinance etc. That they would encroach upon the civil power, that there would be no end of their encroaching. Others magnifying their learning, piety, and exceeding services for the Parliament . . .'

Into this new world of covenant and conscience there flit, now and then, the determined survivors of an earlier age. The utmost concession they will make to the new order, it seems, is to find out who now dispenses the privileges that are their inalienable right. 'Friday. 3 April . . . The Lady Deincourt asked Countess of Chichester obtain from Sir Thomas Fairfax, the general being in Truro in Cornwall, a safe conduct for her, with servants, coach, goods etc., to remove from Oxford to London. The House wondered that the general had granted it, ordered to give her a pass to send her back with her servants, coach, goods etc., to Oxford. Notice taken that she had been very malignant against the Parliament. Deny that she was Countess for her husband made Earl after the great seal was assumed by the Parliament . . .'

Parliament had assumed the great seal in 1644, and the Chichester creation was one of King Charles's gestures of defiance. So there was more than malice in John's remark. But he was distracted from his interest in the ladies by the greater outrage of a man 'charged with blasphemy and heresy. Outrageous horrible expressions against the Trinity of persons in the Deity, and the Godhead of our Saviour. I abhor extremely to mention any of them . . .' He was probably referring to the persecution of Quakers. On April 6 he reported the ladies still recalcitrant and undaunted:

'The Lady Deincourt refused to obey the order Friday last, pretending sickness and that her sister Mrs Porter and many other Papists and most violent malignants tolerated in London, that herself had been moderate etc. Order she may not be endured to disobey the order on Friday . . . Order for shipping away of Mrs Porter to her husband in France or Spain.'

Old Sir Edward of Ridlington stood for good order and fair government. His saintly son was in arms to achieve these things, guided by his Christian principles. James of Sapcote sat speculating about the form such government should take, in 'a versatile timber house' off Birdcage Walk in London. Young John of Kelston used his influence in Somerset, where he could, to prevent the wrongs and oppressions that follow in the wake of war. And in Parliament his father, the elder John, reflected and complacently recorded the growing strength of the unloveliest quality of man. He was at the intolerant centre where the bitter sects competed in their claims to be the mouthpiece of their terrible god.

On Thursday, April 23, 'Lieutenant General Cromwell came into the House. Public thanks given him by the Speaker'. The same evening John's election as a Burgess was resolved to have been unlawful, and he went out of the House. He returned in July as a Member for Somerset, in the same month that Sir James of Swakeleys entered Parliament as a representative of Rutland county.

Sir James may have thought that his military duties were over, and that the only task remaining was to refashion the fabric of government. His last military duty had resembled those of young Captain John at Bath. It was to save property in his own county from unnecessary damage. The great house at Burley in which his family had once entertained King James was occupied by a garrison, and in response to a plea from Rutland the Committee of both Kingdoms empowered Sir James to 'remove fortifications without further spoiling house or stables'. That was in May. On June 24 Oxford capitulated, and King Charles escaped in disguise to the Scots at Newark.[215]

The moment had come for constitutional discussions between a king and the representatives of his two kingdoms. James of Sapcote hurried to the spot, 'attending out of curiosity the Commissioners appointed by Parliament to bring King Charles I from Newcastle nearer to London'. This is the account of Toland, informed by Aubrey's notes and the details given him by James's sister after his death. By this time James was uncertain of his welcome with the King. 'He was by some of 'em named to wait on his Majesty, as a person known to him before, and engaged to no party of faction. The King approved the proposal, yet our author would never presume to come into his presence except in public, till he was particularly commanded by the King; and that he, with Thomas Herbert . . . were made Grooms of the Bedchamber at Holmby.'[216]

One of the clearest differences between the English and Scottish characters began to show itself at this time, particularly in the Scottish King himself. Questions of religious doctrine reflect this difference like a mirror, and the images are as sharply in contrast as the writings of John Knox and the judicious Hooker. Between the first and second civil wars this difference was to turn the English and the Scots from allies into bitter enemies.

For in England the end proved to be a political one. The Presbyterians in Parliament who thought the war had been fought to impose their doctrines in place of Archbishop Laud's discovered that the army which won it had no intention of enforcing their particular creed. In Scotland, on the other hand, the most opportunist politician was bound to the religious covenant. The army, so far from being an opponent of presbyterianism, was its greatest strength. In England religion was assisting a political revolution; in Scotland politics were assisting a religious revolution. It was the tragedy of King Charles that he brought a

JAMES HARINGTON, 1611-1677
Author of 'The Commonwealth of Oceana'
attributed to A. Van der Venne

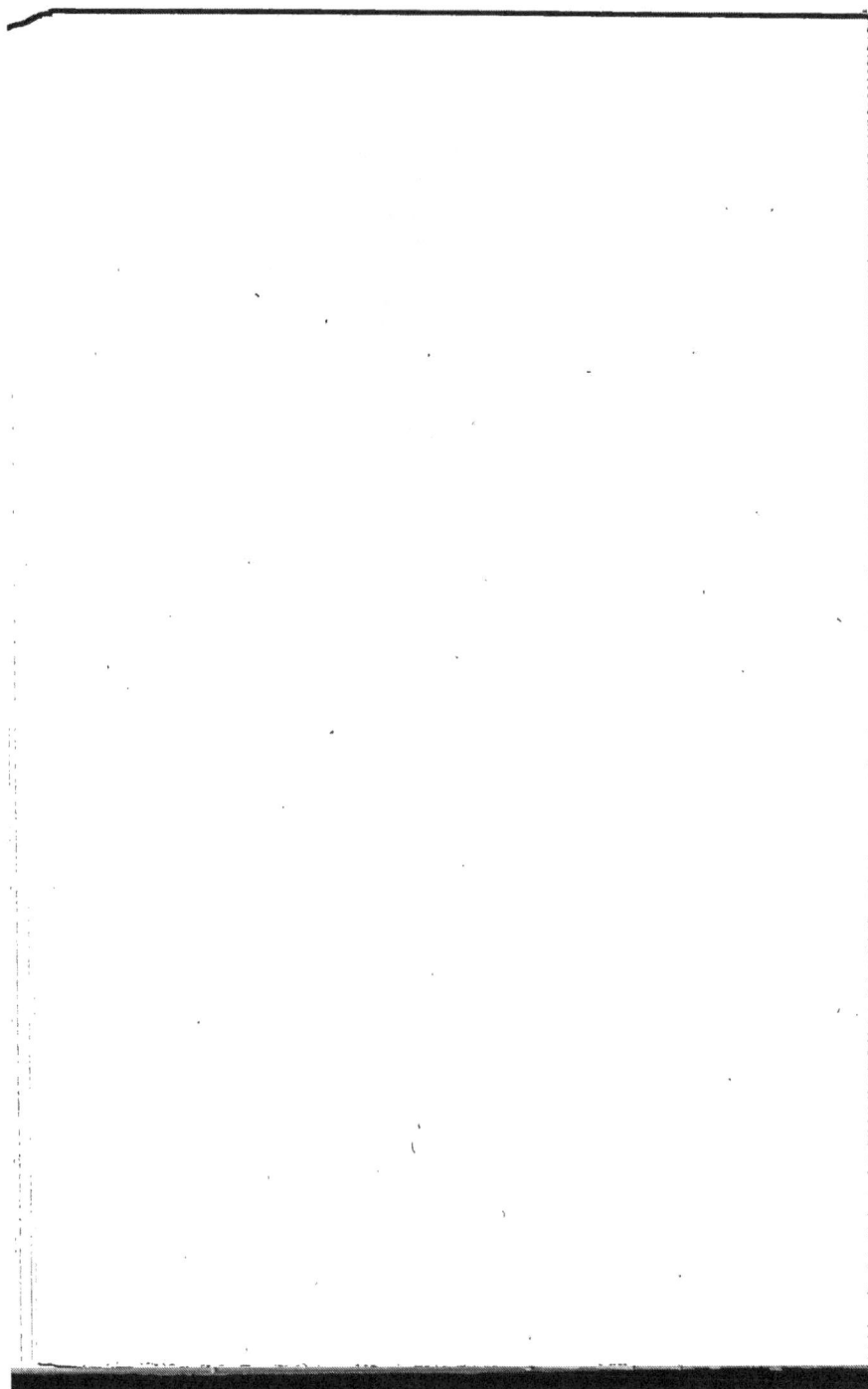

Scotsman's dogmatic conscience to the problems that each of these revolutions raised. It opposed him to both, so that he failed to side wholeheartedly with either against the other when the rift between England and Scotland gave him his opportunity.

At Holmby House Charles had the leisure to ponder these problems. It is impossible not to pity him, so tortuous and vacillating, yet so rigid in his beliefs. He had James of Sapcote with whom to discuss the question of government. But since his conversations with the Scots at Newcastle the religious question weighed more heavily on his mind. He could gain the support of the Scots if he would accept presbyterianism; but this raised the issue of doctrine. James of Sapcote could not help him here; but guarding the King was Sir James of Swakeleys. Surely Charles must have been referred from one cousin to the other.

'I desire to be resolved of this question,' wrote the King to Sir James, 'why the new reformers discharge the keeping of Easter?' The humility with which he argues his case is touching. 'When anybody can show me that herein I am in error, I shall not be ashamed to confess and mend it; till when you know my mind.'

Sir James had thought about these things. 'Your Majesty's reason upon which your query is built hath a great mistake even in the foundation of it', he began. He then explored eighteen biblical references with a skill that Charles could hardly have heard equalled at Newcastle. Sir James concluded, 'but for the observation of Easter to be an annual festival to Christians, I find not anything in the Holy Scriptures: and your Majesty is pleased to place it only upon the Church's authority.' Many historians have written that it was for that 'only' that Charles died.[207]

The spring of 1647 was an anxious one at Holmby, for captive and captors. Sir James had been appointed by Parliament in the new year, with Pembroke, Denbigh, and seven others to bring the King south from Newcastle. They had reported to Speaker Lenthall on February 16: 'by the providence of God which hath gone always with us, from the first step to the last in this journey, the king is come well to Holmby'. But there was anxiety in their report. 'We have here 900 horse and dragoons, with quartering which in a little compass cannot but be very burdensome unto the country, and therefore entreat you to give special directions for their pay.'[217]

This was the issue between the whole army and Parliament while the King lay at Holmby. The army gained the victory by refusing to disband without being paid its arrears, and by seizing the person of the King. While the army negotiated from its position of strength with the Parliament men, Charles escaped to Carisbrooke in the Isle of Wight. At last he decided to throw in his lot with the presbyterians.

Out of personal loyalty and affection, James of Sapcote went to Carisbrooke with him. So he was able to give Charles some timely advice about another of his cousins when John of Kelston, M.P. for Somerset, arrived at Carisbrooke. John 'desired to have some discourse with his Majesty', according to Anthony Wood's account, but Charles, having heard from James 'that he was a canting and prophetical presbyterian, thanked him ... for his good intentions, without discoursing with him on any point'. Whereupon Harington, wishing his Majesty much happiness, withdrew. According to another account, Charles remarked at his departure that John's pride would have showed through the hole in a stocking. But his visit was not wasted. It helped to show how sincere was the King's conversion to the creed over which, in 1648, the English and the Scots fought one another.[218]

By the August of 1648 the royalists, the presbyterians and the Scots were defeated. Charles was removed to Hurst Castle, where once more James of Sapcote accompanied him. But now his devotion was mistaken for support of the King's acts and opinions, and he was summarily dismissed. He must have hung about in the hope of being of further service to the man he loved, but not as a King. 'As they were taking the King to Windsor,' says Toland, 'he begged admittance to the boot of the coach, that he might bid his master farewell; which being granted, and he preparing to kneel, the King took him by the hand and pulled him in to him. He was for three or four days permitted to stay. But because he would not take the oath against assisting or concealing the King's escape, he was not only discharged from his office, but also for some time detained in custody, till Major-General Ireton obtained his liberty.'

Meanwhile a high court of justice had been set up to try the King: for the second civil war had convinced Cromwell that it would never be possible to bind Charles to any agreement that he would not repudiate at the first opportunity. The court was to consist of 135 commissioners under the presidency of Bradshaw. The men chosen consisted largely of army officers, Members of Parliament, and country gentlemen. Sir James of Swakeleys, who combined all these attributes, was one of their number, and on January 23 he sat in trial on the King. But he did not attend when sentence was passed, nor sign the death warrant.

King Charles had been moved to St James's for his trial, and here once again James of Sapcote sought him. The farewells this time were final. On the scaffold outside the banqueting hall of Whitehall palace Charles gave his devoted cousin a last memento. It is said to be the gold toothpick case that remains, ironically, in the possession of Sir James of Swakeleys' descendant to this day. The execution was hidden from the public by a high barrier surrounding the scaffold, but James, who was within this barrier, was so distressed by the sight he witnessed that Aubrey says he 'contracted a disease by it'.

He was thirty-seven years old, and he had seen a great deal at close quarters of government and misgovernment. He now retired to his study in Birdcage Walk, where his friends noticed that he was often writing, they knew not what.

But Sir James was drawn increasingly into the tasks of government. He did not seek office for its prizes. Work was thrust upon him because he was industrious and efficient. He and many of his colleagues stand as examples to the men of earlier and later ages who carved huge fortunes out of their offices. Sir James was one of the saints, the integrity of whose government foreign observers noted in admiring dispatches.

He was nominated to the Council of State, constituted by Act of Parliament immediately after the death of the King. He was named to go to Scotland. He was placed on the committee to consider means of raising public money. He busied himself over the preservation of timber, the upkeep of the militia, the problems of the common sewer, the mint. In April Parliament decided to settle £3,000 a year on the two younger children of the late King, and to entrust them for their education and maintenance to Sir Edward Harington of Ridlington. Sir James was asked to report whether his father would consent to this arrangement.[219]

Unfortunately the reasons for his refusal have not survived. Perhaps Sir Edward remembered what a burden his uncle's royal charge had imposed on the family fortunes. Or perhaps he could not face the labours of such a task; for he was an old man, and died four years later.

It was in the May following the King's death that Sir James enjoyed a deliverance recorded, not in his own divine meditations, but in a graphic letter from the Council of State. It illustrates the problem which the continuance of a standing army presented in a country that was not properly equipped for such a luxury. The Council wrote to a Colonel Stubber:

'We heard of the miscarriages of your soldiers while in Kent, and since their going thence we have had complaints of them from many places where they passed. How people of meaner condition were oppressed by the common sort of them will easily be judged by the carriage of some of their officers to Sir James Harington M.P., at whose house near Uxbridge four soldiers quartered last Saturday night. The behaviour of two of them named Monday and Hack, serjeants in Captain Sydenham's company, was most insufferable, threatening to press into his lady's chamber, now lying-in, because they could not be satisfied in what they pleased to ask, and would not take quarter-money under 1/4 a day. As to the Act of Parliament, they said they esteemed it not so much as a straw under their feet, and generally threatened to ruin and spoil things when they could not have what they asked. Sir James is forced to continue at home to preserve his house from their spoil, and can neither attend the House nor this Council. What other people suffer from them, that have not the heart or way to make their grievances known, you may well judge.

'The alienating of men's minds from the present government by the barbarous carriage of these men (whose deportment is as if they had conquered the nation) will be greater disservice to the commonwealth than they will be able to make good by all the service they are like to do in Ireland. You are to send Monday and Hack up hither in custody, to be proceeded against as such disorderly people deserve, who, instead of being instrumental to keep discipline in the army, are themselves the chiefest among those that break it. You are also to repair forthwith to your regiment and command all your officers to do the like, and to march constantly with them, and remain with them in their quarters, and see that exact discipline be observed and quarters duly paid, and that they march peaceably, so that the country may not be oppressed, nor the Parliament and Council troubled with complaints, and compelled to use force to keep the country in peace.'[219]

The members of the Council, whose authority was based on naked force, knew the danger of power unharnessed, and knew how to express it in prose. The Mondays and the Hacks were diverted to Ireland, where the great historian Geoffrey Keating had just completed a history of his unhappy country in classical Irish from sources soon to be scattered and destroyed.

Sir James was made President of the Council of State in 1652, and joint Master of the Mint in the following year, when he inherited the baronetcy on his father's death. One of Mazarin's agents reported of the Members of the Council: 'they live without ostentation, without pomp, and without mutual rivalry. They are economical in their private affairs and prodigal in their devotion to public affairs, for which each man toils as if for his private interest. They handle large sums of money, which they administer honestly, observing a strict discipline. They reward well and punish severely.' In this decade of efficient government at home and successful war abroad no Cecil built his Hatfield. But the rare virtue these commonwealth men possessed in public office has impressed posterity less than a flamboyant display of doubtful honesty. Sir James Harington, third baronet, has not even an entry in the *Dictionary of National Biography*.[220]

While Sir James was labouring to make the government of England an expression of gratitude acceptable to God, for His many blessings, James of Sapcote remained locked in his library. At first he was left alone, out of respect for his sorrow. But his acquaintance had been large and his company much sought in earlier years, and in due course inquisitive eyes noticed the growing pile of writings which proved that James was not wholly abandoned to melancholy. And the day came when he had finished his work and confessed its theme to his friends.

'He no sooner discoursed publicly of this new doctrine, being a man of universal acquaintance,' wrote Toland, 'but it engaged all sorts of people to busy themselves about it as they were variously affected. Some, because they understood him, despised it, alleging it was plain to every man's capacity, as if his highest merit did not consist in making it so. Others, and those in number the fewest, disputed with him about it, merely to be better informed; with which he was well pleased, as reckoning a pertinent objection of greater advantage to the discovery of truth (which was his aim) than a complaisant applause or approbation. But a third sort, of which there never wants in all places a numerous company, did out of pure envy strive all they could to lessen or defame him.'

So *The Commonwealth of Oceana* became known to the world. It proposed that Cromwell should establish James's model republic and then retire, just when he was tightening the reins of absolute government with the establishment of major-generals and the order against scandalous books. Cromwell was an empiricist, and he had by this time satisfied himself that parliamentary government did not work. He had picked exactly the right men to sit in Parliament, but because he did not know the need for effective control of the House by a strong front bench, his ideal Members had turned out to be rogues. Cromwell angrily dismissed them. And he was not impressed by the theories of *Oceana*. The printing of it was suppressed and the manuscripts seized, and Cromwell laughed, 'the gentleman had like to trepan him out of his power, but what he got by the sword he would not quit for a little paper shot'.[221]

It is interesting that the republican James Harington acted in these circumstances exactly as his royalist forebears had done in the past. He went straight to the court and up the private stairs to harangue the sovereign in person. He addressed himself to Mrs Claypole, Cromwell's favourite daughter, in the palace of Whitehall that he had once lived in himself as a courtier. 'While he attended, some of her women coming into the room were followed by her little daughter about three years old, who stayed behind them. He entertained the child so divertingly that she suffered him to take her up in his arms till her mother came; whereupon he stepping towards her, and setting the child down at her feet, said,

' "Madam, 'tis well you are come at this nick of time, or I had certainly stolen this pretty little lady."

' "Stolen her!" replied the mother, "pray, what to do with her? For she is yet too young to become your mistress."

' "Madam," said he, "though her charms assure her of a more considerable conquest, yet I must confess it is not love but revenge that prompted me to commit this theft."

' "Lord!" answered the lady again, "what injury have I done you that you should steal my child?"

' "None at all," replied he, "but that you might be induced to prevail with your father to do me justice, by restoring my child that he has stolen."

'But she urging it was impossible, because her father had children enough of his own, he told her at last it was the issue of his brain which was misrepresented to the Protector, and taken out of the press by his order. She immediately promised to procure it for him, if it contained nothing prejudicial to her father's government. And he assured her it was only a kind of political romance, so far from any treason against her father that he hoped she would acquaint him that he designed to dedicate it to him.'[221]

And so he did when, in 1656, *The Commonwealth of Oceana* was published.

An analysis of the political views expressed in the *Oceana* would require a volume. Toland emphasized its most famous thesis in his introduction of 1700. 'That empire follows the balance of property, whether lodged in one, or a few, or in many hands, he was the first that ever made out . . . 'Tis incredible to think what gross and numberless errors were committed by all the writers before him, for want of understanding this plain truth.' James showed how Henry VII had weakened the medieval baronage, how property, and therefore power, had become distributed gradually since then amongst the larger ranks of a gentry. 'By these degrees came the House of Commons to raise that head, which since has been so high and formidable to their Princes, that they have looked pale upon those Assemblies.'[222]

James's solution was that the class of ruling gentry should be perpetuated by the equal division of property among sons, and the limitation of the dowries of daughters. There should be perpetual Parliaments, election by secret ballot, payment of Members. In this first detailed model constitution to be published in England, everything possible was done to prevent the aggrandizement of the few, or the transfer of power to the masses.

When Cromwell died there was suddenly the chance that this 'little paper shot' might carry the day. His death occurred on 3 September 1658, the anniversary of his victories at Dunbar and Worcester, and when his power had never seemed greater. But it did not descend to his son. An alliance of army officers and republicans (many of them Haringtonians) brought the Protectorate to an end the following May. The restoration of the Republic was declared, and the Long Parliament was returned to power.

On May 19 a new Council of State was constituted by Act of Parliament. Thirty-one men were nominated, any nine of whom constituted a Council, provided six of these were Members of Parliament. Sir James Harington of Swakeleys was once again made President.

Things were very different from those eager hopeful days when he had first held high executive office, and the Orders bearing his presidential signature reflect the anxieties with which he wrestled. Only four days after the Council first met, it was writing to the captain of the militia troop in Gloucester: 'Council is informed of a very dangerous design against the public peace by adherents of Charles Stewart and other ill-affected persons, and of meetings held, and arms secretly sent down from London in trunks by carriers.'[224]

The following day it wrote to the governor of Portsmouth: 'in the present dangerous and unquiet state of affairs, both at home and abroad, the Committee of Safety saw fit to appoint you governor of the important garrison of Portsmouth; and Council, confiding in your vigilance and faithfulness, continues you in that command, and has sent you a commission to continue'. The Commander-in-Chief of the forces in Scotland, General Monk, received an equally ominous warning.

'Council having heard of various designs by the members of Charles Stewart's party to raise new war against the state, and that arms are distributed in various parts of the kingdom to that end . . . desire you to watch the malignants in Scotland, concluding that there is a correspondence with those in England.'

The Commander-in-Chief of the forces in Flanders was reinforced. 'We . . . are sensible of the wants of your garrison, and your charge for their supply. We have ordered some proportion of all the things wanted to be sent to you at once.' Before the month was out, such warnings as these, bearing the ill-fated signature of President Harington, were being carried through the length and breadth of England. To Wiltshire, Gloucester, Somerset, Cornwall and Shropshire went the panic message; 'having heard of the enemy's preparations to disturb the public peace, and principally in the Western counties, we desire you . . . to watch the enemy's movements most carefully'. The High Sheriff of Northumberland read: 'Council hears from Sir Charles Howard that, taking advantage of the unsettled state of government, a hundred ill-affected persons . . . expelled his tenants and retain forcible possession, threatening to kill all who oppose them.'

Worse was reported from Middlesex. 'Council hearing that a rude multitude from Enfield Town have broken down the hedges and ditches of the enclosure, and threaten to cut down houses and throw down all the enclosures there, desire you to examine the business, and proceed according to law to suppress tumult and protect proprietors from violence.'[224]

Sir James must have been relieved to hand over the Presidency on June 7 to Sir Archibald Johnston. His cousin had shown, in the

Oceana, how power had passed with property to the gentry. It was beginning to look as though both might pass to a different, and larger, order of society. And this was a danger that many might consider more frightening than the return of a Stewart.

The author of *Oceana* saw in the present troubles an ideal opportunity for the adoption of his political principles. They would secure government where it belonged, by the natural process of historical evolution, not in king or people, but in the gentry. In Haringtons of the mid-seventeenth century variety, in fact.

He summarized these principles in a masterly table of political aphorisms. He wrote tracts, serious and flippant, in reply to critics. But his strongest asset was his skill and charm as a con-versationalist, and he exploited this by arguing publicly in the London coffee-houses. In November 1659 he formed the Rota Club in Westminster of which Aubrey was a member. 'He had every night a meeting at the (then) Turk's head in the New Palace Yard, where they take water, the next house to the stairs.' This whole area has been transformed since the fire that destroyed the old Palace of Westminster. 'The discourses in this kind were the most ingenious and smart that ever I heard, or expect to hear, and bandied with great eagerness. The arguments in the Parlia-ment House were but flat to it . . . The room was every evening full as it could be crammed.'²²⁵

Pepys went there on 17 January 1660 'and heard very good discourse. It was in answer to Mr Harington's answer, who said that the state of the Roman Government was not a settled govern-ment, and so it was no wonder that the balance of prosperity was in one hand, and the command in another, it being therefore always in a posture of war'. James's remarks on this subject must have been particularly disagreeable to the late Protector Oliver Cromwell. His inhabitants of *Oceana* detest war 'as a thing very beastly', and 'count nothing so much against glory as glory gotten in war'.

James was trying to settle the problems of government, using only the weapons of the mind. But these were not the weapons that now controlled events. The army which had united with the Parliament men to destroy the Protectorate put a stop to its sit-tings in October 1659. The following February General Monk arrived in London.

Pepys strolled into the Rota Club just in time to witness its dissolution, and 'heard Mr Harington and my Lord of Dorset and another Lord talking of getting another place at the Cockpit, and they did believe it would come to something'. But the tide had turned against experimental forms of government. 'The club broke up very poorly, and I do not think they will meet any more.'

James had to wait for the slow process of historical evolution to transform his ideas into reality, some in 1688 in England, some in France and America a century later, and others, such as the secret ballot and family allowances in an age that has not even seen fit to reprint his works. Meanwhile, 'upon the unexpected turn upon General Monk's coming in, all those airy models vanished'. And the house of Harington was doomed.

NEMESIS

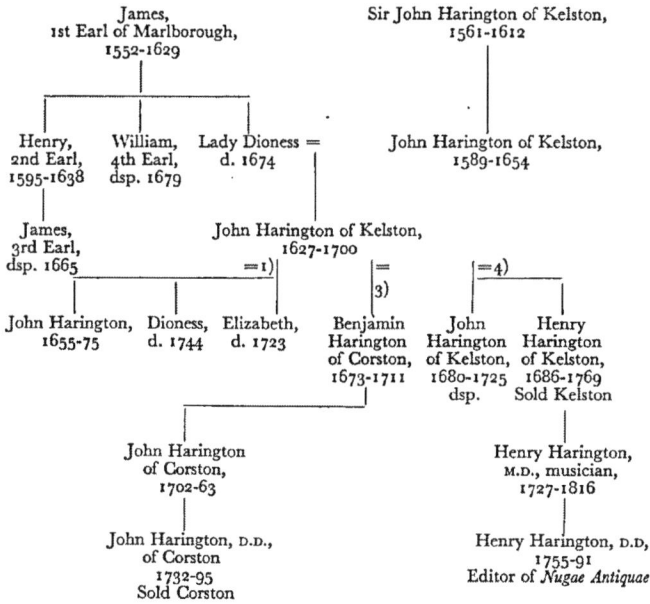

James,
1st Earl of Marlborough,
1552-1629

Sir John Harington of Kelston,
1561-1612

Henry,   William,   Lady Dioness =   John Harington of Kelston,
2nd Earl,   4th Earl,   d. 1674   1589-1654
1595-1638   dsp. 1679

James,   John Harington of Kelston,
3rd Earl,   1627-1700
dsp. 1665   =1)   =   =4)
                                                 3)

John Harington, Dioness,   Elizabeth,   Benjamin   John   Henry
1655-75   d. 1744   d. 1723   Harington   Harington Harington
                                         of Corston, of Kelston, of Kelston,
                                         1673-1711   1680-1725 1686-1769
                                                     dsp.   Sold Kelston

         John Harington   Henry Harington,
         of Corston,   M.D., musician,
         1702-63   1727-1816

         John Harington, D.D.,   Henry Harington, D.D,
         of Corston   1755-91
         1732-95   Editor of *Nugae Antiquae*
         Sold Corston

FOURTEEN

NEMESIS

JOHN HARINGTON, the third of Kelston, was saved from this doom by a timely death. As one of the Parliamentary Presbyterians with whom King Charles had at last allied himself, John could not have been held to have approved the death of the King. But still less could James of Sapcote; and this availed him nothing.

After the King's death, John seems to have abandoned public affairs for the learned interests that he pursued with such a sterile enthusiasm. On 11 October 1652, for instance, 'having an earnest desire to know the Arabic letters', he wrote to 'the incomparable his highly honoured friend John Selden Esquire', asking whether he might borrow an Arabic copy of 'St Matthew's gospel or the book of Genesis, or any other part of the old or new testament, whatsoever you shall please to favour me with'. John stood at the crossroads of the age of scholasticism and dogma that was passing, and the new age of inquiry and experiment. Fuller could describe him as learned and religious, and he said this with approbation. But the mutilated pages of Wyatt's manuscript are the only monument to John's piety and learning.[226]

The literary activities of his son during these years must have given him considerable pain, unless they were concealed from him altogether. After his youthful exploits in the civil war, young John had gone to Cambridge in 1647. He was still only nineteen years old. It was not politics nor yet religion that filled his thoughts, but matters more frequently uppermost in the minds of young men of his age, and particularly among his own forebears. He confided to his sister Elizabeth: "Twas in the day of that sweet time when the gaudy earth seems newly teeming with the fruits of Flora, and paints her young cheeks like a bride; when the Sun her lover smiles, and runs his nearest course to court her. 'Twas at the hour when the larks shrill notes called forth their Lady Morn; dropping her pearls like favours on the gazing mortal.'[227]

He not only confided these sentiments to his sister in several
letters of considerable length. In 1651 he offered them in verse
and in print to a larger public. 'Judicious reader, for I hope thou
art such, as I truly wish thee, thou hast here an historical poem . . .
'Tis writ in shorter verse, thing rare, unusual for these longer
subjects; one reason whereof, 'twas meant at first a sheet or two
only, though afterwards more won upon me.' Perhaps they won
upon him because he had kept copies of his letters to Elizabeth.

> That time o'th'year when th'gaudy Earth
> Seems new lain in of flowery birth:
> When paints her cheeks young like a bride
> As her first youth's created pride
> Strove t'imitate: when Flora traces
> Courtesan-like, with all her graces,
> Arts, sweets of essence; whilst the sun
> Her lover smiles, and hastes to run
> Near course to court her. . . .[118]

Young John liked to elide the smaller parts of speech and
possessed a romantic nature. There is nothing more to be said of
him as a poet, except perhaps that he married four times and left
twenty surviving children at his death.

In 1654, when he was twenty-seven years old, John succeeded
his father as Member of Parliament for Somerset, and married his
first wife in November. But he did not succeed to Kelston, which
his father left at his death to the Lady Dioness his widow. In
1655 Oliver, Lord Protector of the Commonwealth, appointed
him 'to be Captain of a troop of horse consisting of one hundred of
such well-affected persons as shall voluntarily list themselves under
you in the County of Somerset'. The Council of State appointed
him a Captain of a Militia company in the April of 1660.[119]

But these commissions are insufficient in themselves to explain
the wrath of Edward Hyde, future Earl of Clarendon, at the
Restoration towards the gallant, genial, and romantic John. Even
the report of an agent in the west (dated 23 May 1659), in which
John's name heads a list of people who had 'been cruel persecutors
of friends for truth's sake', is hardly adequate to explain it. It
looks more likely that John was singled out for attack because his
name was Harington.[120]

Clarendon wrote to Lord Poulett, whose father had complained of the dereliction of John's father at the Bridgewater Sessions, in 1660. His letter bears traces of a personal animosity in the King himself which is strangely at variance with the usual generosity and clemency of his nature.

'My Lord, we, having received such information as respecteth the former proceedings of many rebellious families in your county of Somerset, do humbly desire your immediate compliance with his Majesty's commands of giving us a true account to our office of all such as may have been employed in the late troubles, by commission civil or military, under the Usurper, or the other kind · of imposed rebellious *authority* as then called. Among some others, information is delivered of John Harington, son to the late Member for the City of Bath, bearing arms by virtue of commission from the Usurper in 1655, whose father was Commissioner of the Parliament to the late King at Carisbrooke castle, and a staunch member of that party, with several more of that name. His present Majesty's good intentions toward all who have not signalified themselves by any notorious deeds of rebellion need not be doubted, as will more amply appear by some Act of indemnity. But examples, in justice to his royal blood and family, as well as to an injured nation, are required . . .'[221]

The only charge against John himself in this letter was that he had held a military commission during the Interregnum; as a very large number of people had done. It is significant that Clarendon's anger was directed mainly against John's dead father and others 'of that name', and what is interesting about his detailed knowledge of the part they played is that he omitted any mention of it whatsoever from his *History of the Rebellion*. He apparently considered the Haringtons worthy of exemplary punishment in life, and in death oblivion.

His attempt to defame John failed: the people of the west knew him better. Lord Poulett replied coldly to Clarendon: 'I have submitted your letter to Mr Harington. Whatever his father's principles led him to, his son is no object of wrath for his Majesty's displeasure. The enclosed certificate will yield you a true account of his and our duty and sufferings. He did bear commission from Oliver Cromwell, but at our request, to protect us from ruin and plunder. His own honesty did make him about to refuse acting, but we dreaded the consequences to ourselves and families. His compliance rendered him exposed to loss of friends and relations in battle, and loss of fortune in many acts of goodness. This county is under great obligations to this gentleman, and our duty obliges us to render him our best services to protect him from his Majesty's displeasure. The King's cause was no sufferer in this matter; and such a singular and nice circumstance as fighting against conscience, and yet for conscience' sake, does give Mr Harington great title to pardon, nay rather, thanks and rewards. We who subscribe this are ready to submit to any pains and penalties for this man's sake, whose honourable family and descent, as well as his own good name and character in our county, claim our best acknowledgments. Pray, Sir, let these reasons urge your endeavours to spare his family, and intercede for Mr Harington's free pardon, which will confirm the duty of all poor sufferers of this county of Somerset to his Majesty's best services on all occasions. In hopes whereof, I remain your servant to command, Poulett. P.S. The city of Bath was much protected and preserved by Mr Harington's accepting Oliver's commission, which else had been exposed to plunder and ruin, which he totally prevented by his good endeavours and friends, to his great loss and injury, as the Earl of Marlborough his father-in-law [son of the Lord Treasurer, so his uncle, as we should call him] can testify to the Council.'[222]

Lest Clarendon should dismiss his evidence as the partiality of a single person, Poulett enclosed a certificate, couched in similar terms and signed by twenty-three others. On the bottom of his copy of it John recorded gratefully in his neat, artistic hand: 'to the above certificate I am indebted for my life and fortune, which otherwise had been forfeited by the laws of the land, and hereby I obtained his Majesty's most gracious pardon under the Seal of England, having engaged in arms on the Parliament behalf at the earnest desire of my friends to save the county of Somerset as much as my endeavours would admit from spoil and rapine. Praised be God'.[223]

John was safe, but there were 'several more of that name', as Clarendon had darkly hinted, whom the admiration of their friends could not save. Sir James of Swakeleys had sat in trial on the late King, and his cousin had published the most devastating attack on monarchy in general and on the dynasty of the Stewarts in particular ever printed. During the months after Cromwell's death when the royalist cause hung in the balance, one of the Jameses was using his administrative skill, the other his skill in argument, to prevent the Restoration. And it hardly admits of doubt that in the odium that gathered round the name of Harington in royalist circles the Jameses became inextricably confused. On each was laid the guilt of both, and it was enough to have spilt over, in the mind of Clarendon, to the Kelston branch. James of Sapcote spelt his name Harrington, as though in an attempt to distinguish himself from his cousin, and his family continued to use this spelling until the extinction of the Sapcote branch. But it did not help. Even King Charles had to be told that Sir James and the author of *Oceana* were different people; and his reply was less characteristic of him than of his father.

The foundations on which King Charles's personal animosity towards the Haringtons was built appear faintly in the letter-book in which John Viscount Mordaunt preserved his correspondence of the years 1658-60. On 3 October 1659 Mordaunt wrote to the Duke of York: 'Sir, the divisions grow so high upon the account of government that monarchy and popular jurisdiction divide the whole nation, and the Council of State, as well as the pretended Parliament . . . Vane designs Lambert for the single person, and Haselrig is so fixed to Mr Harrington's commonwealth that he will lose all his ill-purchased estate in defence of it.'[234]

In the same month he wrote to the King himself: 'Haselrig now appears a zealous champion for liberty, Parliaments, and a republic. He is seconded by Neville and Mr Harrington's cabal.' To the future Lord Clarendon Mordaunt wrote: 'Sir Henry Vane and Thurloe are reconciled. Harrington's new commonwealth promoted vigorously in debates.' James had provided the opponents of monarchy with an alternative that he showed to be not merely preferable, but in the long run inevitable. For a year, while the royalists waited abroad for the climate of opinion in England to alter in their favour, James opposed the trend of popular fervour with his clear and penetrating logic. For him there could be no forgiveness.

Retiring to his house, James continued to write about and discuss republican principles. A royalist suggested to him that he should apply his theories to monarchy, and in his disinterested way he drew up a scheme which was submitted to one of the King's ministers and presumably destroyed. He composed his ablest statement, to be published after his death as 'A System of Politics'. Then, 26 November 1661, he was arrested and committed to the Tower of London, 'where none were allowed to come to his sight or speech'.[235]

Toland's account of what followed was probably given him by

James's sister, Dorothy Bellingham. 'His sisters were inconsolable, and the more so, the less they knew what was laid to their brother's charge. One of them, who on another occasion had experienced the King's favour, threw herself now at his feet, and petitioned him to have compassion on her brother, who through a great mistake was fallen under his Majesty's displeasure. For as she was sure that none of his subjects exceeded his loyalty, so his Majesty might see he was not the man designed, since the warrant was for Sir James Harington, whereas her brother was never honoured with such a title by his Majesty's ancestors, and he would not have accepted it from Oliver. To this the King made answer that though they might be mistaken in his title, he doubted he might be found more guilty of the crimes alleged against him than he wished any brother of hers to be.'

The charge against James was that he was involved in Colonel Salmon's plot, the precise aims of which are buried beneath the exaggerated rumours of the time. Wildman and Praise-God Barebones, who were certainly implicated, were thrown into the Tower at the same time as James, who was accused of having conspired with them. It was an improbable fabrication.

After several weeks' close confinement, the King permitted an examination of James, at his sisters' request. It was conducted in the Tower by the Earl of Lauderdale, Sir George Cartaret, and Sir Edward Walker, the author of *Oceana* standing, a prisoner before them. Lauderdale opened the proceedings sadly:

'Sir, I have heretofore accounted it an honour to be your kinsman, but am now sorry to see you upon this occasion; very sorry, I assure you.'

'My Lord,' replied James, 'seeing this is an occasion, I am glad to see you upon this occasion.'

'Sir,' continued his cousin, 'the King thinks it strange that you, who have so eminently appeared in principles contrary to his Majesty's Government and the laws of this nation, should ever since he came over live so quiet and unmolested, and yet should be so ungrateful. Were you disturbed? Were you so much as affronted, that you should enter into such desperate practices?'

James, who was still totally ignorant of the charge against him, inquired what these practices might be, and on learning of the conspiracy, showed that he had seen neither Wildman not Barebones for about two years. He then began to speak his mind.

'This plainly is a practice, a wicked practice, a practice for innocent blood; and as weak a one as it is wicked. Ah, my Lord, if you had taken half the pains to examine the guilty that you have done to examine the innocent, you had found it. It could not have escaped you.'

Lauderdale rose, and one of his colleagues reminded him that it was late, but James was not finished with them.

'You charge me with being eminent in principles contrary to the King's Government and the laws of this nation. Some, my Lord, have aggravated this, saying that I, being a private man, have been so mad as to meddle with politics: what had a private man to do with government? My Lord there is not any public person, not any magistrate, that has written in the politics worth a button. All they that have been excellent in this way have been private men, as private men, my Lord, as myself. There is Plato, there is Aristotle, there is Livy, there is Machiavelli ... Did Alexander hang up Aristotle, did he molest him? Livy for a commonwealth is one of the fullest authors. Did not he write under Augustus Caesar? Did Caesar hang up Livy; did he molest him? Machiavelli, what a commonwealths-man was he! But he wrote under the Medici when they were Princes in Florence. Did they hang up Machiavelli, or did they molest him?'

The commissioners sat silent while the first great exponent of the historical method in England justified his thoughts and actions to them. Well might they have reflected later, as Aubrey did: 'the arguments in the Parliament-House were but flat to it'.[116]

But Clarendon, it seems, was determined that another Harington should not slip through his fingers, and particularly the one whose interpretation of the causes of the civil war was so much more penetrating than his own. James was still kept a close prisoner without being brought to trial, and at a conference of the Lords and Commons Clarendon persisted in the charge that he was implicated in the conspiracy.

Perhaps James was, to some extent, the victim of the spite that springs from disappointment. His cousin, Sir James of Swakeleys, was nowhere to be found. One James Harington had been sentenced by Act of Parliament: the other had been thrown into the Tower. The situation must have been exasperating to those who wished to make an example of the Haringtons before an injured nation.

A single letter survives from this period, from Sir James to his wife. It is dated 19 March 1661, and addressed to 'his loving wife the Lady Harington at her lodging in Fleet Street'. It seems that Sir James had gone into hiding in London, while Catharine sought favour at court, if not for him, at least for herself and her numerous offspring. (Sir James praised God 'that has given me by one wife sixteen olive-branches; and them circumstantiated with divers remarkable favours'.) It is a moving letter to read, from a devoted husband forced to inform his wife that he is no longer able to support her.

'My Dear. I am surprised by the last letter. But however, God and the King's will be done, for to both of them I do freely submit myself. But for me to make any proposition is not proper, because not in my power to perform. For such is my condition, as till my estate be cleared I am not able to raise any monies, because I can propound nothing for security thereof. But that my noble Lord Lauderdale (to whose favours I am so exceedingly obliged, though I have for the reason abovesaid been necessitated to be hitherto thereof neglective) may clearly understand my condition, accordingly know how to represent it to his Majesty. I have here expressed the particular of my estate and debts, which pray thee present with my humble service to his Lordship: with this assurance, that if upon the diligentest enquiry can be made they be not found to be really true, then let me not find any favour: and if truth, as for such I here assert them, I humbly spread my sad condition therein before his Majesty for his gracious mercy and compassion towards an ancient family, and numerous issue. For praying God for a blessing on thy endeavour, and for his Majesty's temporal and eternal happiness, I remain thy most affectionate husband.'

The enclosed list of assets and debts shows the annual rental of Ridlington in Rutland to have been £140, Swakeleys in Highgate £30, and Merton near Oxford, his mother's portion, £600. His debts amounted to £8,113, and after paying the interest on them he was left with £284 a year.[287]

Or rather, he would have been but for the statute of 1661, in the thirteenth year of the reign of Charles II. In this Act of Parliament Sir James and five others were 'degraded from and made incapable of all and every the Titles of Honour, Dignities, and Pre-eminences which they or any of them now have, or which at any time hereafter may descend unto them. And that neither they or any of them shall at any time hereafter have, bear, or use the Name, Style, Addition or Title of Lord, Baronet, Knight, Esquire or

Gentleman, or any of them; nor shall use or have any Coats or Escutcheons of Arms whatsoever, nor any other legal Title or addition whatsoever, but shall be for ever reputed and are hereby declared to be Persons of Dishonour and Infamy'. Even Clarendon may have been satisfied, unless he noticed too late that this Act, unlike the older Acts of Attainder, said nothing to prevent the title and coat of arms from descending to the heirs of the Infamous James.

'And further that the said William Mounson, Henry Mildmay, James Harington, Robert Wallop and John Phelps and every of them shall upon the seven and twentieth day of January which shall be in the year of our Lord 1661 [that is, 1662 in the revised calender] or as soon after as they shall be apprehended, carried to the Tower of London, and from thence drawn upon sledges with ropes about their necks and according to the manner of persons executed for High Treason quite through the streets of London unto the gallows at Tyburn, and from thence in like manner be brought back again to the Tower of London; and there, or in such other prison as his Majesty shall think fit, continue prisoners and suffer pain of imprisonment for and during the term of their natural lives.'

Pepys once saw the sledges being prepared for this annual entertainment; but Infamous James never contributed to it. He had taken refuge, under the name of Edwards, with the royalist printer, Dugard, who had printed the *Eikon Basilike* attributed to the royal martyr. Dugard had suffered imprisonment for publishing this and other books, and might have been tried for his life had not James saved both him and his press. So Dugard later deposed in defence of his kindness to James.[228]

His gratitude was discovered when one Captain Short arrived at his house with a squad of soldiers, and in the course of their search discovered the Infamous James. But James had previous experience of this kind of situation from the days when he resided at Swakeleys. He refused to yield himself without a warrant, the importance of which is not difficult to impress upon the military mind. When Captain Short returned with it, both Dugard and James had disappeared. Nothing remained for Captain Short but to make the deposition which led to the apprehension of Dugard. Perhaps his sense of humiliation was softened a little by the touching tale of humanity and loyalty that he had to tell.

While James escaped abroad, his property of Ridlington was

settled on the Duke of York as part of the reward for his many impecunious years of exile. But somehow his wife Catharine managed to save the properties of Swakeleys which had belonged to her own family and Merton which had belonged to that of her mother-in-law. The only evidence of the resource with which she tackled the problem of supporting her enormous family is 'The case of the distressed Lady Harington; together with her Petition, humbly presented to this Honourable House', and preserved among the Somers tracts.

In it she skipped the usual references to the antiquity of the Harington family, and began instead by mentioning her plain estimable father 'Sir Edmund Wright, who was the Lord Mayor of London in the beginning of the troubles, and appeared upon all occasions for the late King, and continued loyal to his dying day, suffering both fine and imprisonment for him'.

She then gave a list of the family property, exactly as her husband had outlined it to her. But she was careful to add that her portion was only hers for life, passing then to her eldest son 'who was always in his judgment for a king and kingly government, and never in the least measure disloyal'.

She referred to 'her miserable husband' as briefly as possible, and concluded by begging 'that, whilst her husband's fault is remembered, her father's sufferings, and her own and children's innocency, may not be wholly forgotten; and that all such in this Honourable House as are either fathers, husbands or children would seriously consider the case of her and her twelve innocent children . . .' This figure is mysterious, for they had now been married for over thirty years, and the total of olive-branches certainly reached sixteen in the end.

'The God of mercy, who hath declared his promise, and pronounced his blessing to the merciful' was invoked last in Catharine's petition, 'of which to make you all partakers shall be the prayers of your Honours' most miserable and distressed suppliant and her numerous issue, who cast themselves at your Honours' feet for mercy to her whole family'. This petition may not have achieved any result whatever. But Catharine had certainly triumphed by the October of 1662, and the petition is the only remaining evidence of the skill and spirit with which she entered the fray.[339]

Her husband was parted from her, and from his children for about eight years, during at least part of which time he was living at Antwerp. 'O gracious Creator, with what a deluge of misery is wretched Man overwhelmed. In how deep an abyss of sorrow is he plunged. Cannot riches, honours, pleasures, wisdom, the content and completement of the whole world's felicity, excite or beget one true smile of joy in the soul? Nay, do they not with man stray from the end of their creation, administering (instead of solace) vexation and infelicity? O who but man hath ruined man; who but himself is the thief and betrayer of himself? What occasioned the parting of this good from the creature, but the departing of man from thee his Creator?' The pious James wrote directions to his children from Antwerp, to protect them against a similar ruin. And he praised God for having humbled him.[240]

His mind strayed back to a hundred homely incidents of happier days, which enliven his divine meditations quaintly:

'No sooner was nature plentifully refreshed, but that at the sight of a great venomous spider, which lay dead at the bottom of the pot, we had reason to fear that our refresher would prove our destroyer, and our drink our poison . . .

'Whether this black and ugly creature was as full of malice as poison, and therefore burst herself in the beer in a kind of revenge . . . I know not. Nor had we time to be coroners, since our present danger did not admit of any delay, as to the seeking for, and taking an antidote; our fear (as is usual) not neglecting or betraying such means and succours as reason offered, *viz.* The taking a good draught of oil of olives, which by the blessing of our gracious God drowned both our fear and danger, we both remaining without the least distemper, in perfect health.'

James of Swakeleys did, with these meditations in prose, what the fourth John of Kelston had done with his pastoral letters to his sister. He turned them into verse. Like John, he composed so many lines of bad poetry that he could hardly help hitting upon a good one now and then.

> All actings here are ordered from above,
> Although they seem eccentrical to move;
> Like watches' wheels, turned by a spring unseen,
> In this world's play, Dame Fortune hath no skein.
> The down of snow, and the white candied balls
> Of hail do not irregularly fall.[240]

James was speaking of 'God's merciful preservation of some of our family from being killed or hurt by a fowling-piece, full laden, and unawares discharged by an unskilful person, carelessly meddling with the cock thereof in the room wherein they were diversely employed'. James was nothing if not courageous in his choice of poetic theme.

> Thus was a piece ordered to wound the wall
> When carelessly discharged, missing them all
> Within that room; unto the wonder, joy
> Of our whole family, freed from annoy.
> All kinds of death are fearful, most of all
> That which is sudden, since by it doth fall
> Souls, with men's bodies, oft into a tomb
> From whence there is no resurrection.
> How great was then this mercy, Lord, that spared
> Some unconverted, others unprepared.[140]

It is surprising to learn that any of James's family could have been unprepared, let alone unconverted.

In 1667 the great Clarendon, architect of the Restoration, joined him in exile. He did not share James's contempt for the vanities of human glory, or interpret his disgrace as the dispensation of a merciful God. He spent his exile in adding his autobiography to the history of the Rebellion that he had composed during the Interregnum in Jersey. It would be unchristian to wish that James's feelings had been as far from grace as his own. On the other hand, James's military dispatches during the civil war make it clear that he might have written an account of those events complementary to Clarendon's, of the greatest value to historians, and not less to the glory of God than his providential poems.

While James was enjoying the most merciful of all his deliverances, it went ill with his cousin of Sapcote. For five months he was kept in close confinement, and only with difficulty did his sisters obtain permission to visit him in the Tower. They took a doctor with them who found James weakened by his imprisonment, and some tenants who would not pay their rent, except in the presence of their landlord. In an attempt to ease his conditions, the sisters gave a present of £50 to the Lieutenant of the Tower.

James gave his sisters a petition to present to Parliament, that he might be given a trial. 'May it ... please this honourable

House to take tender consideration of the sufferings of an Englishman hitherto innocent; and that the long continuance of him in prison without trial may be hereafter the case of others, and a precedent for the like case: and that this honourable House would please to move his Majesty that your petitioner may be proceeded against by a legal way of trial, or that he may have his freedom; so that he may no longer languish in prison to the ruin of his health and estate.' James could not be brought to trial because no evidence had been found against him in the investigations of the Wildman plot. And his sisters could not find one Member willing to present his petition in the House of Commons.[241]

So they moved for a writ of Habeas Corpus. There was a simple answer to that before the Habeas Corpus Act was passed. 'His warder came one day to his sisters at Westminster', says Toland, 'and acquainted them that between one and two o'clock that morning their brother was put on board a ship to be transported he knew not whither, without any time given him either to see his friends, or to make provision of money, linen, or other necessaries. Nor could his relatives for a whole fortnight, either at the Tower or in the secretary's office, learn what was become of him, till they received a note from himself on board one of the King's ships then lying under Hurst castle, informing them that he believed he was bound for Plymouth. About a month after, he sent 'em word by another letter that he was landed on a kind of rock opposite to Plymouth, called St Nicholas Island.'

Here the author of *Oceana* went harmlessly mad. The cause of his insanity remains a mystery. Aubrey had recorded that the death of King Charles I made him ill, and his condition in the Tower had already alarmed his sisters. The confinement of St Nicholas Island undermined his health further, but as a result he was removed to Plymouth where he was 'used with extraordinary respect by the deputy-governor of the fort, Sir John Skelton, who frequently invited him to his table, and much loved his conversation'.

But a certain Dr Dunstan prescribed a drug called guaiacum, which James took in his coffee as a cure for scurvy. 'He drank of this liquor in great quantities,' says Toland 'every morning and evening. But after using it for some time, his sisters to their no small amazement, received no more answers to their letters. At length advice was brought 'em from his landlady that his fancy was much disordered, and desiring somebody might come to look after him. Immediately one of them addressed herself to the Earl of Bath, then chief governor of Plymouth, and informed him of his prisoner's sad condition. This noble lord, who laid many obligations on him before, and gave frequent orders for his good usage, went hereupon to intercede for him with the King, representing the danger of his life if he were not removed from that unwholesome place to London, where he might have the advice of able physicians. And the King was accordingly pleased to grant a warrant for his release, since nothing appeared against him, supported by good proof or probable presumptions.'

It was too late. 'The next day the Lady Ashton, with another of his sisters, took their journey towards Plymouth, where they found their poor brother so transformed in body and mind that they scarce could persuade themselves it was the same person. He was reduced to a skeleton, not able to walk alone, slept very little, his imagination disturbed, often fainted when he took his drink, and yet so fond of it that he would by no means be advised to forbear it . . . A rumour at Plymouth, that Harington had taken some drink which would make any man mad in a month; the surliness of his doctor, and something blabbed by a maid that was put against his will to attend him, made his sister suspect he had foul play lest he should write any more Oceanas.'

A month later he was well enough to travel, and before he returned to London he stopped in Surrey to drink the Epsom waters. But though his physical health improved, his mind was permanently impaired. Aubrey describes him in those last years 'in the Little Ambry (a fair house on the left hand) which looks into the Dean's Yard in Westminster. In the upper storey he had a pretty gallery, which looked into the yard . . . where he commonly dined and meditated, and took his tobacco'.

He married at this time, and saw many of his old friends, and wrote the note to Aubrey in a shaky hand which alone survives of his correspondence, in the Bodleian Library. His madness was of a quaint kind as Aubrey described it, being 'a fancy that his perspiration turned to flies, and sometimes to bees . . . 'Twas the strangest sort of madness that ever I found in anyone. Talk of anything else, his discourse would be very ingenious and pleasant.'

So tragically died, in 1677, the last Harington to befriend or vex a king of England, and was buried beside Sir Walter Ralegh in the church of St Margaret, Westminster.

Meanwhile the house of Kelston, having survived the malice

233

of Clarendon, was tottering into ruin of its own accord. The widowed Lady Dioness survived her husband by twenty years, and although she did not keep close residence at Kelston herself, she denied the house to her son. Yet no member of the family ever had greater need of it than he. Before his mother's death in 1674, John the fourth had been married three times, and his wives had borne him fourteen children.[241]

A solitary letter written by the aged Lady Dioness survives among the papers which the British Museum acquired from her descendant Miss Philippa Harington in 1946. It is addressed to her eldest grand-daughter, aged thirteen, in 1669: 'Dear Betty, I received both your letters and am very glad to hear that you are well and that you like the country. I did always think that your aunts would be kind to you, otherwise I should not have been willing you should have gone so far to them. My desire is that you will principally take care to serve God, who is able to make all persons and places good to you; then that you will shew all dutiful respects to your aunts, who I doubt not will continue their love to you. Dear Betty, I know no news worth the writing but that I do love you and shall always pray for you while I am

Your most affectionate loving grandmother D H.'

It is an unremarkable letter except for the tender concern it contains for a girl who had lost her mother when she was only four years old.[242]

The survival of the Lady Dioness was the first affliction of the house of Kelston. The private weakness of her brother provided another. The earldom of Marlborough had descended to the Lord Treasurer's grandson, and when he was killed in a sea-battle against the Dutch in 1665, it reverted to his uncle, who became the fourth earl. He had no children, and Lady Dioness was his sole heir; but he drank.

In his portrait, the fourth earl makes a pathetic contrast with his father the first earl, resplendent in his robes of office. The fourth wears the severe collar and plain dress of the puritans, and his eyes are sad. Behind his head is a little coronet, but the paint has been applied heartlessly to his nose. Some of his last letters were preserved at Kelston, scrawled in a huge grubby hand, as though by a child unused to pen and ink.

His evident terror was the widow of the second earl. He complained once that he had been 'turned out by my sister the countess at seven o'clock in the evening'. He did not say why.

In 1677 he wrote to John Harington: 'Mr Justice. Yesterday I received a letter from Mrs Twitty, wherein amongst other things she writes that your good aunt is upon coming down to Bath, and withal wishes me to be careful. This news so bad puts me into a great anxiety, so that I know not what to do. For God's sake send me your coach this afternoon, that I may come over to you to have your advice in this confusion I am in. I vow rather I would meet this devilish aunt, I would hang myself or run away into Ireland. So I rest

Your poor unfortunate uncle and servant Marlborough.'[142]

The request for the loan of a coach might have had no particular significance if this second letter from Marlborough to his nephew John, written in 1678, had not survived: 'I pray send to your daughter Dioness to send me those eighteen guineas that she hath of mine, for I intend, God willing, to take my journey Monday next. I hope I shall see you here tomorrow to dine with me, if you can send me I pray five pounds.' John's second daughter Dioness was an unmarried girl of twenty at this time.

The end came two years later, and is best expressed in a letter of condolence that John received from a friend. 'Honoured Sir. I am extremely sorry to learn that my lord is so ill and that he is not like to recover. When I heard he drank much brandy I expected no other but not so soon . . .'[143]

The Lady Dioness had died six years earlier. The heir to the properties of Marlborough, had there been any, would have been John's eldest son. He was already the heir to the Speccott inheritance of his mother, John's first wife. One day he would be the fifth John Harington of Kelston.

But within a few months of the death of Lady Dioness the final blow had struck his house. Young John Harington the heir had died, nineteen years old and unmarried. The Speccott inheritance had passed to his sisters, dear Betty, and the younger Dioness, who would carry it as soon as they married to their husbands. It was astute of Marlborough to ask Dioness for eighteen guineas, and to content himself with five pounds from her father.

In these embarrassing circumstances John established himself at last as the fourth lord of Kelston, and four years later he took the step which completed the ruin of his house. He was fifty-one years old, the age at which that all-worthy knight his grandfather had died, and he took a new wife who brought him no inheritance and raised another nine children on his encumbered estate.

The real date of Kelston's dissolution is not the year in which Bishop Pococke rode out from Bath to watch the house being demolished. It is 6 October 1693.

As long as the Lady Dioness was alive, John had lived at the manor house of Corston, a property across the valley from Kelston that his father had bought. Here he left the family that he had reared before he inherited Kelston, including Benjamin, the new heir at the death of his eldest son. He wanted to see another John Harington live at Kelston after him.

In 1693 another son, John, born to his fourth wife, was thirteen years old and Benjamin his heir was arranging to marry Elizabeth Lyde. Her marriage settlement of £2,000 was paid in September and on October 6 John the fourth of Kelston put his shaking signature (very different from the neat hand of earlier years) to a deed which settled on Benjamin the manor of Corston. It was all Benjamin ever received of his patrimony. When in 1700 John died, at the age of seventy-two, Kelston passed to the son of his fourth wife.

James of Sapcote had proposed that all children should receive an equal share of their parents' estates. The principle of primogeniture that he attacked has had an incalculable effect on the structure of society and its influence never appeared more dramatically than when the principle was abandoned in the house of Kelston. John did not abandon it as a convert to the opinions of his remote cousin. He did so as a man in his dotage, pressed by the claims of a young family. In so doing he extinguished a family tradition that had persisted with extraordinary vigour for six hundred years.

How complete the extinction has been the modern visitor to Kelston may judge. The little village, not four miles from Bath, is hardly changed since Queen Elizabeth's reign. The rectory still stands, though with additions, in which Ethelreda's husband placed young Thomas Harington as Rector. Sir John Harington's stables, ale-house, and orchard wall, and the beautiful dovecot still surround the tiny church. But of the great house, only the burnt grass in dry weather shows the faint foundations. The church contains but one Harington memorial, no tombs of Sir John or Sweet Mall are to be seen, and the names of their descendants only remain on a few plain and weathered slabs in the graveyard.

For in the middle of the eighteenth century both Corston and Kelston were sold, and in its new owner Kelston suffered a peculiar and dreadful fate. His name was Sir Caesar Hawkins, Baronet, a physician to George III, and a village tradition says that he wished to establish his new Hawkins dynasty at Kelston without being embarrassed by the memory of the Haringtons who had preceded him there. So Bishop Pococke, riding out from Bath, saw his workmen destroying the huge dilapidated house of Kelston stone by stone until nothing was left but the level grass. And now nothing remains of the Hawkins family at Kelston save this act of vandalism, recounted from time to time by villagers to living Haringtons, when they visit the scene of their family's vanished splendour.

The descendants of the senior and junior branches have played useful parts in English life since Kelston and Corston were sold. They have served honourably in the armed forces, the Church, the administration. Their contribution might be thought more worthy of a civilized society than that of their ancestors before 1700.

But it has been undistinctive. It is the contribution of an English professional class possessing little personal family tradition within the larger excellence of the middle-class tradition. George III, meeting the Lord Mayor of Bath; an Indian Viceroy, chatting with one of his generals or judges, could hardly have been aware that they were in the company of men living consciously in the tradition of Lord John of Aldingham. Their earlier counterparts had never been allowed to forget it.

In the case of Sir James of Swakeleys, third baronet and senior representative of the family, the tradition lingered longer. Whether Sir James was ever again able to settle in England and help to perpetuate that tradition will never be known. His wife Catharine died in 1675 and was buried in Merton church beneath this inscription:

> She that now takes her rest beneath this tomb
> Had Rachel's beauty, Leah's fruitful womb,
> Abigail's wisdom, Lydia's faithful heart,
> Both Martha's care, and Mary's better part.

Sir James died in 1680, and it is a family tradition only that he too was buried at Merton. The property that had been preserved by his wife was augmented by careful management until the succession of their great-grandson Sir James, sixth baronet, in 1717.

This Sir James became addicted to field sports. At Merton,

237

which had reached his family through the Doyly marriage and been preserved in it by the devoted Lady Catharine, he introduced a pack of harriers. These he presently replaced with a pack of foxhounds. One day, says a family tradition, he asked his servant Irons if the harriers were not a fine pack:

'Yes, but they cry "oak and ash, oak and ash" ', replied the old man. Later he showed Irons his foxhounds and asked him the same question.

'These cry "land and all, land and all" ', said Irons: and he proved to be right. In 1740 Merton was mortgaged, and in 1747 Sir James quitted his home.

He joined Prince Charles Edward in France, and among the escapades that the author of *Pickle the Spy* related of him was a plot to begin an insurrection at Lichfield races in the September of 1747. When Sir James, sixth baronet, died in 1782 the *Annual Register* described him as 'nearly allied to the two royal houses of Scotland and Portugal'. But one of his sons entered the church, the other the army. The descendants of the senior branch also were slipping at last into the estimable ranks of the professional classes.

Here we must leave them, grateful for the many dutiful services they have performed for our country, grateful too, perhaps, that they have never reverted to any of their earlier courses. But above all, we should respect the name of Harington for the odd and distinctive way in which its representatives have enriched the traditions of their country. For the traditions of a country are the sum of every local and personal contribution to them, and there is no family in England by which they have been more splendidly endowed.

Nor has even a royal dynasty left a more gracious or extended memorial to its greatness in this island. The tomb of Lord John at Cartmel Priory remains one of the wonders of the fourteenth century, as that of his descendant at Porlock remains a wonder of the fifteenth. The tomb of John Harington and Alice his wife in Exton church is among the most beautiful of sixteenth-century monuments, and the seventeenth-century masterpieces of Nicholas Stone at its east end combine with it to make this tiny church buried among the trees a marvel hardly less astonishing than Angkor.

Compared with these sleeping figures, the places where they dwelt convey little of their spirit. The ruins of Gleaston, Exton

238

walls, where tall nettles and wild strawberries contend, Swakeleys where cricketers lounge and Sergeants Monday and Hack pressed their unwelcome presence, in these places no ghosts walk any more. Only at Kelston, in spite of all Caesar Hawkins could do, you will still encounter Sir John Harington. For he was the apotheosis of the English countryman, and he loved this quiet valley through which he would ride with his dog Bungay at his heels, learning the wisdom that dwells with clouted shoes. And country people do not forget.

REFERENCES

REFERENCES

[1] Henry Harington's first edition of his family's papers was published in 1769 and 1775. A second edition in three volumes appeared in 1779

[2] H. R. Trevor-Roper, *The Gentry 1540-1640*, Economic History Review Supplement

[3] *Surtees Society*, vol. CXXVI

[4] J. R. C. Hamilton, *Excavations at Jarlshof*, plate XXII

[5] Corrected in *G.E.C.*; see also *Harleian Society*, vol. LXXXI

[6] See Canon S. Taylor, *Cartmel, People and Priory*

[7] The property of Sir Richard Harington, Bart. Rigge's paper on the opening of the tomb, *Trans. of Cumberland and Westmorland Ant. Society*, Pt. 1, vol. V, 1881

[8] Longleat MSS 11102-8, 11148. Information given by the Librarian, Miss Coates, Longleat

[9] Whittaker, *History of Whalley*

[10] Victoria County Histories, *A History of the County of Lancaster*, vol. VIII

[11] *Chetham Society*, vol. I

[12] All information about Sir Nicholas Harington is taken from J. S. Roskell, 'Knights of the Shire for Lancaster 1377-1460', *Chetham Society*, New Series, vol. XCVI; R. Somerville, *Duchy of Lancaster 1265-1603*; 'John of Gaunt's Register 1379-83', *Camden Society*, Third Series, vols. LVI-VII

[13] Maurice Bond, transcription in *Antiquaries Journal*, vol. XXXV; also reproduction, but the seals are not distinguishable

[14] J. H. Wylie, *The Reign of Henry V*

[15] John Page's Journal, *Archaeologia*, vols. XXI-II. Gregory Skinner's Chronicle, *Camden Society*, New Series, vol. XVII

[16] See also Chadwyck Healey, *History of West Somerset*

[17] J. S. Roskell, 'Knights of the Shire for Lancaster 1377-1460', *Chetham Society*, New Series, vol. XCVI

[18] J. S. Roskell, *The Commons in the Parliament of 1422*

[19] *Rolls of Parliament*, vol. V, p. 191

[20] Will of Sir Thomas Harington, *Surtees Society*, vol. XXX; see also Whitaker, *Richmondshire*, and *Piccope*, vol. IV

[21] J. Hunter, *History of Doncaster*, vol. II

[22] Sixteenth-century copy of Sir James Harington's Will; B.M. Add. MSS 46,373, unfoliated

[23] Whitaker, *History of Whalley*

[24] *Rolls of Parliament*, vol. VI; see also Pollard, *The Reign of Henry VII*

[25] *Statutes*, 19 Henry VII, Chapter 40

[26] For the subsequent history of Hornby Castle, see *Chetham Society*, New Series, vol. CII

[27] James Wright, *History of Rutland*

[28] The Laund marriage contract and deeds connected with the purchase of Horn Manor are the property of Sir Richard Harington, Bart

[29] Victoria County Histories, *A History of the County of Rutland*

[30] B.M. Add. MS. 32647, fol. 53

[31] Ibid., fols. 57-8

[32] Ibid., fol. 71

[33] Ibid., fol. 59

[34] Ibid., fol. 61

REFERENCES

[35] B.M. Add. MS. 32647, fol. 64

[36] Ibid., fol. 63

[37] Ibid., fol. 74

[38] B.M. Add. MS. 27632, fol. 3; warrant from the Duke of Norfolk to Sir John Harington, Joint Treasurer to the English army in France, dated 6 June 1545, included in a commonplace book to which three successive John Haringtons of Kelston contributed. The error in D.N.B., that John Harington of Kelston (chaps. 6 and 7) held the office of Treasurer may spring from the preservation of this Exton document among the Kelston papers

[39] H. R. Trevor-Roper, *The Gentry 1540-1640*

[40] Machyn's Diary, *Camden Society*, vol. XLII

[41] Brewer, *Letters and Papers of Henry VIII*, vol. III, pp. 244, 863

[42] B.M. Add. MS. 46373, unfoliated

[43] *Privy Council Calendar 1542-7*, p. 491

[44] The property of Miss Philippa Harington

[45] *Harleian Society*, Visitation of York

[46] *Cal. S.P. Dom. 1547-80*, p. 358

[47] The property of Mr John Harington More

[48] *The Letters and Epigrams of Sir John Harington*, ed. N. E. McClure, pp. 66-7

[49] *Nugae Antiquae*, ed. Park, vol. I, p. 385

[50] Ibid., p. 313

[51] Ibid., vol. II, pp. 323-4

[52] Ibid., ed. Harington, vol. II, p. 84; vol. III, p. 304

[53] B.M. Add. MS. 36529 passim; Egerton MS. 2711 passim

[54] Ibid., 46382 unfoliated

[55] *Nugae Antiquae*, ed. Harington, vol. III, pp. 244-5

[56] F. J. Poynton, *Memoranda of Kelston*

[57] *Cal. Pat. Rolls 1555-7*, pp. 95-6

[58] *Nugae Antiquae*, ed. Harington, vol. III, pp. 259-60; Sir John Harington, *Orlando Furioso*, notes to Canto 19

[59] E. M. Tomlinson, *A History of the Minories*

[60] *Camden Society*, vol. XLVIII; J. A. Muller, *The Letters of Stephen Gardiner*

[61] *Nugae Antiquae*, ed. Park, vol. I, pp. 364-5; see also vol. II, pp. 67-71

[62] Ibid., pp. 135-7; cf. J. E. Sandys, *Shakespeare's England*, vol. I, where the erroneous date 1550 is repeated

[63] *Nugae Antiquae*, ed. Park, vol. I, pp. 51-2, 135, 140-3

[64] Ibid., pp. 63-6

[65] B.M. Add. MS. 36529, fols. 67-8

[66] *Nugae Antiquae*, ed. Park, vol. II, pp. 333-4; first published in *Paradise of Dainty Devises*, 1600

[67] Ibid., pp. 324-5

[68] B.M. Add. MS. 36529, fol. 32

[69] *Cal. Pat. Rolls 1560-3*, pp. 155-6, 510-11

[70] F. J. Poynton, *Memoranda of Kelston*

[71] B.M. Add. MS. 36529, fol. 69

[72] Ibid., 46382 unfoliated letter from G. F. Nott to Henry Harington, 1810; *Orlando Furioso*, notes to Canto 29

[73] *Nugae Antiquae*, ed. Park, vol. I, pp. 105-8

[74] B.M. Lansdowne MS. 13, art. 38

REFERENCES

[75] Ibid., 18, art. 36, letter from Lady Lucy Harington to Lord Burghley 4 February 1573; see also Poynton, *Memoranda of Kelston*

[76] G. F. Nott, *Poems of Wyatt*

[77] *Orlando Furioso*, notes to Canto 19

[78] B.M. Add. MS. 46381 unfoliated

[79] John Chapman, *World Review*, March 1948

[80] *Nugae Antiquae*, ed. Park, vol. II, p. 96

[81] Ibid., p. 157; *Metamorphosis of Ajax*, ed. 1927, p. 27

[82] *Nugae Antiquae*, ed. Park, vol. I, pp. 127-8

[83] Ibid., pp. 131-5

[84] S. P. Dom. Elizabeth 144/4

[85] *Metamorphosis of Ajax*, ed. 1927, p. 6; ed. 1814, Apology, p. 21

[86] *The Letters and Epigrams of Sir John Harington*, ed. N. E. McClure, pp. 61-2

[87] B.M. Add. MS. 46381 unfoliated

[88] F. J. Poynton, *Memoranda of Kelston*; B.M. Map 5005 (7)

[89] *Nugae Antiquae*, ed. Park, vol. I, pp. 177-8

[90] *Letters and Epigrams*, pp. 311-12, 175, 218, 298

[91] *Nugae Antiquae*, ed. Park, vol. I, pp. 174, 175-6, 169

[92] Ibid., pp. 167, 172-3

[93] Ibid., vol. II, p. 215

[94] Ibid., vol. I, p. 166

[95] *Acts of the Privy Council*, vol. XXII, p. 504

[96] Sir Walter Raleigh, *Some Authors*, whose chapter on Sir John Harington remains the outstanding assessment of him in print

[97] *Nugae Antiquae*, ed. Park, vol. II, pp. 163-4

[98] *Metamorphosis of Ajax*, ed. 1927, pp. 65-6

[99] *Nugae Antiquae*, ed. Park, vol. I, pp. 209-10

[100] *Letters and Epigrams*, p. 66

[101] *Metamorphosis of Ajax*, ed. 1927, pp. 104-5

[102] Ibid., ed. 1814, Apology, p. 19

[103] Ibid., ed. 1927, pp. 102-3

[104] *Nugae Antiquae*, ed. Park, vol. I, pp. 239-40

[105] *Letters and Epigrams*, p. 187

[106] Ibid., p. 163

[107] *Nugae Antiquae*, ed. Park, vol. I, p. 236

[108] Ibid., pp. 203-4

[109] Ibid., pp. 245-6

[110] Ibid., pp. 242-3

[111] *Letters and Epigrams*, pp. 221-2

[112] *Nugae Antiquae*, ed. Park, vol. I, p. 259

[113] Olive Eckerson, *My Lord Essex*; H. R. Trevor-Roper, *The Gentry 1540-1640*

[114] *Nugae Antiquae*, ed. Park, vol. I, p. 292

[115] Ibid., p. 267; see also *Orlando Furioso*, 1634, notes to Canto 12; and G. B. Harrison, *Last Elizabethan Journal*

[116] *Nugae Antiquae*, ed. Park, vol. I, pp. 309-10, 317-19

[117] Ibid., pp. 312-14

[118] Ibid., vol. II, pp. 248-50

[119] Ibid., vol. I, pp. 320-4

[120] Ibid., p. 338

REFERENCES

[121] *Nugae Antiquae*, ed. Park, vol. I, p. 333

[122] *Letters and Epigrams*, ed. McClure, from which all the letters quoted in this chapter are taken

[123] Poynton, *Memoranda of Kelston*; Lady Rogers's Will

[124] *Nugae Antiquae*, ed. Park, vol. I, pp. 325-31

[125] Ibid., p. 335

[126] Victoria County Histories, *A History of the Country of Rutland*

[127] See J. E. Neale, *More Elizabethan Elections*, Eng. Hist. Rev., vol. LXI, pp. 32-44, and *The Elizabethan House of Commons*, pp. 129-39. These describe in fascinating detail the elections to the House of Commons of John, first Lord Harington of Exton, and his brother Sir James of Ridlington

[128] *Nugae Antiquae*, ed. Park, vol. I, pp. 371-5

[129] *Orlando Furioso*, Canto 10

[130] *Nugae Antiquae*, ed. Park, vol. I, pp. 367-70

[131] *Metamorphosis of Ajax*, ed. 1927, p. 68

[132] *Letters and Epigrams*, ed. McClure, pp. 128-9

[133] *Nugae Antiquae*, ed. Park, vol. I, p. 353

[134] B.M. Add. MS. 5842, fol. 214

[135] Wake, *Rex Platonicus*

[136] *Letters and Epigrams*, p. 87

[137] B.M. Sloane MS. 1446, fol. 46

[138] J. D. Milner, *Burlington Magazine*, vol. XLVI, p. 167

[139] B.M. Harleian MS. 7011, fol. 78

[140] Ibid., fol. 80

[141] *Nugae Antiquae*, ed. Park, vol. II, p. 310

[142] Ibid., vol. I, pp. 392-5

[143] Ibid., vol. II, pp. 312-14

[144] *Nugae Antiquae*, ed. Park, vol. II, pp. 309-10

[145] B.M. Landsdowne MS. 91, fol. 35

[146] Ibid., fol. 37

[147] Ibid., fol. 39

[148] *Venetian Calender 1607-10*, p. 216

[149] Ibid., pp. 388-9

[150] *Nugae Antiquae*, ed. Park, vol. I, pp. 389-90

[151] *Venetian Calender 1607-10*, p. 278

[152] Ibid., pp. 215-16

[153] *Nugae Antiquae*, ed. Park, vol. II, p. 406

[154] *Venetian Calender 1610-3*, p. 524

[155] *Cal. S.P. Dom. 1611-8*, p. 170

[156] *Nugae Antiquae*, ed. Park, vol. II, pp. 317-18

[157] *The Private Correspondence of Jane, Lady Cornwallis*, ed. 1842, p. 29

[158] *Cornwallis Correspondence*, Introduction

[159] Ibid., p. 26

[160] S.P. Dom. James I, pp. 109-80

[161] *Cornwallis Correspondence*, p. 65

[162] Ibid., p. 129

[163] S.P. Dom. James I, pp. 122-99

[164] Chancellor, *Annals of the Strand*

[165] *Cornwallis Correspondence*, pp. 23, 27, 24

[166] Ibid., pp. 33, 36

REFERENCES

[167] Ibid., pp. 43, 47
[168] Ibid., p. 58
[169] Ibid., pp. 44, 76
[170] Holles Diary, *Camden Society*, Third Series, vol. LV
[171] *Cornwallis Correspondence*, p. 57
[172] Ibid., p. 28
[173] Ibid., p. 25
[174] Ibid., pp. 24, 122
[175] Ibid., p. 57; S.P. Dom. James I, 111/34
[176] Ibid., p. 61
[177] Ibid., p. 50
[178] Ibid., p. 37
[179] S.P. Dom. James I, 122/90
[180] *Cornwallis Correspondence*, p. 86
[181] Ibid., p. 125
[182] Ibid., pp. 118-19
[183] Ibid., p. 100; S.P. Dom. James I, 130/15
[184] S.P. Dom. James I, 140/57
[185] Ibid., 129/5
[186] Ibid., 143/63; *Cornwallis Correspondence*, p. 45
[187] *Cornwallis Correspondence*, p. 25
[188] Ibid., p. 40
[189] S.P. Dom. James I, 109/80, 109/89, 109/102, 109/133
[190] *Cornwallis Correspondence*, pp. 78, 82
[191] Ibid., pp. 145-8
[192] S.P. Dom. Charles I, 36/46
[193] F. J. Poynton, *Memoranda of Kelston*
[194] S.P. Dom. Charles I, 291/137
[195] *Nugae Antiquae*, ed. Harington, vol. II, pp. 260-2; see also Poynton, *Memoranda of Kelston*
[196] *Cal. S.P. Dom. 1633-4*
[197] S.P. Dom. Charles I, 347/15
[198] Ibid., 349/2
[199] Ibid., 349/117
[200] Ibid., 351/37
[201] Ibid., 352/33
[202] Sir James Harington Baronet, *Horae Consecrae, or Spiritual Pastime*, printed in London 1682
[203] *The Oceana of James Harrington Esq.*, ed. Toland, 1737
[204] Aubrey, *Brief Lives*
[205] S.P. Dom. Charles I, 412/92; Aubrey, *Brief Lives*
[206] Ibid., 446/40
[207] Sir James Harington, *Horae Consecrae*
[208] *Cal. S.P. Dom. Jan-Sep. 1644*
[209] *Cal. S.P. Dom. Oct. 1644 – June 1645*
[210] *Camden Society*, Third Series, vol. LV
[211] *Nugae Antiquae*, ed. Harington, vol. II, p. 248
[212] Ibid., p. 278
[213] Ibid., p. 279-81

REFERENCES

[214] B.M. Add. MSS 46,374, unfoliated

[215] *Cal. S.P. Dom. 1645-7*

[216] James Harrington, *Oceana*, ed. Toland 1737, p. xvi; also *Wood*, III, 1115

[217] B.M. Add. MSS 19,399, fol. 1

[218] *Wood*, vol. III, p. 895; F. J. Poynton, *Memoranda of Kelston*

[219] *Cal. S.P. Dom. Feb. 1649 – Feb. 1650*

[220] Firth, *Oliver Cromwell*

[221] See S. B. Liljegren, *Oceana* (Heidelberg, 1924), which throws doubt on this account by Toland

[222] *Oceana*, ed. Toland 1737, pp. xix-xx

[223] See Russell Smith, *Harrington and his Oceana*

[224] *Cal. S.P. Dom. May 1658 – June 1659*

[225] Aubrey, *Brief Lives*

[226] B.M. Egerton MSS 2711, fol. 94

[227] *Nugae Antiquae*, ed. Harington, vol. II, p. 85

[228] *The History of Polindor and Flostella*, by J. H. 1651

[229] B.M. Add. MSS 46,373, unfoliated

[230] S.P. Dom. Interregnum 203/13

[231] *Nugae Antiquae*, ed. Harington, vol. III, pp. 1-2

[232] Ibid., pp. 4-6

[233] B.M. Add. MSS 46,373, unfoliated. Printed in Harington's *Nugae Antiquae* with errors among the names of signatories

[234] *Camden Society*, Third Series, vol. LXIX

[235] *Oceana*, ed. Toland 1737, p. xxxi

[236] Ibid., pp. xxxi-iv

[237] B.M. Add. MSS 23,206, fol. 30

[238] *Cal. S.P. Dom. 1661-2*

[239] *Somers Tracts*, Seond ed., vol. VII

[240] Sir James Harington, *Horae Consecrae*

[241] *Oceana*, ed. Toland 1737, pp. xxxvi-vii

[242] F. J. Poynton, *Memoranda of Kelston*

[243] B.M. Add. MSS 46,376, unfoliated

INDEX

INDEX

INDEX

253

INDEX

INDEX

Waller, Sir William, 199-200
Wallop, Robert, 228
Walsingham, Sir Francis, 110-11, 117, 128
Warwick, Neville, Earl of, 47, 49
Wars of the Roses, The, 42, 43-61
Westminster Abbey, 187
Westmorland, Earl of, 41
Wildman, 225, 233
William, King of Scots, 64
William, Prince of Orange, *see* Orange
Wolsey, Cardinal, 98
Wood, Anthony, 197, 210
Worcester, Battle of, 215
Wotton, Sir Henry, 160

Wright, Catharine, 177, 189, 226-7, 229-230, 237-8
Wright, Sir Edmund, 189, 229
Wroth, Master, 94
Wyatt, Sir Thomas, 87, 88, 94, 180, 181, 220

YORK, ARCHBISHOP OF, 48
York, Richard, Duke of, 46, 47, 48, 49, 50, 51
York, Duke of (1659), 224, 229
York, Elizabeth of, *see* Elizabeth, Queen of Henry VII

ZOUCHE, LORD, 72

255

CPSIA information can be obtained
at www.ICGtesting.com
Printed in the USA
LVHW050245080322
712833LV00004B/172

9 781014 894106